In this compelling book, Kuja cha
sion and calls us to something de
invites us into a posture that will
ultimately more transformative. R(
you will be challenged.

—**Craig Greenfield**, author of *Subversive Jesus* and founder of
Alongsiders International

A bold and courageous examination of unconscious motivations for mission, whereby we discover the way of interior freedom that allows for more
effective service in our world. A timely clarion call for the integration of
contemplation and action.

—**Phileena Heuertz**, author of *Pilgrimage of a Soul: Contemplative Spirituality
for the Active Life* and co-founder of Gravity, a Center for
Contemplative Activism

In *From the Inside Out*, Ryan Kuja helps us to right-size our egoic ventures
of fixing the world to seeing its people through wildly curious, deeply wise,
and always loving eyes. No matter your current worldview, *From the Inside
Out is sure to expand its boundaries of beauty and reconciliation. This transformational book will be required reading for all Make Way Partners staff
and mission volunteers.*

—**Kimberly Smith Highland**, author of *Passport Through Darkness* and
founder of Make Way Partners

A timely contribution to the conversation about mission, which master-
fully weaves together stories from the author's own experience, biblical
reflection and theological insight. Even as he challenges widespread mis-
conceptions of cross-cultural mission, Kuja's intention is to awaken a fresh
and liberating engagement with God's redeeming work in the world.

—**Emmanuel Katongole**, Associate Professor of Theology and Peace Studies,
University of Notre Dame and author of *The Sacrifice
of Africa*

In these pages, Ryan courageously talks about the power of story and the grace of redemption. This book is not simply about theory or general recommendations. It is told through the lens of someone who has done the hard work of questioning in order to find a new way forward. Ryan wrestles with what it truly means for us to live into incarnational ministry by first calling us to look at our history and personal stories before seeking to impose ourselves on the narratives of others. This book gives me hope for the future of missions, both locally and globally, and is a teaching tool for a new way forward. It will take you on a journey of self-discovery that is convicting, inspiring, and ultimately redemptive.

—**Romal Tune**, Senior Advisor to the President, TMS Global and author of *Love Is an Inside Job: Getting Vulnerable with God*

Ryan Kuja brings together a rich analysis of cultural, theological, and spiritual formation issues along with rich reflections of the Bible and his own experience among the marginalized. Ryan skillfully deals with the many blind spots in the life of the agent of transformation, such as communication of our beliefs, culture, personality, and perceptions of our histories. He reinforces that foundational to any model of mission or development is the *transformation of the agent of transformation*—"integrity in integral mission." I recommend *From the Inside Out* to anyone who sincerely seeks to invest themselves in contexts of poverty—so they may heal the poor and themselves.

—**Jayakumar Christian**, Director and CEO, World Vision India and author of *God of the Empty Handed*

From the Inside Out is at once heartbreaking and hopeful. Through theological exploration, therapeutic insights, and personal stories from his experiences around the world, Kuja confesses the Western church's missionary movement's devastating sins of colonialism, ethnocentrism, and dehumanizing theologies, while offering a new way forward for Christian missions marked by memory, mysticism, mutuality, and imagination. A new era of expressing and embodying the good news of Jesus is possible, but first Western missions must repent and undergo a conversion itself. This book is a critical tool towards that end.

—**Ben Katt**, host of *RePlacing Church* podcast and regional leader, Resonate Global Mission

Through depth, honesty, humility and storytelling bound together in theological insight, Ryan shares, not as an expert, but with the authority of one who has tried and failed and in doing so discovered the grace to keep going. This book invites all of us to embrace the courage to open ourselves to the healing only God can bring, and in doing so offer that healing to our world.

—**Michael Hidalgo**, author of *Changing Faith: Questions Doubts and Choices about the Unchanging God*

In a world of unrest and uncertainty, Ryan Kuja awakens us to a hopeful vision of God's dream of restoration. *From the Inside Out* offers engaging stories and practical anecdotes for what it looks like to live purposefully with the transforming mission of God as our goal and the Spirit of Christ as our guide. A worthwhile read for anyone ready to wholeheartedly engage.

—**Christiana Rice**, co-author of *To Alter Your World: Partnering with God to Rebirth Our Communities* and missional leadership coach & trainer, Thresholds

Ryan Kuja has created a tool that is both field guide and textbook for missional practitioners by using tools of hermeneutics, cultural and social analysis, history, and personal experience "in the field." Hermeneutics gives us first century field-tested experience from the great mission strategist and apostle, Paul; history gives us warnings of unintended harm imposed on receiving cultures as practitioners bring their own "Main Street" to cultures where streets may not even be paved; cultural analysis gives tools where listening comes first and proclamation is embodied in humility; and Ryan's personal experience brings a passionate missioner whose desire to faithfully serve the *missio Dei* has been tried, tested, and tempered by listening well to biblical text, cultural setting, and the unfolding story of his own pilgrimage of fierce faith. This is not a heavy academic tome with which you will argue but an invitation to listen deeply and well in the pursuit of your own faithful practice of mission.

—**Keith R. Anderson**, President Emeritus, The Seattle School of Theology and Psychology and author of *A Spirituality of Listening*

In *From the Inside Out*, Ryan Kuja bravely faces the fractures in the foundation of Christian mission, and asks the kinds of questions that are essential for the future of our faith.

—**Amy Peterson**, author of *Dangerous Territory: My Misguided Quest to Save the World*

From the Inside Out

From the Inside Out

Reimagining Mission, Recreating the World

Ryan Kuja

FOREWORD BY
Dwight J. Friesen

CASCADE *Books* · Eugene, Oregon

FROM THE INSIDE OUT
Reimagining Mission, Recreating the World

Cascade Books
An Imprint of Wipf and Stock Publishers
199 W. 8th Ave., Suite 3
Eugene, OR 97401

www.wipfandstock.com

PAPERBACK ISBN: 978-1-5326-1639-6
HARDCOVER ISBN: 978-1-4982-4015-4
EBOOK ISBN: 978-1-4982-4014-7

Cataloguing-in-Publication data:

Names: Kuja, Ryan, author. | Friesen, Dwight J., foreword.

Title: From the inside out : reimagining mission, recreating the world / Ryan Kuja ; foreword by Dwight J. Friesen.

Description: Eugene, OR : Cascade Books, 2018 | Includes bibliographical references.

Identifiers: ISBN 978-1-5326-1639-6 (paperback) | ISBN 978-1-4982-4015-4 (hardcover) | ISBN 978-1-4982-4014-7 (ebook)

Subjects: LCSH: Missions—Theory. | Missionaries.

Classification: BV2063 .K85 2018 (print) | BV2063 .K85 (ebook)

Manufactured in the U.S.A.   05/21/18

For Katie—

Wife, companion, best friend, life partner, grounding presence, encourager, container—and far more than the sum of these.

And for those living on the margins of the global village who invited me to open my eyes.

He was reluctant to open it, for once such a thing is opened, it cannot be shut again.

—Alan Paton

Contents

Foreword | ix

Acknowledgments | xv

Chapter 1: Missionary, Save Thyself | 1

Chapter 2: The Sins of Mission | 14

Chapter 3: Myth, Memory, and Constellations | 27

Chapter 4: McMission | 45

Chapter 5: Poverty, Shame, and Creation | 62

Chapter 6: Crossing Borders | 80

Chapter 7: Aliens, Athens, and Incarnation | 96

Chapter 8: Called | 111

Chapter 9: Your Brain on Mission | 130

Chapter 10: Missionary Republic | 143

Chapter 11: Wounded Healer | 162

Epilogue | 178

Bibliography | 181

Foreword

*F*ROM THE INSIDE OUT is among the first repentant works emerging from the modern Western Christendom missionary movement. It's a project that doesn't set the West's vision of salvation, justice, peace, or church at its heart; nor does it operate from a colonizing perspective demanding that those different from me and mine become like me and mine. As its title suggests, *From the Inside Out* inverts our imagination of Christian mission and does so reflective of the "Truth" of Christ as inseparable from the "Way" and the "Life" of Christ. For far too long Christians—especially those marked by the evangelical movement—have assumed that Christian mission was little more than translating "Truth." *From the Inside Out* guides us toward a more integrative dance.

In these pages one can feel a radical reorientation of Christian missionary imagination simmering throughout. A reorientation as simple as it is profound. I hear this project reframing Christian mission as participating in the dance of story redemption.

The Story Redemption Dance

While sometimes we might wish God would replace, remove, or refurbish parts of our story, personality, and systems of oppression, it's simply not what God does. God does something far more radical: God redeems. That thorn in your side, that limp in your step, that cross you pick up, that shame-filled part of your past that you've never told anyone about, your ongoing addiction which you work so hard to keep hidden . . . these are the very broken places through which God delights in revealing shalomic hope. As Joseph said in reflecting back on the trauma he experienced at the hands of his brothers, "What people meant for evil God means for good." God redeems!

ix

Vital to God's redemption is the redemption of stories we tell our-selves. *From the Inside Out* reimagines Christian mission as participating in God's work of redeeming three interanimating narrative strands: (1) our personal story shaped by the cultural contexts in which our sense of self developed, (2) the story of the place where we inhabit, and (3) God's gospel story. These three stories need each other, for when they are held in dynamic relationship, each opens up to God's redemptive dream for creation.

The Redemption of Your Personal Story

You are a living story. We each have a narrative that we live out of, and live into. Our narratives are vital to our sense of self. I'm not simply talking about the collection of vignettes we might share when enjoying the company of friends or family, though those stories are very important as they often offer a gateway to discovering our deeper personal narrative. Rather, I'm talking about the story that undergirds why you do the things you do, in the way you do them; the story that lies beneath your hopes and your shame. I'm talking about the story you occasionally experience as a roadblock to even deeper intimacy in your closest relationships; that core account shaping how you make sense of your existence. That story is yours. And your story is to be blessed and embraced, listened to and loved. It is absolutely unique and your story is in need of redemption. The great psychiatrist Irvin Yalom writes, "Every person must choose how much truth [s]he can stand," suggesting that we all edit our personal stories to make sense of the complexity of our lives. We emphasize certain parts, we leave out other parts. We live out of the stories we tell ourselves about who we are.

Given that you are looking at this book, you likely tell yourself a story about yourself which compels you to live as a blessing to others. Your internal narrative whispers to you that the way you serve and love God is by serving and loving others. Where does that story come from? Why do you serve? Do you know? What does serving others do for you? Can you own the fact that you need to do what you're doing to satisfy a complex desire and/or shame formed symbiotically with your equally complex narrative? You are never simply obeying Christ, or serving the poor, or participating in God's mission: there is always more going on. Sometimes your story binds you, condemns you, even woos you to become less, to hide, to exaggerate your importance, or _____ (fill in the blank), because you've felt the pull to the dark side in your story. We all see ourselves through a glass darkly. You have devised this self-story to cope or make sense of your life. Your personal story is in need of redemption, and that is why your story must dance with at least two other stories.

For those seek to follow in the Way of Christ, it can be shocking when we discover how easily our good intentions can unwittingly become harmful to the very people we are seeking to serve and love. Recall Jesus in the Upper Room narrative in the Gospel according to John. Famously Jesus Christ, God incarnate, gets up from the table, takes a basin and towel, and humbly washes the feet of his disciples. Right before Jesus gets up from the table the Gospel tells us, "Jesus knew that the Father had given him authority over everything and that he had come from God and would return to God. So he got up from the table. . . ." Authentic service requires growing in knowledge of who you are, of your deepest story. From the Inside Out.

The Redemption of the Story of Your Place

This brings us to the second narrative strand of the "Story Redemption Dance"; the story of the place we inhabit. The story of the place in which we live, serve, and participate in God's mission is richly complex. Similar to your personal story, the place where you are has a deep story. In the speed of modern life it is easy to go about our lives hovering above our place without attending to the gloriously unique story of our place. As you attend to the particular story of the place you live, you will develop a growing awareness of the culture(s) that form your perspectives, beliefs, values, languages, likes/dislikes, and so much more. You are being formed both by the place you inhabit, and by the way you inhabit it. What stories do you tell about where you are? How do you live where you are in light of that story? Are you there to discover it? Fix it? Save it? *From the Inside Out* helps us to see some of the harm we will cause to our place if we assume we've mastered our place's story, or assume its story doesn't matter as long as we proclaim the gospel.

The greatest gift of the place in which God has located you is that it is teeming with people who are not like you, with cultures unlike yours, faith unlike yours, systems of relating unlike yours, and so on. This real difference is not only present when you move across the globe but is even present in your culture(s) of origin. Coming to know the story of the place where you are is an ongoing process for the place where you are is living, changing, forever becoming. If a place is treated simply as a cross-cultural experience then we run the risk of commodifying that place for our plea-sure, and our ministry there will likely colonize more than liberate. When God plants us in a place, that place becomes our teacher.

As we come to know and love and bless the story of the place we are, we begin to see not only its beauty and the ways it reflects God's shalomic imagination, but we also begin to see the way your unique story and the unique story of the place resonate. You begin to discover what your respon-sibility to do or to be is uniquely. Equally as important you will discover those things that are beyond your responsibility, or ability. Embracing lim-its can be excruciatingly painful. Yet God has given us limits. And limits are a gift that fosters a life of prayer, collaboration with diverse others, and cre-ates much needed space to lament injustices and proclaim with prophetic imagination the good news of Christ within that particular place.

The Redemption of God's Story

Which brings us to the third narrative strand that is in need of redemption: our understanding of the story of God.

I'm not sure why so many of us struggle to admit this most basic fact. God is God and we are not. If God is infinite, omniscient, omnipotent, and Creator of everything, then it only makes sense that whatever faith tradi-tion, theological understanding, spiritual experience, Divine encounter, or even reading of Scripture informs the God-story you hold, it is in need of redemption. God is bigger than our understandings, while more intimately close to us than we are to ourselves. Our understandings are limited, bi-ased, particular, and culturally informed. And while can know something, we can't know everything.

Your experience of God's story is yours, though it has been cultur-ally framed and given language and meaning. Your telling of God's story is important. Your understanding of God's story is what holds you when you are worried. It comforts you when you're afraid. It emboldens you to act with resurrection hope when despair might seem more natural. It frames how you think about salvation, and participate in mission . . . and it is in need of redemption. *From the Inside Out* powerfully demonstrates the ways missionaries and other faith-based sojourners in cultures different from their own come to discover more of God's story through the very people and places they are called to serve. This *inside out* inversion of Christian mission suggests that Christian mission itself is in need of redemption, and that *inside out* transformation just might be the only way to authentically bear witness to the transformative power of God in Jesus Christ.

From the Inside Out and the Outside In

What makes this book such a radical reimagination of mission and the missionary is that it incites us to imagine our desperate need of those God is inviting us to "serve." It helps us anticipate the expansion, and even the redemption of our understanding of God through the mutual sharing of life. There is no better person than Ryan Kuja to wisely guide you into this story redemption dance.

If you will lovingly attend to the deepest story *inside* you, your ministry will flow *out* from an integration of stories, which will liberate you to receive the gift of God's diverse world that is *outside* your experience and like God did in Christ, you will welcome it *in*. Formational work from the *inside out* is the only way to receive the *outside in*.

Like many women and men who have come before him, Ryan's experience of the Creator compels him to serve others, especially the poor and the powerless. Ryan has followed the Spirit's leading all over the globe, often locating himself in some of the most perilous places on earth. While to some it may sound crazy for someone to move into regions of the world fought over by competing guerilla armies, with no running water or electricity; to those who have been marked by resurrection hope, it's less crazy and more a dare to embody shalomic imagination. That's Ryan.

Ryan is also among the most courageous people I've ever met. Surely his courage is evidenced not only by his willingness to follow Christ into missionary service, but more oddly by his willingness to stop. His openness to intentionally pausing to make time to ruthlessly integrate his own story requires a fearlessness few possess. To interrogate the cultural biases and assumptions that constrained him to do mission in the way he did it, and to soberly assess the impact his "service" was not only having on those he served, but also having on his own formation. That takes guts. And Ryan didn't stop there. He integrated his story, listened deeply to the stories of the places he'd been, and opened himself to encounter the story of God afresh, and now at the time of writing this Ryan has reentered the world of mission . . . and he is doing so differently. That's courage.

By the time I met Ryan Kuja he was already in the throes of interrogating how his deepest assumptions compelled his missionary calling.

This book emerges out of God's love of him and his love of God, his missionary experience, courageous reassessment, and willingness to pass on what he's learning.

You're going to love this book. Not only is it well written and filled with remarkable stories, but it explores some of the questions about life in the Way of Jesus that you've probably felt. And Ryan leans in with a heart of love for God, others, mission, and the shalomic Way of Christ . . . he's no skeptic throwing stones at some missional strawman. He's a missionary seeking to be a person of integrity who lives faithfully present to God, to the people and place he's with, and to his unique story. You'll feel his quest to be an authentic human being in the world, and if you're like me you will feel emboldened to continue in your own quest for faithful presence.

Blessings as you journey *From the Inside Out,*

Dwight J. Friesen

The Seattle School of Theology & Psychology

Acknowledgments

A PICTURE EMERGES AS I bring to mind those who have generously offered themselves during the process of writing this book. It is an image of myself in the center of a large circle of people who have given their wisdom, support, guidance, and insight. It is a wide circle indeed, comprised of many faces who provided a center in which I could stand, and eventually articulate what had been stirring inside for many years.

Of the numerous faces, one stands out in a special way. My beloved wife, Katie, painstakingly read and reread, edited and reedited, and listened to me in moments of enthusiasm and despair while helping me turn intuitions, ideas, and research into a coherent project. I could not have written this without her support, and her giving me the time and space I needed to create something worth publishing.

A significant section of the circle's circumference is comprised of faculty and staff at The Seattle School of Theology and Psychology, who invited me to think across disciplines and to embark on the work of integrating my experience serving across cultures as well as guiding an academic synthesis of mission, theology, psychology, and spiritual formation. Initially, when this book was still a distant hope, The Seattle School provided the challenge, space, and container for me to write and research, dialogue about and wrestle with difficult questions, questions I never knew I had to ask.

I am particularly grateful to Dr. Dwight J. Friesen, who posed a question to me while we were talking in his office one day about my final research project for the Master of Arts in Theology & Culture program. As I was explaining the vision I had for the project, Dwight interjected, "Do we need to write a book?" which he hastily appended to, "I mean, do *you* need to write a book?" Implied in his question was an invitation to go deeper and explore the things I had been wrestling with and processing regarding global mission and justice work over the previous decade. Had he never asked that question, this book might never have been completed. I am thankful for his guidance of the research project that was the seed of what you now hold in your hands. I am also grateful to Dr. Forrest Inslee for reading an early draft of the manuscript, providing valuable insight about what to pursue and what to let go of.

Also at The Seattle School, Dr. Ron Ruthruff challenged me to confront my neocolonial assumptions and question my understanding of calling in order to "embody the gospel across cultures in more beautiful ways." Dr. Chelle Stearns's theologizing taught me far more than systematics. She invited me into a deep love for contextual theologies relevant to the places where I have lived and worked, and in doing so, insisted that I become a theologian of my own.

Dr. Dan B. Allender's words in the classroom and in his office evoked what had remained unnamed in me, both the beautiful and the tragic. He also taught me the skill of reading personal narrative with kindness while naming deep harm and profound blessing, and summoned me to continue pursuing healing in myself and in the world. Dr. Keith R. Anderson, whose pursuit of me—or perhaps my pursuit of him—led to conversation, which led me to begin seeing with new eyes issues of vocation and calling, listening and spiritual direction, and building an "altar in the world."

Dr. J. Derek McNeil, who took me under his wing, gave me both his time and presence, and reconfirmed my deep love for engaging cross-culturally. In his office, he listened to my stories of joy, heartache, confusion, and hope and consistently reminded me what humble, dedicated, wise leadership looks like, not only for an institution, but for a soul. Dr. Roy Barsness's knowledge of the self and wisdom toward the psychotherapeutic process facilitated a new posture in terms of how I listen to the stories of the people I sit with. Dr. Caprice Hollins taught me how to have uncomfortable conversations about race, ethnicity, and culture while guiding me into knowing myself as a racial being living in a racialized world. And Tom Cashman, a man of constant prayer and earthy wisdom, who as a professor introduced me to the Celtic Christian tradition, and as my spiritual director for several years, listened attentively as I fitfully navigated through relationships ending, geographical transitions, and a variety of seasons of discernment. His insight into discerning the presence of God in the midst of this was invaluable.

I also want to thank my editor, Dr. Charlie Collier, whose feedback helped turn a manuscript into an actual book. His insight, addressing big-picture issues as well as minutiae, was invaluable.

I also would like to express gratitude to the many friends who encouraged me to keep writing, to keep pursuing my heart, to keep moving forward. I am grateful for each of them, especially Joseph Byrd, spiritual director for a season and friend for a lifetime; Romal Tune, who told me it was a matter of when, not if; and Seth Taylor, whose confidence bled over when I had little of my own.

To each of you, named and unnamed, I am indebted.

Author's Note

Some names and identifying details have been changed to protect the privacy of individuals.

1 ————————————————

Missionary, Save Thyself

Our missionary activities are only authentic insofar as they reflect participation in the mission of God.

—David Bosch

If you have come here to help me, you are wasting your time. But if you have come because your liberation is bound up with mine, then let us work together.

—Lilla Watson

Haunted

THE FIRST TIME I witnessed an infant die from poverty was in South Sudan. His eyes were sunk deep into his head, skin lay slack over his limbs, ribs protruding sharply. His name was John. Malnutrition robbed him of his life while stealing a son from his parents, a brother from his sister, a promising young life from the community. His mother wailed the tears of mourning before laying her son in a grave. I had previously been exposed to the deep injustice of poverty, but never its unmitigated power to act as executioner.

The first time I can remember witnessing poverty was in my living room as a seven-year-old boy. While watching television, infomercials for Christian Children's Fund would occasionally come on, images of undernourished black babies with distended bellies crying outside of a shack somewhere in Africa interrupting my cartoons. I remember sensing a conviction that this was not how things were supposed to be, that something was deeply amiss. I promised myself that when I grew up and had money of my own, I would do something to help.

Of course, I was too young to understand the complex nature of poverty. It would be nearly two decades until I'd come to learn about and personally witness the multifaceted systems of injustice that allow poverty to persist. All that mattered to that little boy as those pictures flashed across the TV screen was that when he was old enough he do something about it.

Thirteen years later I stepped off a Boeing 747 onto the tarmac in Cape Town, South Africa, a starry-eyed twenty-year-old embarking on a journey of serving the urban poor and studying at a local university. My new residence was in a seedy neighborhood of the city called Mowbray. I spent time with my homeless neighbors, sharing meals and driving them to appointments in the old Mercedes-Benz I had purchased for a thousand dollars. I volunteered with at-risk youth in a nearby township—a densely populated urban area built at the periphery of cities by the apartheid government for non-whites. And I surfed the world-class waves of the Atlantic and Indian Ocean coastlines nearly every day.

Jeremy, one of my homeless neighbors, hung out near the house often. His face was always dirty and grime usually covered his hands. Addicted to sniffing glue, his eyes had a constant glazed-over look and his clothes emanated a distinct odor. The cruel reality of living on the streets was written all over his face and body. Jeremy loved KFC, which happened to be located just around the corner, so we'd often walk up the street to eat chicken together. Other times we would hang out at the house, eating and talking. He told me about the death of his parents when we was a young boy and how he went to live with an uncle who ended up physically abusing him. He spoke candidly of the beatings he endured before escaping for a life on the harsh, unforgiving streets of Cape Town.

Following my time in Cape Town, I packed up my suitcase, loaded my surfboard, said farewell to Jeremy and my other friends, and set off in the old Mercedes, toward the Cape Flats and into the Great Karoo, across mile after mile of South Africa's vast interior, crossing the Orange River and past Bloemfontein, one of the nation's three capital cities. Eventually, the road passed through the glimmering lights of the Johannesburg-Pretoria metropolis, finally crossing the border into Mozambique just south of Kruger National Park. I spent a few months in the capital city, Maputo, helping out at an orphanage run by Catholic sisters.[1]

---

1. Psychological research related to child development has demonstrated that

My time on the African continent soon began to draw thin and before I knew it, I was boarding a plane home to complete the last year of my bachelor's degree. Back in the United States, I reflected on the year I had spent in South Africa and Mozambique, the stunning places I'd had a chance to see and the thousands of miles I drove in that old Mercedes. Most of all, it was the friendships I'd made along the way, especially with Jeremy, that stood out.

But back at home, I also felt discontent. There were more people to help, projects to start, things to do. And in the future, I didn't want to just spend time with people on the margins. I wanted to be a change agent. I wanted to help in more concrete ways that had measurable results. I wanted to make a real difference.

Following graduation from college, I moved to the United Kingdom to study humanitarian assistance at Liverpool School of Tropical Medicine in preparation for a career in the field of international relief and development. After completing the program, I left for South Sudan to work with a faith-based humanitarian aid organization. I found myself in a remote village—referred to by local staff as the "bush"—near the banks of the White Nile, in one of the least developed places on earth. Statistically, it was among the poorest regions in the world with staggering rates of malaria, malnutrition, and tropical diseases like leishmaniasis and schistosomiasis. Infant and child mortality rates were shockingly high; one in four children would die before their fifth birthday. There was a mere 2 percent child immunization coverage and maternal mortality was the highest in the world.

My job involved setting up feeding centers for acutely malnourished children, some of whom were literally starving to death as a result of food insecurity. The seven-year-old watching cartoons had grown up; the vow I made as a boy had been actualized.

It was in that village I witnessed poverty steal the breath from John's lungs, take a vibrant young body and turn him into a tiny corpse. The images I had first witnessed on television as a child had become the face of John.

The injustice of poverty began to haunt me.

---

short-term volunteering in orphanages can contribute to attachment disorders and negative long-term outcomes for children. Also, orphanages are not the best option for caring for orphaned and vulnerable children. For more on this, please see Greenfield, *Urban Halo*, and "Why Are We Still Building Orphanages in 2016."

Who Is Saving Who?

While living in the bush, I got to know a Dinka man named Abijek who lived in a nearby village and was employed by the organization as our daytime guard. He kept an eye on the goings-on in and around the compound where our team was based, which was comprised of little more than a flimsy straw fence surrounding the camping tents where we slept, four or five mud huts known as *tukuls*, and two white canvas storage tents used to store program supplies.

Abijek was a worker, always going far beyond what was required of him. He could have sat idly in a chair all the day long, leisurely keeping watch. But Abijek never did that. Instead, he worked hard eight to ten hours a day, six days of the week, doing whatever needed to be done, from repairing the *tukuls* to fixing the straw fence after a wind storm to hauling gravel across the village to a project site. And he never once complained about anything—not even when he got stung by the irksome scorpions that had a way of sneaking up at inopportune times, like when sitting on the pit toilet while sick with a gastrointestinal infection (which was not infrequent in the bush of South Sudan). The rest of us would yelp, shout, and curse when we made contact with the business end of those deviant little desert creatures. But not Abijek. He emanated a distinct radiance that reminded me of the saints of old, his face often emitting a resplendent glow. His ebullient energy would have been magnificent even in a place of abundance, but here, amid the paucity of resources and the stench of starvation, it was nearly inconceivable. Yet, the most astonishing thing about Abijek is that he was also deaf and mute.

One afternoon he was organizing the little mud hut where the food for our team was stored, arranging boxes of off-brand pasta and cans of mixed vegetables, the nonperishables that formed the backbone of our diet since there was no electricity, which meant no refrigeration, which meant no way to keep anything cold in the scorching hot climate. His forehead was dripping with sweat as he bent over to place things low on the shelves and got on his tippy toes to reach up and place things high above his head. I was in the *tukul* with him sorting through the food when I noticed the expression on his face shift, from one of getting a task done to a look of distraction. He pointed outside and motioned for me to follow him. We walked out and, surprisingly, the Land Cruiser was there. Some of the team members had returned unexpectedly, which in itself wasn't a big deal. They had finished their work early in the village to the north and had come back to the compound prior to when they were expected. Nothing noteworthy. But Abijek had somehow sensed that the vehicle had returned. He knew it was there. I hadn't even heard the truck pull up. Neither of us could see it from our position in the mud hut. Abijek just knew. He walked out to greet the passengers as if nothing strange had just happened. And to him, it wasn't strange. He perceived through something of a sixth sense, something the rest of us who can hear and talk just don't seem to possess.

Another afternoon, not long after John's death, as Abijek was about to head home for the day, he walked over to me and made the sounds he always made when he was excited about something. He motioned for me to follow him and began walking toward the group of huts at the back of the compound. His pace got faster with each step he took. I was barely able to keep up with his swift strides without breaking into a jog. He continued to wave his hand and beckon me along as I followed, easily gaining ten paces on me as he made a beeline for the *tukul* where we ate our meals, a make-shift mess hall in the bush. He turned quickly to his right as he ducked under the low entryway, where a door should have been, except there wasn't, because one doesn't come by doors in this part of the world all that often. He walked over to the table that was piled high with a disarray of random papers, books, and food. With an intent single-mindedness, he reached for a Bible that was lying there and immediately flipped it open to the book of Romans. He scrolled down the page with his index finger, the dirt on its tip leaving a light brown mark scrawled across the page.

He pointed at the words of the next sentence, underlining them with his fingernail, nimbly tracing an invisible line beneath the words of Romans 8:1: "Therefore, there is now no condemnation for those who are in Christ Jesus." His face was again radiating that familiar countenance of sheer pleasure.

I read the words once and then a second time, nodding my head in agreement, trying to join him in his excitement in whatever it was he was trying to reveal to me. I assumed that he was attempting to show me that he was, as a Christian, free of condemnation. I told Abijek that I agreed with him and with the words.

He again pressed his index finger against the page, with more force upon each repetition, the radiant expression on his face beginning to shift into a look of sternness. He knew I was missing the message.

But what *was* the message?

I had heard this verse preached on and talked about and argued over. I had heard it a hundred times before, it had become just empty text. So what was Abijek's fuss about? His effort to reveal some profound truth or insight to me was turning into an exercise in futility. And he didn't have the ability to raise his voice and shout it out, to yell to me, "This is what I am trying to tell you. Wake up and see!"

A few more seconds passed and he closed the book, set it back down on the table, and walked out, his pace sluggish, his radiant countenance having eroded into the face of a man in disquietude. He began his long walk home for the evening, and I walked toward my tent.

The time I spent in South Sudan was marked by deep emotional and spiritual pain. And Abijek, the mender of the human spirit that he was, somehow could sense my pain, shame, and distress just as he had sensed the Land Cruiser. This man living—surviving—in one of the most economically marginalized places in the world was trying to set *me*—a Westerner there to help his people—free.

I had come to South Sudan to serve, save, and sacrifice—what I call *The Three S's of Mission*—and Abijek blew the whole thing up in a radical reversal of roles. He was the saved, I was the lost. He was the one serving me. He had the ability to love more fully. He was the one who had the words of life.

Abijek was like a silent prophet crying out in the wilderness, "Missionary, save yourself!"

The injustice of mission began to haunt me.

Searching for Answers

Something was deeply amiss. I began to question everything about mission and aid work, the particular ways I was helping the poor, and the source of the perplexing pain I was experiencing interiorly. I ended up leaving South Sudan and began another journey of seeking answers.

I commenced therapy and spiritual direction and over time, I began to encounter my psyche and soul in new, intimate ways I never previously had. I began to name what had until then remained unnamed, including post-traumatic stress disorder from a violent event that had happened several years earlier (which we look at more in the final chapter).

In the midst of this psychotherapeutic and spiritual process, the insights that were emerging led to more questions. Had I somehow betrayed those I tried to help—and myself—by avoiding the difficult parts of my story and the pain of my past? Had I acted more as a catalyst for patronizing charity than biblical justice? Was part of the reason why I was engaging in mission to fulfill my personal need for meaning and purpose? If I was truly called to this work of cross-cultural ministry, why was I so burned out?

The time eventually came when I needed to travel overseas again to seek out more answers to the new questions that were arising. I returned to South Africa several times. During one of those trips, I stayed in a rural village along the Indian Ocean coastline for several months, home of the Xhosa people, to conduct an independent research project for a class in graduate school.

There, I met an American missionary, Cindy, who had moved to the village from North Carolina with her husband and children. She was friendly and outgoing, inviting me over for coffee on several occasions and letting me use the internet connection at her house. After a few conversations with Cindy I began to sense that beneath her kindness was a woman who believed she had all the answers for the indigenous Xhosa who had lived there for over five hundred years before she arrived. Her patronizing posture revealed the belief that she was whole and they were broken. She thought the Christians in the village, if they were to be *real* Christians, would have to adopt the version of the gospel that she knew to be the truth and interpret the biblical text as she had been taught back in North Carolina. Cindy criticized the ecclesiology of the whole African church. Over the course of a few months, I heard Cindy critique everything and everyone—except for herself.

While on a trip to Haiti to collect more data and speak with more missionaries and faith-based seekers of justice, I met an American doctor who had started a project outside of Port-Au-Prince. From the moment I met him at the airport baggage collection area, he exhibited a firm grandiosity and condescending attitude. After spending a week with him, some clear patterns had emerged. He was certainly committed to serving, to doing good and making a difference, which was commendable. Yet, those good intentions came alongside a hunger for power and control, and an adulation of the authority that his white skin and abundant financial resources leveraged in the local community. Though he was there to serve the poor, he was serving his own ego and unmet needs just the same.

Over the next few years, I also found myself in India, Nicaragua, and El Salvador. Everywhere I went, I encountered more faith-based sojourners from North America doing various types of mission work with the best of intentions, all the while remaining unaware of their true impact on local people and their own need to know themselves, their own need for saving and transformation. Over and over I saw people committed to all sorts of good work—community development, anti-human trafficking, clean water, education for youth, discipleship, church planting—who were unintentionally, and often unconsciously, acting out the white savior narrative, grasping for power over others, using the poor as objects of their compassion, and believing they could transform people without having been transformed themselves. As I spoke with these people, members of the body of Christ acting on a sense of calling and a vision for doing good in the world, as I took notes on how their projects operated, and witnessed how they engaged relationally, there was a mirror being held up in which I saw my own reflection.

The injustice of mission haunted me even more.

I came to see that people who sense a call to cross-cultural work of all sorts—discipleship, community development, aid work, short- and long-term mission, anti-human trafficking work, social entrepreneurship, and other forms of advocacy (who I refer to throughout the book as faith-based sojourners)—often head off somewhere to make a difference without the psychological self-knowledge, spiritual maturity, theological groundedness, and cultural competency necessary to do the good they hope to do, to be the catalysts for justice that they have the potential to be. Many end up furthering harmful relational patterns, a narrow version of the gospel rooted in American Christianity, neocolonial assumptions, and a savior complex rather than the redemption and flourishing of the kingdom of God.

I wrote this book for people who are currently engaged in, as well as those who are interested in pursuing, all sorts of cross-cultural justice and mission work, the faith-based sojourners who seek to make a difference down the street or across the globe. I would be remiss, however, if I didn't also say that I wrote it for myself. Completing this project became an integral piece in coming to terms with my own disillusionment, pain, haunting, and the shattering of the dreams of the seven-year-old boy who believed in his heart that he could do something to help.

Gratefully, the boy believes that once again because the grown-up, through that long, liminal period of searching and asking hard questions, came alongside him to deal with the complex reality of engaging cross-culturally. The dream of the boy lives on, but the guidance of the mature grown-up is indispensable.

Idealism and the childlike urge toward compassionate action are laudable starting points, but they can only take us so far. Good intentions are where we begin. They are not an invitation to get on a plane and show up somewhere ready to "help." Knowing ourselves as cultural, spiritual, and psychological beings is an absolute necessity. As we enter into the process of awakening, we come to see the ego, or false self, that is continuously operating, either in the foreground or in the shadows; that much of what is dubbed "mission" is not rooted in the gospel or God's dream for the world; that colonialism isn't over, it's just gone underground, impacting how we think about the poor and engage issues of justice. We come to see the subtleties, the complexities, the factors that lie underneath our desire to do good that can inadvertently perpetuate harmful patterns.

I am a lover of the church and its commitment to mission and the work of justice. Despite the critique—or more accurately, precisely because of the critique, wrestling, questioning—I begin with affirmation, a deep *yes* to mission and various forms of cross-cultural engagement. I follow that yes with a *no* to that which has little to do with God's work toward the flourishing of the world and all within it. The no is the prophetic interrogation of the actions, attitudes, and imaginations that are false, the subterfuge that infects us in subtle and not so subtle ways, impacting the way we participate in the work of cross-cultural ministry, often in ways that cause unintended harm to the materially poor as well as ourselves.

Developing cross-cultural and missional competency is a journey, an ongoing process more than a place to arrive at. It is the work of a lifetime. Avoiding the deep questions and in-depth reflection is something North Americans are good at it; inner work seems optional in a society fixated on accomplishment, success, and achieving great things. Relatively wealthy Westerners have the privilege to not tend to the deeper questions of mission and global justice. But choosing that option that our privilege allows for also means forfeiting the opportunity to fully and authentically join God's work in the world. Engaging with the inner landscape of psyche and soul in whatever form that may be—psychotherapy, spiritual direction, contemplative prayer, etc.—does not mean forgoing the outer work of justice. It is not an excuse to eschew action for contemplation or allow a focus on psychospiritual growth to preclude commitment to mission. Inner work and outer work are two sides of the same coin. They are not opposites, but complementary. Practices that cultivate a more robust spirituality as well as psychological and emotional health lead us, as individuals and communities, into a deepening engagement with the world, which we will explore further in later chapters.

Each of us shares much in common. Our stories are all connected because, though unique and unrepeatable, we have each been shaped by the same forces: the Western imagination, colonial narratives, American Christianity, personal tragedy and wounds, the desire for personal meaning and purpose, and the neurobiology of our brains. I learned this the hard way, through the path of failure that eventually, after many years in the wilderness of disillusionment and despair, began to birth new understandings, fresh ways of seeing myself and the materially poor, new forms of prayer and contemplation, and healing in the context of community.

My wish is that you resonate with and locate yourself within the words that follow. But my real hope is that something in these pages gives rise to dissonance, disruption, and provokes a questioning and deep reflection on what most of us have been taught regarding mission, justice, and cross-cultural ministry. To examine something deeply is to risk disturbing the status quo, to put to hazard our comfortable ideas and ideals and trade them for a risky yes to the uncertainty of the God who forever is inviting us into the new. To examine—and to both question and love what we find—is to move toward greater truthfulness and integrity and come to embody the gospel across cultures in more beautiful ways.[2]

There is too much at stake in the work of cross-cultural ministry and mission to continue with the status quo, to keep going as we have been as if there aren't new ways forward that are in deeper resonance with God's mission.

For the sake of the world, we question.

For the sake of the gospel, we examine.

For the sake of the dignity of the image-bearers we serve—as well as ourselves—we inquire.

Authentic curiosity and questioning stem not from a desire to critique, but from a deep love and commitment to the church, the poor, the world. Love involves curiosity, a desire to encounter the depths, a longing to know completely, in a way where nothing remains hidden. The act of love shines

---

2. "Embodying the gospel across cultures in more beautiful ways" is a phrase, as well as an intention, I first heard from Dr. Ron Ruthruff, associate professor of practical theology at The Seattle School of Theology and Psychology.

light on what is secret, what has remained concealed. Love unearths what is hidden and caresses it, accepts it, allows it space to breathe. In a certain way, this book was born out of my process of unearthing—sometimes gently digging and other times ferociously excavating—the concealed, bringing it to the surface, often failing to love what was found, always awkwardly attempting to know the recovered. I hope it might invite you into a similar movement of unearthing for the sake of greater love.

The Mission of God

The biblical text emphasizes God's action in the unfolding of history, revealing a God who acts on behalf of the slave, the prisoner, the orphan, the widow—all who are marginalized by society. The story of God revealed in the Bible from Genesis through to Revelation is a story of justice for the oppressed, freedom for the captive, life for the dead, equity for the poor, joy for the downtrodden. This is what God has been doing since the beginning and what God continues to do. Mission is about entering into this unfolding story and becoming part of God's work of mending our broken world.

Having been created in the image of God we are bearers of a kind of divine DNA that gives rise to the impulse to heal, restore, redeem, and reconcile. This is hardwired into our core, something we sense as a primal desire to participate in God's ongoing creation of a world in which peace and flourishing are realities for all people, where every community, every person, every creature—the whole of creation—exists in a state of wholeness according to the Creator's design, which the Hebrew people called shalom. Shalom is "what the Kingdom looks like and what Jesus requires of the Kingdom's citizens. It's when everyone has enough. It's when families are healed. It's when shame is renounced and inner freedom is laid hold of. It's when human dignity, bestowed by the image of God in all humanity, is cultivated, protected, and served in families, faith communities, and schools and through public policy. Shalom is when the capacity to lead is recognized in every human being and when nations join together to protect the environment."[3] We are called to be shalom-makers, co-creating with God a world of equity, justice, wholeness, and peace.

"Mission," writes the iconic South African missiologist David Bosch, "is not primarily an activity of the church, but an attribute of God. . . To participate in mission is to participate in God's love toward people, since

3. Harper, *Very Good Gospel*, 14.

God is a fountain of sending love."[4] If we follow this line of thinking, the church exists for the purpose of mission rather than the other way around. Mission is not an activity the church participates in. The very essence of the church, its being, is missionary. The church isn't called to *do* mission but to *be* mission—to be the embodiment of God's mission on earth. Bosch acknowledges Karl Barth as "one of the first theologians to articulate mission as an activity of God himself."[5] Mission is God's turning toward the world in love for the flourishing of humanity and all of creation.

As God sent Jesus, so we are sent to incarnate shalom in the fractured, broken world that is our home. As Christians, our mission is not secondary to our being. The concrete ways we carry this out and participate in serving the purposes of God will be in consonance with God's very being and nature.

All of the active roles we take to serve others and bring heaven to earth are seen through this larger picture of *missio Dei*, God's mission of redemption, restoration, and catalyzing shalom. If this is the case as the Christian tradition posits, then the practical steps we take to participate in God's mission should center on this in-breaking of justice and shalom. The story of God working in history is precisely the story we are called to participate in, to be co-creators with God in bringing heaven and earth together. Mission is first and foremost God's mission. The church is called to participate in what God is doing. In this sense, the church and mission cannot be parsed out, separated one from the other.

But there is a problem, as we saw earlier. The body of Christ—the church—has over the course of time often failed at aligning itself with God's being and thus the *missio Dei*. All too often, Jesus followers haven't participated in ways that catalyze true transformation or bring about greater flourishing. Over the course of history, up to and including today, mission and justice work haven't always been about mission or justice; they haven't always been a reflection of God's being and the foundation of sending love at the heart of the Trinity.

There is a fissure in the foundation of mission, a crack nearly as old as Western civilization itself.

---

4. Bosch, *Transforming Mission*, 390.
5. Ibid., 389.

Reflection Questions

1. In your personal experience serving at the margins, what have you encountered that has caused you to ask difficult questions about mission work, even questions that may not be welcomed by church leaders or your peers?

2. In what ways have your original paradigms about mission collapsed? Is there something new wanting to be born in place of the old?

3. As you reflect on the concept of the *missio Dei*, how might thinking about mission as something we are called to *be* rather than something we are called to *do* shift how you understand the biblical imperative to pursue justice and shalom?

2

The Sins of Mission

The cross is a sign of what happens when one takes God's account of reality more seriously than Caesar's.

—STANLEY HAUERWAS

Unfortunately, evangelicals in mission still tend to proceed as though their major problems are methodological. They are not. They are theological.

—DAVID J. HESSELGRAVE

I Pledge Allegiance

DURING THE TIME OF the Roman Empire, a succession of rulers known as the Caesars sat on the throne. Considered to be divine kings, each Caesar was regarded as a lord and savior, a son of God who would bring about a universal reign of peace and prosperity. Like all empires do, the Romans utilized violence, war, and territorial expansion to ensure the power of Caesar and the economic, political, and social control upon which their kingdom rested.

Crucifixion was a tactic utilized to kill, shame, and dehumanize those who they saw as a threat to their power. They used it to deliver the longest, slowest, most excruciating death possible, one that would terrify onlookers into submission and obedience. It was a political weapon which gave a very clear message: stir up dissent and this is where you will end up. Crucifixion was an integral part of bringing about Rome's vision of a universal reign that would come by way of imperial expansion across the face of the earth.

This reign, led by Caesar the son of God, exalted the power of the empire that the Romans believed was their destiny.

Early in the first century AD, a Jewish rebellion rose up in Judea against the Roman occupiers in an effort to assert their right to liberty and their belief that no Caesar was their lord, that God alone was King. In retaliation, fifteen thousand Roman troops descended on Judea to squash the uprising. Two thousand people were crucified on a single day. Others were taken by the army and sold off into slavery. Jews in Judea feared for their lives.

In the midst of this period of barbarism, "in the time of King Herod of Judea,"[1] as Luke's Gospel puts it, a Jewish teenager named Mary was visited by an angel who spoke to her, saying, "You will conceive and give birth to a son, and you are to call him Jesus. He will be great and will be called the Son of the Most High. The Lord God will give him the throne of his father David, and he will reign over Jacob's descendants forever; his kingdom will never end."[2]

The angel Gabriel spoke this politically and socially charged message, using words like *reign, kingdom,* and *throne,* describing to Mary the deeply subversive event that would soon unfold in the midst of the Roman occupation and its violent campaign of terror in Galilee, where she lived. The angel brought a message from the God of the universe revealing that she would conceive and give birth to a son who would have a kind of power that the empire could never even imagine. He would reign on the throne as the son of God, a divinely instituted ruler whose kingdom would be eternal. The angel's words were simultaneously an indictment of the present injustices going on in Judea as well as a promise of liberation through the one she would conceive, this Jesus, who would deliver her people from every form of oppression.

God chose Mary, a young, unwed Galilean Jewish girl colonized by the Romans to bear God-in-the-flesh inside of her womb. Soon after this divine encounter, Mary tells her cousin Elizabeth of the angel's visitation:

> My soul glorifies the Lord
>
> and my spirit rejoices in God my Savior,
>
> for he has been mindful
>
> of the humble state of his servant.
>
> From now on all generations will call me blessed,

1. Luke 1:5 NIV.
2. Luke 1:31–33 NIV.

for the Mighty One has done great things for me—

holy is his name.

His mercy extends to those who fear him,

from generation to generation.

He has performed mighty deeds with his arm;

he has scattered those who are proud in their inmost thoughts.

He has brought down rulers from their thrones

but has lifted up the humble.

He has filled the hungry with good things

but has sent the rich away empty.

He has helped his servant Israel,

remembering to be merciful

to Abraham and his descendants forever,

just as he promised our ancestors.[3]

In these words known as the Song of Mary or the *Magnificat*, she references the realities of being colonized, of being ruled by the powerful and the proud, those who had control of her people—the empire. And she said it would be, by God's intervention in Jesus, reversed. The hungry would be filled, the humble lifted up. The tides would turn in favor of the dominated, the abandoned, the sinned against, the crucified, the poor, the occupied.

About thirty years later, under the reign of Caesar Tiberius, Mary's son commenced a ministry of peace and reconciliation. He healed the sick, raised the dead, and taught about the kingdom of God—the new reality about which the angel had foretold that was contrary to the ways of violence and exploitation of the kingdom of Rome.

A social, religious, and political dissenter, he conversed with prostitutes and shared meals with tax collectors. He healed on the Sabbath and reinterpreted religious purity norms. He preached sermons that rattled the religious establishment. He was an ally of a kingdom other than Caesar's and as a result, the Romans saw him as a threat to their power. After three years of healing the sick, restoring sight to the blind, and prophetic teaching, the Roman military hung him on the execution stake that thousands before him had bled and died on.

The story as we know continues. Jesus was resurrected three days later, defeating the powers of death. Not long after, his close followers left

3. Luke 1:51–55 NIV.

Jerusalem and traveled throughout the expansive Roman Empire, sharing the gospel, the good news about Jesus' life, death, resurrection and the everlasting kingdom that he was installing on earth. They started communities to live out together this message which was subversive to, and in direct opposition of, the kingdom of Rome and the lordship of Caesar.

In the Roman Empire, there was no separation between religion and politics; they were both part and parcel of everyday life. Religion was politics and politics was religion, forming a seamless underlying social fabric that was intentionally designed to control the citizens and ensure allegiance was pledged to the emperor. The original followers of Jesus didn't conform. They adhered to the church—the countercultural, anti-imperial community in the midst of the empire. The focus of the church was on how people lived together and were in relationship to one another in a way contrary to the empire's values of hierarchy, dominance, violence, and scapegoating. The first Christians were experimenting with living together in contrarian ways that aligned with the gospel rather than the dominant culture.

Becoming a follower of Jesus in the first century was dangerous. The choice to commit oneself personally and communally to the crucified Messiah was one of the most radical, risky things someone could do. It was so hazardous because it was such a profoundly political statement that rebuked the state. To follow Jesus was to explicitly *not* follow Caesar. To confess "Jesus is Lord" was to commit to the kingdom of God and to eschew the kingdom of Rome. To say yes to the way of Jesus was to say no to the way of empire. To embrace the church community was to reject the imperial community, which meant to be labeled a dissenter and risk being killed for it.

At that time, committing one's life to Jesus wasn't a simple private affair. Following Jesus wasn't about going to heaven, finding salvation in an ethereal afterlife, or having prayers answered. It was a commitment to a way of life centered around the church, small communities that together participated in society in a radically different way based on how they understood Jesus' ministry, death, and resurrection. Church wasn't a place people went on Sunday to worship the risen Christ. The early church was found in communities that sought to take care of one another, serve one another and the broader community, and together embody the life of Jesus anew.

The original Jesus followers were concerned with how the *polis*—the body of citizens—would live in community and share life together. *Polis* is the root of the word politics, which more than being only about government has to do with how citizens of a society share life together and function corporately, what they choose to do—and not do—which has a particular set of consequences for the citizenry. The early church had a different organizing principle than the Roman Empire in which it was embedded. Church communities were centered on "being a new creation in Christ, filled with the Spirit, possessing gifts of the Spirit and overflowing with the fruit of the Spirit, controlled above all by love; they are communities that should be pure and holy, mutually supportive and interdependent, completely united, transcending the oppositions and tensions between different groups within the community, and with every kind of barrier that would divide them in normal society broken down."[4] The original church was an alternative *polis* existing right in the midst of the Roman *polis*. The church body sought to imitate the way of simplicity, communion, and prophetic reversal of structural violence, poverty, and injustice that Jesus was catalyzing. This was the kingdom of God, the new reality being born in the midst of the old social order, which was good news for the most oppressed, broken, and disenfranchised.

Jesus Born Again

Nearly three hundred years after Jesus was executed by the Roman military, Constantine the Great became the emperor of Rome. His brother-in-law, Maxentius, was a bitter enemy and their rivalry lead to war on many occasions. In AD 312, Constantine had a vision. It is said he saw a cross appear in the sky and Jesus spoke to him of his eminent victory over Maxentius in battle. Constantine's defeat of his brother soon after led him to believe divine intervention from the Christian God had allowed him victory. Constantine converted to Christianity.

In the years following Constantine's conversion, Christianity was made the official religion of the Roman Empire. It became the only religion permitted. One now became a Christian simply by being born into it rather than risking death to commit to a subversive way of being in the world. Three centuries of relatively small groups of Jesus followers risking their lives for the kingdom of God in subversion of the kingdom of Rome was subsumed by the empire itself. The radical, nonviolent, Spirit-filled alternative was usurped by the state. Power, greed, violence, and the perversion of the original Jesus movement resulted.

4. Chester, "Pauline Communities," 105.

In a church in the city of Ravenna, about two hundred miles north of Rome, there is an ancient mosaic depicting a regal-looking man, kingly and mighty in appearance, dressed in the attire of a Roman military officer. It looks like it could be the Roman Emperor. The figure holds an object in his hands which reads in Latin, "I am the way, the truth, and the life." It is a picture not of Caesar, but of Jesus.[5] In another church in Italy, Santa Podenziana in Rome, there is a mosaic which depicts Jesus dressed in an expensive toga, sitting on an imperial throne. Again, he could be mistaken for the emperor. Beside Jesus are his disciples who have the appearance of the Roman aristocracy.[6] These two mosaics personify Jesus as one who had created a new empire of which he was divine head. The original Jesus movement which was patently anti-imperial—that acted in subversion of Rome, that declared the emperor wasn't lord, that professed allegiance to an alternative way of being together opposed to the violence and sin of the state—had vanished. The image of the ragtag group of fishermen and tax collectors who gave up everything to follow Jesus and be conduits of the kingdom of God had been lost. The subversive teacher who ate with sinners, welcomed the outsider, overturned the tables of moneychangers, healed the sick, and who was labeled a criminal of the state and executed, was intentionally recast in the image of the empire—of power, wealth, imperial rule, economic hegemony, and political dominion.

God's son had been born again as Imperial Jesus.

As Jesus was remade into the image of divine emperor, a near duplicate of Caesar, theological reformulating was needed to validate the economic and political aspirations of the church. This wasn't a difficult task to accomplish given that Rome was the seat of ecclesial leadership. One aspect of this new theology involved Augustine's doctrine of the just war. The Roman church needed moral justification in order to continue the Christendom project that Constantine had initiated, using any and all means necessary, including war.

Imperial Jesus became the resolution to many of the questions that were arising in terms of how to spread Christianity—and the church's economic, social, and political aspirations. He was a convenient Messiah who played to their ideologies and ambitions. He even began to lead the fight against "infidels" and enacted Holy War on behalf of the church's interests. Imperial Jesus became the one who would spread the universal peace and

---

5. Cohen, "Legitimization Under Constantine," lines 134–38.
6. White, "Legitimization Under Constantine," lines 244–59.

prosperity of the newly fashioned Christian Empire. And the church began to develop imperial theology to undergird its imperial aspirations.[7]

The Cross and the Sword

In 1492, Christopher Columbus stumbled upon the Bahamas while searching for a sea route from Europe to Asia. The indigenous Arawak people, who had inhabited the Caribbean for centuries, "emerged from their villages onto the island's beaches and swam out to get a closer look at the strange big boat. When Columbus and his sailors came ashore, carrying swords, speaking oddly, the Arawaks ran to greet them, brought them food, water, gifts."[8] They presented parrots, balls of cotton, spears and other items. According to Columbus himself, "they were well-built, with good bodies and handsome features. . . . They do not bear arms, and do not know them, for I showed them a sword, they took it by the edge and cut themselves out of ignorance. They have no iron. Their spears are made of cane. . . . They would make fine servants. . . . With fifty men we could subjugate them all and make them do whatever we want."[9]

Columbus and his men wasted no time in getting to their task of exploring for gold and spices: "On the first Island which I found, I took some of the natives by force in order that they might learn and might give me information of whatever there is in these parts."[10] From the outset the colonizers used violence to control and subjugate the Arawaks, who "faced Spaniards who had armor, muskets, swords, horses. When the Spaniards took prisoners they hanged them or burned them to death. Among the Arawaks, mass suicides began, with cassava poison. Infants were killed to save them from the Spaniards. In two years, through murder, mutilation, or suicide, half of the 250,000 Indians on Haiti were dead."[11]

A Dominican friar who participated in the original conquest of the West Indies, Bartolome de las Casas, eventually began speaking out

7. I'm not arguing for or against just war theory or trying to make a case for or against the merit of Constantine, Augustine, or the Christianization of the Roman Empire. Rather, I'm trying to paint a picture of some of the key events in the history of Christianity and that eventually led to the first wave of European colonialization.

8. Zinn, *People's History of the United States*, 1.

9. Ibid.

10. Ibid., 2.

11. Ibid., 4.

against the subjugation by the Spanish. He became a potent voice for social reform and outspoken advocate for indigenous rights. Las Casas wrote, "Our work was to exasperate, ravage, kill, mangle and destroy; small wonder, then, if they tried to kill one of us now and then. . . . The admiral, it is true, was blind as those who came after him, and he was so anxious to please the King that he committed irreparable crimes against the Indians."[12] The Spanish, continues Las Casas, "grew more conceited every day," and rather than walking, "rode the backs of Indians if they were in a hurry . . . they also had Indians carry large leaves to shade them from the sun and others to fan them with goose wings."[13] The newly arrived colonists, Las Casas goes on, "thought nothing of knifing Indians by tens and twenties and of cutting slices off them to test the sharpness of their blades."[14] He narrates an account of when "two of these so-called Christians met two Indian boys one day, each carrying a parrot; they took the parrots and for fun beheaded the boys."[15]

Imperial Jesus had been brought by Columbus and his compatriots to the so-called New World. In the midst of this brutality, Columbus wrote in a report back to the Spanish crown, "Thus the eternal God, our Lord, gives victory to those who follow His way over apparent impossibilities."[16] The Spanish visitors had instigated a reign of terror in the name of Jesus Christ, the Messiah who had ushered in a reign of justice, freedom, and flourishing for all.

The cross and sword went hand in hand, literally and metaphorically, each escorted by the other in fulfilling the colonial task—both wielded in the name of the One who had lived and taught the way of forgiveness, nonviolence, and peace. The Christian symbol that represented the suffering Messiah had been co-opted by European imperialists and reverted back into a symbol of power, dominance, and colonial rule. It had once again become a Roman cross, returning to its past as a symbol of humiliation and shame. The vision of peace and prosperity through the sword entered a contemporary manifestation in the Americas. The way of empire was renewed, allegiance pledged to the crown of Spain rather than the kingdom of God. Western colonialism robbed the cross of Christ, the nonviolent

12. Ibid., 6.
13. Ibid.
14. Ibid.
15. Ibid.
16. Ibid.

Prince of Peace,[17] and returned it to its original imperial means of controlling the subjects of the foreign throne and bringing about expansion of its territory. The violence of the sword had muted out the message of the reconciling love of the cross. The Way modeled and taught by Jesus was replaced by the way of the imperial ego. The potential expansion of God's kingdom and the *missio Dei* taking root through expressions of cross-cultural shalom was aborted.

The crack in the foundation of global mission began to appear. In 1493, a year after Columbus's first voyage to the New World, Pope Alexander XI wrote a document, known as a papal bull, declaring that lands not inhabited by Christians were free to be "discovered" by Christian rulers on behalf of their European monarchs. He declared "the Catholic faith and the Christian religion be exalted and be everywhere increased and spread, that the health of souls be cared for and that barbarous nations be overthrown and brought to the faith itself."[18] This document was one of the centerpieces of the Doctrine of Discovery which authorized European claims in the Americas. Indigenous brown- and black-skinned people across the world—anyone who was not Western, white, and Christian—were theologized into uncivilized, uncultured, and regressive nonpersons and labeled enemies of Christ. Violence toward indigenous persons was codified by papal decree, ethnocentrism sanctified through holy writ.

The first wave of European colonization, supported by the church's doctrine, led to the eventual conquest of the whole of the Americas. The living out of this theology was practical, egregiously so. The church had institutionalized racism and ethnocentrism through theologizing colonialism into doctrine.

Imperial Jesus continued to grow up. The fissure in the foundation of mission widened.

The Sins of Mission

Led by the church, the colonial aspirations of Spain and other European imperial powers were rooted in the hope of Westernizing indigenous people who they considered to be less than fully human while simultaneously pursuing economic gain and political control. Over a period of a few hundred years, there was hardly a region on earth *not* colonized by a European

17. Isa 9:6.
18. Alexander VI, *Inter Caetera*.

nation; over the course of modern history, most of the people living in most of the countries on earth have been subjected to colonialism and its project partner, Imperial Jesus, who served the colonists' task of remaking others in their own image.

In the late 1800s lived a Belgian monarch, King Leopold II. Although he was a king, he was dissatisfied with his life and political role in Europe, and he thirsted for new ventures. As a palliative for his existential woes, Leopold convinced the major European players to allow him to stake out a new territory in the Congo River basin in central Africa. He claimed it was his goal to improve people's lives by civilizing them. To this end, he set up an official philanthropic organization—which the United States and several European nations signed their approval of—and under the guise of altruism launched his personal project. What happened next reads as a microcosm of the transgressive history of colonization: mass executions, slavery, the spread of disease, forced labor, and exploitation of natural re-sources. During the period following Leopold's snatch of the Congo River basin, in the area now known as the Democratic Republic of Congo, half of the population perished.[19]

Leopold epitomized the evil perpetrated by the colonizers during the second wave of European colonization beginning in the mid-1800s, a period which includes the Scramble for Africa. In a frenzied push for economic gain and political power, nearly the entire continent was seized and partitioned, King Leopold only one example of the nefarious nature of conquest and domination of indigenous people during this period.

New international boundaries were drawn on the world map and names such as Portuguese East Africa, Portuguese West Africa, German South West Africa, and British East Africa popped up seemingly over-night. By the turn of the twentieth century, there were only two nations on the continent, Ethiopia and Liberia, that hadn't been subject to long-term imperial rule.

The foreign mission societies began to thrive during this period. Eu-ropean missionaries were being sent across the continent and beyond to evangelize native people and civilize the savage. Fortunately for the colo-nists, the church had the Doctrine of Discovery and Imperial Jesus, theo-logical undergirds for its colonial strategies.

The push by Europe to expand their overseas claims went hand in hand with the expanding Catholic and Protestant mission societies and

19. For more on King Leopold II, see Eichstaedt, *Consuming the Congo*.

their aims. So began an epoch of global mission growing up alongside co-lonialism, bedfellows in a task done in the name of the Jesus who emphati-cally subverted the imperialism of his day and who called his followers to be peacemakers, to put their swords back into their sheaths.[20]

The atrocities and human rights abuses of Columbus and Leopold are over and done with, horrors from the annals of time. So why talk about the scandalous past? Why dwell on what was and not move forward into a vision of what could be? Of course we aren't like the conquistadores. We're not traveling for economic gain or political power. We aren't scrambling to exploit people. We obviously don't want to dehumanize and hurt. We want the opposite. We want to help. We want to serve. We want to be part of the solution. And indeed, we can.

Yet, the ghosts of history haunt, not only the descendants of indigenous people of the Americas and Africa, but you and me—Western Christians. Leopold's ghost prowls about secretively, not overtly violent like the man he was, though no less deceitful. The ghost is perhaps even more dangerous than the man, the subtly of its discreet tactics more difficult to discern than the explicit harm of colonialism. A phantom from the imperial legacy that exacts a toll on those it chooses to visit—which is each of us—it is Leopold's ghost with which we must wrestle. As we do, we come to see, sometimes frightfully, that we are the inheritors of a project gone awry.

The era of colonial mission is a haunting part of our Christian inheri-tance. We know it happened. We have an awareness of the egregious sins of mission, yet there is a tendency to refuse to speak of these terrors of his-tory perpetrated by our ancestors not that many generations ago. It easily may have been my or your sixth or seventh great-grandfather who brought Imperial Jesus to the African continent to civilize native people who were believed to be of an inferior race. The last thing we want to do is dig up the buried atrocities—genocide, ethnic cleansing, slavery, torture, forced labor—all of which were theologically instituted.

Blaming Christianity for its crimes isn't the purpose of having these difficult conversations. Engaging the truth of the past is not toward a goal of indictment, but reflection. Looking back at where we have come from, we remember how our faith tradition was intimately involved in commenc-ing the Atlantic slave trade. Later, it also became a central voice for ending slavery. Christianity has been used as an instrument of profound beauty and blessing as well as harm and curse.

20. John 18:11.

Gustavo Gutierrez sees theology as "critical reflection on historical praxis."[21] To reckon with our Christian past, our inheritance fertile in blessing and prolific in sin, is to reflect theologically, which we must do as theology provided the foundation from which the original sins of mission grew. To simply say mission needs fixing or alteration today would be to say corrective measures, modification, or methodological alterations are needed. But our problems are not ones of method. They are more elemental than that, not of method but of theology.

To confess is to make known, to bare something, "to allow ourselves to walk from behind the bushes and see ourselves as we are."[22] Confessing the sins of mission means speaking the unspeakable. Yet if collectively we are to move forward as body of Christ and reimagine what it means to engage with marginalized people across cultures, we must prophetically interrogate the past. We have no choice but to engage the theological underpinnings of colonialism and the original missionary movement. We must look into the eyes of Imperial Jesus to see how he still exists tacitly in our imaginations. We must wrestle with the ghost of Leopold that continues to tacitly condone white, Western, Christian supremacy. There is no future of integrity unless we face the past, unless we know and confess our collective history, a history that is still alive, a past that is continually resuscitated in the present.

Yet, colonialism isn't just a history. It is a story. And that story lives on. It is a story that takes away dignity and crushes the image of God within people. It is a story of control of bodies and consciousness, of land and resources, of social and economic domains. *Colonialism is a story of death.* It is subtly written into every line of mission and cross-cultural helping work, one that must be read and reread closely and carefully. To know the narrative thoroughly and honestly is to see the present more clearly. Though colonial mission began a long time ago in a place far away, it is a story we continue to tell and live, usually without realizing it. So we don't confess history as much as we confess a story, a story about now. We are concerned with the place and time that is open to reform, available to be recreated anew according to the *missio Dei.* Now. Here. Today.

Can you and I, Western Christians who are passionate about justice and called to serve the least of these, confront the harm while remaining mindful of the blessing?

21. Gutierrez, *Theology of Liberation*, 12.
22. Bantum, *Death of Race*, 138.

Together, can we transcend the injuries while carrying forward the blessing, reimagining what it means to embody the gospel across cultures in more beautiful ways?

Reflection Questions

1. Accepting the reality of our Christian past is disruptive. Confronting the sins of mission isn't a comfortable or easy task. Neither is seeing how the mistakes of the past still impact the ways we serve the global poor. What do you feel in your body and mind as you confront or re-confront the evil done in the name of Jesus? How have you seen the past impact the present in your life, personally or in your work?

2. European colonialism and its accompanying genocide and ethnic cleansing was theologically corroborated by the church, by people who were followers of Jesus. Where in your life have you seen theological doctrine create harm? Where have you seen doctrine bring life?

3. The original Jesus movement sought to undermine the structures of society that wrought injustice, violence, and oppression. Where do you see this happening in the church today, either at home or overseas? Where do you see its opposite, the church doing damage to the poor and oppressed?

3

Myth, Memory, and Constellations

The past is never dead. It's not even past.

—WILLIAM FAULKNER

In the deathly world of riches, fullness, and uncritical laughter, those who now live in poverty, hunger, and grief are hopeless. They are indeed nonpersons consigned to nonhistory.

—WALTER BRUEGGEMANN

Only the Bushmen

EN ROUTE BACK TO Cape Town from a road trip in the old Mercedes, a friend and I stopped for the evening in a town in the middle of South Africa. Located on the main route between Johannesburg and Cape Town, Colesberg is a small farming town with a few shops and several old guest houses. After checking in at a hostel, we walked down the street to a sleepy little restaurant with an Afrikaans name neither of us could pronounce. We found a few empty seats at the bar and ordered dinner and a beer. The bartender, a white man around fifty years old with a thick mustache to match his thick Afrikaans accent, struck up a conversation, asking us where we were from and what we thought of South Africa. It was normal small talk in a quiet restaurant. Our food came, along with another beer.

Somewhere in the course of the conversation, the chitchat gave way to local politics, and local politics to apartheid—South Africa's institutionalized system of racial segregation—which had officially ended nine years previously in 1994, when Nelson Mandela was elected in the country's first democratically held elections.

The bartender made a few racially biased comments, intentionally making a point about his stance on white racial superiority.

"The Dutch were the first people in the Cape," he said, referring to the area around present-day Cape Town where sailors from the Dutch East India Company stopped over on their sea voyage from Holland to India.

"There were no black people there before the Dutch arrived," he reiterated.

My friend and I questioned him about the factual error of his comment, which turned the sentiment of the conversation from friendly to contentious.

By this time the bartender's wife had taken an ear to what was going on with the young Americans. Visibly agitated, she hovered nearby for a few moments before saying, "Why don't you guys leave. Just leave!"

A bit taken aback, but with the assistance of two glasses of liquid nerve, I ignored her and said to the bartender, "The Dutch weren't the first people in the Cape. When Jan Van Riebeeck rounded the Cape of Good Hope in 1652 and established a Dutch colony, people were there. The Khoikhoi and the San had been living there for centuries." I'd been taking a class on the history of southern Africa at University of Cape Town, so I was armed with knowledge about the area's history that I wouldn't otherwise have been privy to.

It felt satisfying to level his fabrication with reality. I took another sip of beer, content in resting fiction with fact.

The bartender remained silent in thought. After a few moments, his eyes lifted to meet mine. Leaning his head and torso forward across the bar close to my face, he shouted, "There were no blacks here man. Only the Bushmen!"

At that, my friend and I left some money on the counter to cover the bill and walked out.

No Africans when the Dutch arrived in 1652? If Bushmen aren't black people, who or what are they? What kind of farce had he been brainwashed into believing to so glaringly avoid historical fact? I was incredulous. How could it be that people actually think this is what happened, believe white European settlers were the ones who "discovered" the southernmost tip of the African continent?

At first, I was dumbfounded. But over the course of the following months, I'd speak to other white South Africans who held similar ideas and eventually come to see that bartender in Colesberg wasn't an anomaly. I thought he and these others were just plain uneducated, simplistic, and ignorant until I learned that many textbooks in South Africa teach exactly that history—or rather, that mythology. Many schools, especially the Afrikaans-speaking ones, don't teach the history of South Africa at all, but the Afrikaner myth of South Africa. Students are taught that when the Dutch sailor Jan van Riebek rounded the Cape of Good Hope and landed in Table Bay, where Cape Town would be built, all he found was uninhabited land. No one was there. Or, in the case of the bartender, no human persons were there, only the Bushmen, animalistic subhumans. Not even *black people*, only the Bushmen, nonpersons living in a land with no history, a place that was *no place* until the Dutch arrived.

"History," wrote Walter Brueggemann, one of the world's leading Old Testament scholars, "consists primarily of speaking and being answered, crying and being heard. If that is true, it means there can be no history in the empire because the cries are never heard and the speaking is never answered."[1] The cries of the oppressed are never heard and their speaking is never answered in the empire, in places without a history. Empire robs history and identity and silences voices. The latent energy underlying individual and communal capacity, agency, and potential is intentionally suppressed. A people fleeced of their history can be converted into the image and likeness of whoever shows up on their shores. Brueggemann goes on to say, "And if the task . . . is to empower people to engage in history, then it means evoking cries that expect answers, learning to address them where they will be taken seriously, and ceasing to look to the numbed and dull empire that never intended to answer in the first place."[2]

Myth or History: Which One Wins?

The Afrikaners who descended from the original Dutch settlers revered Old Testament stories that reinforced their status as chosen people, such as Moses leading the Israelites to the promised land. They held themselves to be modern-day Israelites and South Africa their land overflowing with milk and honey. Believing that God had given them and their descendants

1. Brueggemann, *Prophetic Imagination*, 13.
2. Ibid.

the whole of South Africa as their promised land, and captive to a sense of manifest destiny, nothing would impede their right to inhabit the land that had been divinely bestowed as their own.[3]

Bewitched by a colonial imagination and seduced by the myth of being the chosen people, Afrikaner political leaders eventually installed the apartheid government which institutionalized racial discrimination. Apartheid was intimately linked to the Christian faith and backed by the leaders of the Dutch Reformed Church, one of the major institutions that assisted the South African government in implementing its discriminatory and violent policies, another instance of empire's theologizing social practices of dehumanization.

The theological terrain of apartheid continues to live on in tangible ways. Although it officially ended nearly a quarter of a century ago, its legacy is present in the social, racial, and gender inequalities that permeate the South African landscape today. Despite the Truth and Reconciliation Commission, which sought to heal the racial wounds inflicted by apartheid, many South Africans are still taught—and caught by—the Afrikaner myth rather than South Africa's history. The bartender that evening in Colesberg was narrating that myth to my friend and me, telling once more the tale of divine election of Afrikaners above all others.

Many Afrikaners remain prisoners of their own myth, afraid of anything that may threaten their identity as the divine elect—including historical reality. History that selectively censors or de-emphasizes what is objectionable sanctions myth through forgetting. Myth-making discerns what to remember and what to forget. The struggle to survive, the victory over the enemy, the hardships overcome are often memories central to the myth of many different cultures. Atrocities committed are usually forgotten.

For example, Afrikaner nationalism in modern South Africa is structured around a central event, the Great Trek. Dissatisfied with the new British administration of the Cape, Dutch-speaking colonists embarked on a large-scale migration from the Cape to the nation's interior in search of their promised land, a homeland where they could live independently and determine their own destiny. Known as the *Voortrekkers*, they were, according to the myth, God-fearing people who overcame adversity while settling the interior of the country. All of that may be accurate as far as it goes. But it doesn't include their commando squads attacking African villages or the indigenous children they captured to work as slaves, who they

3. Kuja, "African Woman's Suffering," lines 17–23.

referred to as "black gold." The story of a devout people of faith surviving by the blessing of God in the face of adversity forms the backbone of the Afrikaner myth of being a chosen group divinely called to prosper together, over and against all others. That myth continues to animate their collective identity to this day.

And that myth is far more powerful than the history, as myths always are. Myths are so powerful because they provide a sense of identity, group belonging, and a sense of collective destiny. In whatever context it is, whether South Africa, the United States, or elsewhere, the myth and the history of a place always exist alongside one another. The myth is what we, members of the dominant culture, are usually most familiar with and what we grow up with. Everyone knows the myth well.

I grew up ten miles away from one of the epicenters of United States history, Plymouth, Massachusetts—"America's Hometown." It is an enduring icon of American history and folklore. The Mayflower anchored there in 1620 carrying about a hundred Puritan separatists from England who had fled religious persecution. The Pilgrims, as they would later become known, established the original colony in New England. The first Thanksgiving took place there. Massasoit and Squanto helped the settlers through wintertime hardships and taught them how to fertilize soil with dead fish.

Growing up, we often took school field trips to see Plymouth Rock—where the Pilgrims allegedly first stepped onto shore—and to visit a replica of the Mayflower docked in Plymouth Harbor, as well as Plymouth Plantation, a living history museum that replicates the original seventeenth-century colonial village. Every year in elementary school, we'd recreate the first Thanksgiving, dressing up as Pilgrims and "Indians" while sharing a smorgasbord of turkey and gravy, mashed potatoes, and cranberry sauce. The teachers told us of the friendship between the Native Americans and the Europeans, how they helped one another to flourish. A picture was painted in our minds of cross-cultural relationships of simplicity and cooperation.

And that is where the lessons stopped and the field trips ended, inside that narrative of mutuality. What wasn't spoken of was the systemic ethnic cleansing of the native population. We didn't hear how two centuries after the Pilgrims landed at Plymouth, up to 80 percent of the Native American population was killed by war or disease, or sold into slavery. The word genocide was never uttered. We never talked about where all the Native Americans had gone. Myth never includes evils perpetrated by the victors. Myth-making requires looking at the past in a way that censors what is objectionable—the massacre of innocents, genocide, ethnic cleansing—and authorizes revisionist history through selective memory. It demands the careful discernment of the content that is to be remembered and revered as well as that which is never, under any circumstances, to be recalled or spoken of. Selective memory simultaneously highlights the honorable aspects of a group's past, emphasizing the collective struggle to survive, victory over the enemy, and persecutory periods that were overcome. These memories are central to the formation of the mythology of the victors. The voices of the disenfranchised of past and present are silenced. History is fictionalized and sanitized, washed in the pseudo-glory of the dominant culture.

I also recall a conversation I had as a teenager with a middle-aged man who was visiting Massachusetts.

"New England is the only part of the country with any history. I'm from California and we just don't have anything of historical interest out there," the tourist said.

In Boston, he could see the *USS Constitution*, affectionately called *Old Iron Sides* due to her ability to withstand immense amounts of enemy fire, docked in the harbor adjacent to the site of the Boston Tea Party. He could walk the street of Paul Revere's legendary ride and set foot in Old North Church where Revere's secret signal, "One, if by land, and two, if by sea," was lit to alert the city of the British army on the night the American Revolution began. He could enter Faneuil Hall, where Samuel Adams delivered iconic speeches.

In many ways, the visitor I spoke with was right. There are fascinating, enduring aspects of American history in the Boston area. Without these events and the places where they unfolded, now icons of important days gone by, the United States of America likely would never have been dreamt of by the founding fathers. Today, we might not have fifty states, or Old Glory, the emblem of the home of the free, land of the brave. Yet, the traveler who offered his thoughts to me all those years ago was also articulating a common assumption: history began with the colonists. The history of the land we inhabit obviously existed before the famous years of 1776 and 1620 and 1492. Yet, the hundreds and thousands of years prior to the arrival of European settlers in which indigenous First Nations cultivated their own lives and land and stories are not seen in the mind of many as history at all, but rather "the days of yore" when everything was sort of stagnant, nothing of significance ever happened, a meaningless epoch devoid of value. The precolonial days are consigned to a nebulous domain of nonpersons living in non-history.

If history begins with the colonists, how much easier it is to live inside the animating myth, the narrative that offers cohesion, belonging, and a sense of unification.

In the United States we have the myth of America as a city on a hill, where all people are equal, where liberty and justice reign. We also have the myth of American exceptionalism which claims the United States is the greatest country on earth, over and above all others through economic, military, and democratic superiority. The American Dream is a significant part of our mythology as well, a national ethos in which anyone from anywhere can achieve whatever they want if they work hard enough—negating any critical look at the impact of systemic factors such as race, class, and educational opportunities. Yet we often don't know, or choose not to know, the history of the United States quite as well as the myth: large-scale genocide that systematically slaughtered indigenous peoples, a great economy built on slave labor and the supremacy of white over black and brown, and a constitution that explicitly protects the rights of white landowning men. Our national mythology, though valuable as far as it goes, misses the realities of economic, class, and racial privilege, as well as the systemic issues that advantage some and disadvantage others.

One current example of how we can be seduced by myth has been unfolding in the Texas public school system. It wants to teach that slavery was never a central issue in the United States, that the Civil War was about states' rights, not slavery (it was about states' rights—their right to own slaves). Five million students in Texas will now use textbooks that intentionally avoid mention of the Ku Klux Klan and Jim Crow laws.[4]

Textbooks assist in creating what a society recognizes as truthful.[5] A history text that circumvents the realities of white supremacist terrorism and a system of government-instituted racial segregation isn't a text on American history, but American mythology. Curriculum that avoids uncomfortable realities provides a layer of protection from having to face a haunting past while intentionally shaping what society sees as truthful and legitimate. Through selective memory, people in positions of power replace history with mythology for the privilege and benefit of their group. As an

4. Brown, "Texas," lines 1–12.

5. Apple, *Official Knowledge*, as cited in Hein and Selden, *Censoring History*, 3–4.

ancient African proverb says, "Until the lions have their own historians, the history of the hunt will always glorify the hunter."

There can be no history in the empire, no history in the colonial project, no history inside of systems of racial and ethnic supremacy—only myth. The myth provides a kind of protection from hearing the echoes of those violated, drowning out their "speaking and being answered, crying and being heard." If the cries are listened to and the reverberations of the speaking from both the present and past are answered, the myth collapses under the burden of reality.

Neither the ancient "numbed and dull" Christian Empire, the original missionary movement, or the colonial project intended to answer. Our task is before us, to prophetically engage history to hear the cries of the poor, the marginalized, the sinned against.

It is the gospel's intention to answer.

Out of Africa

As much as any other region of the world, the continent of Africa has been held in the Western imagination as a place without a history.[6] This blank slate *sans* history shaped colonial rule, post-independence neocolonial governments, and current nation-state politics. It also contributed to the Western mission, aid, and development methodologies employed by all sorts of organizations and faith-based sojourners. With no history, vacant of hundreds and thousands of years of a storied past, Africa is seen as an empty canvas on which the will of foreign agendas can be drawn.

Since Africa is perceived, consciously or unconsciously, as a place without a history, it is also a place without a story, devoid of people choosing to live out their own will and destiny. Every place devoid of a story of its own is fodder for the Western imagination to levy its own desires, ideas, and values onto it, a void onto which its imagination can be directed.

As we know, Africa does have a history. In fact, as the birthplace of humanity, it is where human history began. *Homo sapiens* walked out of Africa to people the earth; no other region has as extensive and impactful a history. Without Africa's stories, there are no other stories. And in terms of the history of Christianity, there are few places that the church has continuously existed as long as it has in East Africa. The Ethiopian Church began 1,700 years ago when Christianity was still in its infancy, more than

6. Katongole, *Sacrifice of Africa*, 70.

a thousand years prior to Europe colonizing the continent. The story of the encounter between Philip the Evangelist and an Ethiopian eunuch who converts to Christianity from the book of Acts sheds light on the origins of the African church. In Greek, Ethiopian means "sunburned face," indicating dark skin. New Testament scholars tell us that that eunuch was actually a black African from Cush, the ancient name for the region south of Egypt comprising present-day Sudan and South Sudan. The areas north and east of Cush were inhabited by people with lighter complexions. It was the Ethiopian eunuch who is credited for being the first Christian evangelist on the African continent. Christianity is an African religion as much as a Western religion.

While Europe and North America have seen a dramatic decline in church attendance, as well as marked decrease in those who identify as Christians, the Majority World has experienced just the opposite. Christianity is exploding across the global South, and the epicenter of its growth is in sub-Saharan Africa. Between 1910 and 2010, the population of African Christians grew from twelve million to five hundred million. Of those living south of the Sahara, 70 percent are Christians and a quarter of the world's Christian population now live on the continent. The center of gravity of world Christianity is no longer located where it once was. The West's domination of Christianity has passed. Christianity was an African religion in ancient times; it is now as well.

Into Africa

Forgetting that Christianity is both an African religion and a Western religion impacts how we do mission, how we understand our role and the people and places we visit. I have an acquaintance, Andrew, who has spent time on the African continent doing discipleship work. He described to me how his work has sometimes been met with suspicion and derision in Kenya, which he called "borderline abuse." He told me how he couldn't understand why local people weren't always open to him and the work he was trying to do for them, but felt that since he was called by God to "the lost," as he put it, he believed God would "open people's hearts" to him.

I do not question the work Andrew is hoping to accomplish for the kingdom or his call to engage cross-culturally. I do, however, wonder about not only his method and approach, but his thin perception of complex issues, including the comingling of Western Christianity and African

Christianity as well as an understanding of how the past has shaped the present. In some sense, it should come as no surprise that there may be suspicion and skepticism in people whose descendants were colonized, stripped of their cultural identities, and more recently, given the message that poverty is their own fault. If there is "borderline abuse," it is not because a group of people is "lost." It is more complex than that. People who have been historically traumatized, held captive by the colonial imagination, told that "we" have the answers to "their" problems and internalized centuries of oppressive influences, are apt to be suspicious of foreigners showing up with answers.

Tragically, what so often happens is that people such as Andrew, who have the best of intentions, are unaware of the deeper dynamics present and so blame people when they respond in less than gracious ways. The mistakes of the past carried out by the colonial church are renewed in the present because we've been unable to talk about the sins of history, to own them and understand how they impact the present. It is easy to unknowingly project the harm of our collective historical narrative onto the Other and then blame them for not accepting our answers to their problems. This is at least partially what Andrew had done in saying he experienced "borderline abuse." He was blaming a group of people who have historically been abused, colonized by our European ancestors, and misnamed their lack of acceptance of his agenda in the place they call home. In some sense, we're all amnesiacs, having been seduced by the myth of mission while forgetting history.

Again, I do not question Andrew's desire to serve and his vision for making disciples. He genuinely wants to do good work in the world for the sake of the kingdom of God. The problem lies in what amnesia has caused us to miss: the history and the story of mission. The classical colonialism has morphed into new forms that are not at all obvious unless we read history—not just literally in books, though that may be part of it—through a deep familiarity with the specific ways the past has shaped the present, how cries have gone unanswered, how amnesia and numbness have set in.

Confession and Lament

The West's impact on the Majority World cannot be overstated. Christianity in Africa, Latin America, and Asia persists in operating under the liability of the Western legacy,[7] partly because these guiding narratives and mythology continue to determine Western approaches to mission and evangelism, relief and development, activism and advocacy. This means mission is in danger of becoming irrelevant even amid its noble aims of promoting the gospel and doing the work of justice—through evangelization, community development, peace building, and humanitarian aid—because of its illiteracy, its inability to read its own history and the histories of the localities it is called to serve.

Past wrongs cannot be erased through forgetting. There is no hope of moving beyond the harm of colonial and neocolonial modalities without memory. To *re-member* the past is to join again that which has been separated. Taking what has been falsely partitioned and placing it back together is the task of finding memory, a common memory based in what happened—the history—in place of the dominant group's appended reinterpretation of what happened, and what continues to happen, for their privilege, power, and benefit—the myth. Engaging in the act of remembering involves a posture toward the past to *re*collect the events and occurrences, both individually and corporately, that hold beauty and blessing as well as violence, abuse, and profound harm. To remember is to choose to battle the temptation of acquiescing to the old theology that biased some humans as subhumans and some persons as nonpersons.

Remembering also creates the space where new images and stories can be held, ones more painful but more truthful. Without memory of the old, new narratives cannot be forged. Without memory, there is little hope for the future; without going back, there isn't room for anything fresh in place of the old. There isn't space for all things to be made new. The conscious act of remembering invites confession, a long-held tradition in the church. Confession involves unmasking, naming what is broken inside the body of Christ, personally and collectively. Confession means allowing ourselves to be disrupted and disturbed by the truth. Reshaping our approaches to mission begins with confessing to ourselves, our communities, and our God that we have been idolatrously secured to false narratives.

Confession is not an end in and of itself. The act of confession can lead to lamentation—the expression of suffering and pain, rather than mere explanation of pain. The act of lament is not limited to our own personal or communal pain in the present, but can, and indeed must, also include the pain of others. Kathleen O'Connor notes that lament "is not depressing; it

---

7. Ibid., 41.

cannot cause sorrow, hostility, or despair. . . . Rather than creating pain, it reveals pain."[8] In lament, confession is embodied emotionally. The experience of sorrow allows us to grieve for the pain of others, as well as have the capacity to respond to that suffering. In responding, we repent—literally, turn around—from the idolatrous worship of the Western pseudo-gods of colonial and neocolonial mission.

We can then begin to tell a more historically accurate story.

We can then live inside a more truthful narrative—the one Scripture tells rather than the one Western mythology tells.

We can then work effectively toward disrupting the myths of mission in our communities of faith and act prophetically against the narratives that are centered on something other than the gospel of Jesus Christ.

To lament the transgressions of history and our own tradition's sins of mission is a threshold through which we must pass if we are to become unstuck, free to mold mission's future out of its contorted imperial shape and back into the shape of Jesus.

History Alive in the Present

The history of colonialism is real; its legacy continues. In fact, it hasn't ended, it's simply gone underground. It shows up in subtler shades of gray now, instead of the black-and-white vulgarity of times past. We have inherited the divine DNA that gives rise to the call and desire to participate in bringing about the kingdom of God and the mutual flourishing of all of creation. We've also inherited colonial DNA that gives rise to imperial tendencies, the desire for power over others and paternalistic attitudes. We carry the blueprint to be catalysts for both shalom and colonialism, for following subversive Jesus and for worshipping Imperial Jesus, for bringing about the kingdom of God and the kingdom of empire, for consenting to the legacy of the original Jesus movement and the legacy of Leopold.

Our mental architecture—the blueprint—is constructed by stories, and stories are powerful shapers of how we see the world, others, and ourselves. Without becoming aware of the narratives that are alive inside of us, we may engage relationally and be involved in projects and programs in paternalistic ways. We can try to help. We can try to serve. We can sacrifice our comforts, our jobs, our finances—even our very lives if we choose to go to places where armed conflict and violence is rife. But in the end, it

8. O'Connor, *Lamentations*, 3.

may not be about justice—or God's mission—until we come to an honest engagement with the narratives that sustain inequality.[9]

If we are to be in resonance with the universe and with God, it means that the narratives we carry into cross-cultural service work must be carefully looked at and examined. All too often, both in days past and present, missionaries and others serving overseas have been unwittingly living by narratives that sustain inequality rather than interrogate inequality and injustice. The narrative of mission that Christians generally adhere to, as we have seen, has its roots sunk deep into the days of the colonial project. In cross-cultural mission and justice work, we are constantly being pulled further into the story of God or the story of empire.

At the core of one narrative is a message about who Africans and other non-Western people are, the soft articulation that the economically poor suffer so greatly because they can't help themselves and need *us* (Westerners) to rescue *them* and solve their problems. The messages often also carry the claim that the Majority World needs development according to the Western template, in line with our way of seeing and our vision of what the world could, should, or must be. These stories we carry end up forming the backbone of how Christian mission is done: the powerful, relatively wealthy, Christian, mostly white North Americans and Europeans go to where the economically poor live and start programs to help. We go evangelize or build houses or drill wells or hand out food or start health clinics with the best of intentions.

We so badly want to make a difference in the lives of the world's most marginalized in whatever way we are called. And I am a firm believer that we can—and indeed must—if we examine closely that original crack in the foundation. Rather than trying to patch it up with a bit of cement while the underlying issue that caused it continues, we need to inspect it like a foundation contractor would, pulling out the deteriorating patchwork that others have attempted to cover while noting the good, solid areas that still remain.

Constellational Thinking

The clearest night sky I have ever seen was in the desert on the border of Botswana and South Africa. The stars danced to a bright celestial

9. Stevenson, "Just Mercy."

symphony. The Southern Cross, Orion, Leo, and all the other constellations shone clear.

The first time a friend pointed out Orion, the hunter, I had a hard time seeing it. I couldn't make out the belt, the shield, or the body. It just looked like a cluster of stars with no discernible patterns. My eyes hadn't been trained to make connections between individual stars, to drawn lines across the black spaces and connect the dots of light to one another.

After some time, I could make out the three stars that comprise Orion's belt. Eventually I made out a body and a shield. After a while, the rough outline of a hunter began to emerge. What had been impossible to see was now quite obvious. If I looked a certain way, links existed where before I couldn't find any, only a disconnected jumble of light specks with no discernible patterns.

When gazing at constellations, we are looking with a different quality of vision, seeing what has always been there, but with a new set of eyes. We are discovering the connections that we'd never bothered to look for. We learn to see what is, upon first glance, difficult to see.

The more I studied the night sky, the more I started to see shapes that I hadn't seen before but had been right there all along, hidden in plain sight. I learned to focus not on the dots of light, but on what was in the space between them, what was in the darkness.

When we gaze at constellations, we aren't making something up, fabricating connections that aren't really there. Rather, when we look with a certain quality of attention and shift to a different sort of vision—to see what is in the space between the light rather than the light itself—with an attentiveness that is both imaginative and analytical at the same time, invisible becomes visible. Lines of connections begin to appear, the same ones people have seen for thousands of years.

So what does looking at constellations have to do with mission?

As I write these words, there is an eighteen-year-old mother, Nyjani, and her two-year-old daughter, Emma, sitting across from me in the living room. They came to the United States two years ago from Democratic Republic of Congo (DRC). Nyjani grew up in Bukavu in the eastern part of the country, a region tragically torn apart by armed conflict for decades.

A militia group armed with AK47s stormed her family's house as they slept one night. They shot her mother, father, and one of her brother's before slicing her sister to death with a knife. Nyjani and her other brother escaped out the back door and ran deep into the forest, where they hid for two days. Once they thought it was safe to return, they began walking back toward town. Along the way, the siblings encountered another militia group. They gang raped Nyjani as her brother looked on, forced to watch. This took place not far from the area Leopold once controlled.

DRC has epidemic levels of rape, some of the highest in the world. Rape is used as a tool of war, in a country regarded as one of the worst places to be a woman. The legacy of colonialism left the nation and the entire region with deep scars that, over the decades, contributed to armed conflict and entrenched poverty; Leopold's legacy is not far off.

Past histories shape present realities in embodied, fleshy ways. In rape. In power dynamics. In poverty that steals life. It is not difficult to connect the dots, to trace the tangible, quantifiable ways that the past has persisted into the present. History isn't over, something for historians and scholars to concern themselves with. The stories of the past—which comprise what we call history—have concrete manifestations in the here and now, in people's lived experiences. History is lived in the present, in different contexts and with new characters and alternative plots.

Would Nyjani's family have been murdered if Leopold never launched a sadistic campaign against the people of the Congo River basin? Would rape be used to control women and violate their bodies so egregiously as a weapon of war if Leopold never exploited the land where her family, over a hundred years later, would cultivate their lives? If history is over, how can the claim be made that a dead European monarch has anything to do with poverty, war, and rape today? Let's look briefly at that, first through a linear approach, followed by a constellational approach.

If you read about the conflict in eastern DRC, you'd hear about how it began in the mid-1990s, following the genocide in Rwanda when millions of Rwandans flooded into DRC. A majority of them were Hutus, the ethnic group that committed the slaughter against the Tutsis. Two years after the genocide, Rwanda and Uganda sent troops into DRC to find the people they suspected did much of the killing, the *interahamwe*. At this time, the main opposition political party with the help of the military of Rwanda and Uganda, ousted DRC's dictator, Mobutu, from power. After that, Kabila, the opposition leader, took the highest seat in the nation and also kicked out both the Ugandan and Rwandan troops, fearful they might gain access to DRC's lucrative mineral resources. A few years later, Kabila was assassinated by one of his bodyguards and his son took office. Over the following years, dozens of armed factions began fighting for control of the mineral mines, killing each other and raping, torturing, and slaughtering civilians.

That is the sequence of events that began nearly 25 years ago, one that eventually led to Nyjani's family being killed by one of those militias and her being raped by another, which led her to flee to the United States as an asylum seeker, and why we found ourselves sitting together in the same room.

The constellational approach tells of a wider series of events that began not in 1994 but over one hundred years before, when King Leopold took control of a large portion of the Congo River basin in 1885. The economic exploitation and egregious colonial violence that Leopold commenced were handed down to the government of Belgium in 1908 when his personal colony became the Belgians' great imperial trophy. Following World War I, the League of Nations requested that Belgium govern Rwanda in order to take it out of the hands of the Germans, who had originally claimed it, as part of their reparations.

The Belgians stepped in and held tight political control of Rwanda. They claimed the Tutsis were the superior ethnic group and gave them the elite positions in government. In 1926, the Belgians introduced an identity card system that labeled Hutus and Tutsis according to their ethnicity. After decades of second-class status under the Belgian crown, the Hutus rebelled against colonial power and the Tutsi elites. Following a national election in 1960 won by the Hutus, Belgium withdrew and Ruanda-Urundi became two separate nations, Rwanda and Burundi.

The Hutu government began to expel Tutsi's from academic positions at universities and acts of violence toward Tutsis became common. They were largely excluded from government processes and had great difficulty accessing employment. In 1986, Tutsis living in exile in Uganda formed an opposition group, the Rwandan Patriotic Front (RPF). In 1989, world coffee prices plummeted. As a major grower and exporter of coffee, a large economic downturn resulted, creating financial difficulties nationwide.

In 1990, the Rwandan military began giving arms to Hutu civilians known as the *interahamwe*, who killed Tutsis throughout the country. The government simultaneously brought a heavy hand to all political dissent and also began persecuting moderate Hutus, including professors, journalists, and business owners. The president, rather than moving forward with a multiparty government as agreed upon, instead continued arming civilians. The anti-Tutsi sentiment increased further.

On April 6, 1994, the president's plane was shot down; some suspected it was at the hands of the Tutsi RPF. Soon after, the slaughter began. Tutsis were massacred all over the country in a process of systemic extermination. Three months later, eight hundred thousand people were dead.

The RPF eventually took power and hundreds of thousands of Hutus fled into DRC (then known as Zaire). From this point, we'd read the last twenty years or so covered above, involving the destabilization of eastern DRC and the militias that tried to control the region.

If we draw lines of connection between the series of events and their potent social, political, and ethnic ramifications, an image starts to emerge in the darkness. The war in eastern DRC that resulted in the rape and murder in Nyjani's story began more than a hundred years before the Rwandan genocide, the event that led to the war in eastern Congo, which led to her rape and her family being murdered. Reading the sequence of events from 1994 on doesn't get to the problem beneath the problem. The linear reading leaves out important lines of connectivity, linkages that allow a fuller, more accurate image to emerge. That telling sees only Orion's belt, and perhaps an arm or a leg, not the hunter. Thinking constellationally asks that we not ignore the linkage to the past so that we might begin to discern the invisible lines of connection and, as the full picture emerges, begin to engage the complex, nonlinear origins of contemporary issues. Nyjani sat in the chair next to me in my living room because Leopold, bewitched by the colonial imagination, initiated a reign of terror, the first bright star in the dark colonial night, from which began to emerge the image of present-day DRC, meaning too, individual bodies and faces and families, teenagers who conceived by rape, some of whom flee for their lives and end up in the United States. Leopold's legacy, and the continuation of it by the Belgian crown, appears in the flesh of violated women. It shows up in the faces of the traumatized, in the violated bodies that bear the violence of poverty, exploitation, assault, calculated disempowerment. That is the story—the history—we are being asked to engage with our minds, and more so, our hearts.

The constellational model isn't perfect, of course. It doesn't necessarily look for pre-Leopold stars in the constellation of Rwandan and Congolese violence; a constellation is not a detailed drawing of the innumerable events, people, and policies that led to wars. Thinking constellationally isn't about finding precise answers but about asking better questions, questions that are based on a circular rather than a linear understanding of how the past impacts the present. It asks how patterns of power across time are related to present situations, whether of armed conflict, rape, pillage, or poverty. Thinking constellationally also reminds us of something fundamental: the colonial ghost is never far off. Even if there isn't a relationship of direct causality (i.e., Leopold and the Belgian crown didn't directly *cause* what is happening in the DRC today), there is a definite connection between the stories of the past and the stories of the present. What is happening currently in eastern DRC is an outgrowth of that imperial domination, the cross and the sword, the control of and violence toward African bodies, though the actors are different and the plot has shifted. The patterns of power have certainly changed form, but they are still present. Most of the current violence is now perpetrated from within by Congolese power brokers hungry for economic and political dominion. Yet, the forces of post-colonial nation-state formation impacted DRC and other countries on the continent and cannot be separated from the imperial legacy. History isn't dead, so it must be remembered, confessed, lamented, and connected to present realities.

Reflection Questions

1. What are your thoughts on Andrew's experience in Kenya? How might you respond in your cross-cultural work if local people rejected your message, your worldview, your desire and hopes for them? Imagine a scene where this happens. What does it bring up in you? Do you feel tension in your body? What visceral feelings come up?

2. In your work across cultures, have you been met with derision or suspicion by local people? If so, what might be some of the deeper underlying factors (either past or present) driving that sort of response?

3. As you think about the difference between history and myth in a given place, what specific ways do you notice selective memory and selective forgetting utilized for power and privilege?

4

McMission

We are not invited to rescue, fix or save people. The heart of ministry is to receive people and then enter into the exquisite mutuality God intends for us all.

—Fr. Gregory Boyle

Our own life is the thing that most influences and shapes our outlook, our tendencies, our choices and our decisions. It is the force that orients us toward the future, and yet we don't give it a second thought, much less a careful examination. It's time to listen to our own story.

—Dan B. Allender

Rescuing and Relationship

I heard the buzzer ring outside the gate one afternoon at the house I was living at in Cape Town. Looking out the big bay window to see who was there, I saw Jeremy, my friend living on the streets who I introduced in chapter 1, standing there cradling something in his arms. He had come by carrying odd things previously, hoping to make some cash from one of my roommates. But I could tell something was different this time. His posture and attentiveness to the object in his hands showed he held precious cargo.

I got up from the couch and walked up the driveway toward him.

"Ryan!" he exclaimed with a thick Afrikaans accent, that came out sounding more like "Lion," motioning me with his hands to come quickly.

"Hey, Jeremy. What you got there?" I asked. I was now close enough to make out fur, light brown and fluffy.

"I have one small dog. Look."

The tiny puppy was probably four weeks old at most. He murmured soft puppy sounds as Jeremy lifted him cautiously and with great care placed him in my hands.

"Where did you get him?" I asked.

With a vague pointing of his finger toward the main street, he replied, "Just up there from one of the guys. But I can't take care of him. And he won't live long out here. Please, will you take him?"

"I can't take care of a puppy right now, either," I told him. "I live with roommates and they won't want a dog. Besides, we aren't allowed to have pets at the house."

"There is a shelter not far from here in Hout Bay," he said, referring to a town on the Cape Peninsula, about a thirty-minute drive to the south. "You can bring him there and they will find him a home."

I couldn't think of any more good excuses to say no so I took the puppy inside. The next day, I dropped him off at the animal shelter.

I often think back to that moment. Jeremy, an addict with a history of trauma and abuse living on the streets, saw in front of him a little dog that was not going to survive without care. Something in Jeremy wanted that tiny dog's life to be better than his. Maybe he saw some of his younger self in that puppy, a child struggling to survive without a safe home or a loving family. Amid his own suffering, Jeremy was present enough to recognize the life and death circumstances that puppy faced, something that mirrored his own living on the perilous streets of Cape Town.

Despite his abusive past, being homeless and hooked on glue, amid an outer context of destitution and violence and an inner reality of deep pain and addiction, he chose to participate in the world in a way where innocence and kindness mattered. In acting according to something so contrary to the violence and abuse he had faced, Jeremy took one wobbly step toward the redemption of his life on the streets, a moment of allowing the door of his heart to be left ajar, if only for a moment. He saw the beauty and innocence that tiny creature represented and made sure the puppy was safe and cared for rather than leaving it to the fate of homelessness, as he had been.

My friendship with Jeremy awakened in me a sense of pleasure in accompanying people on the margins. But there was a part of me that wanted more. I wanted to do something that really mattered. Cultivating friendships with my homeless neighbors and making sure a puppy was safe and taken care of were fine things to do, but in my mind they just didn't matter all that much. I wanted to save lives. My desire was to rescue people in need.

Having grown up in a society that places its highest value on achievement and getting things done, an emphasis on relationship and "being" over rescuing and "doing" made little sense to me then, certainly not in terms of a career of service to the poor, which by that time had become my greatest desire. And the church hadn't offered a vastly different message than society, either. Ministry and mission, as I had been taught, were about helping people in need, doing things for people (usually brown and black people who lived in different neighborhoods or different countries) who couldn't do things for themselves. It was about "us" serving or saving "them."

At that time, I was unaware that the gospel offers an entirely different conception of ministry, mission, and justice than the one I, and most North American Christians, are familiar with.

A SAD Approach

Practical, long-term solutions to poverty and systems of injustice are certainly needed, perhaps more than ever before. North American Christians have the opportunity to interface with Majority World churches, communities, and leaders to establish partnerships that address pressing issues such as access to education, clean water, and primary healthcare services, as well as other types of needed community development and relief programs. Yet much of the current work being carried out by the North American church addressing justice issues in the Majority World are more a reflection of our culture than of gospel-oriented engagement.

Mission tends to look like American society: a race to complete tasks, accomplish projects, and get things done—prioritizing *product* over *process*—rather than bottom-up approaches that prioritize empowerment of the real experts on issues of poverty and injustice—local people. Many are familiar with the Standard American Diet (SAD)—eating food-like substances that aren't really food at all and don't offer any nutritional value, like Fruit Loops, Slim Jims, and my all-time favorite, McDonald's Chicken McNuggets—which the fast food behemoth announced a few years ago are now being made of *real* chicken meat (which leaves one wondering about what they were made of before). Similarly, the typical North American diet of cross-cultural mission is a fast-food style, in-and-out approach driven by speedy results and outcomes. I call it McMission. It has foundations in our culture that is driven by an ingrained desire for achievement and accomplishment. McMission, like the Standard American Diet, consists of utilizing approaches that appear on the surface to be wholesome—sometimes they taste so sweet and look so good—but don't offer much in the way of lasting value.

Christians aren't the only ones implicated in the McMission approach to cross-cultural service work either; people traveling overseas to volunteer or work with secular nonprofits are shaped by the same societal emphasis on getting things done and making things happen. Given that its crux is active participation in the *missio Dei*, mission has the potential to catalyze mutual transformation, both in the lives of the economically poor being served and the relatively wealthy Westerners who are serving. We can be catalysts for bona fide transformation, ameliorating poverty, making disciples, and subverting systems of injustice. But McMission conflicts with this inherent potential since it is more in resonance with American society and often, a mistaken conception of mission, than the gospel. It also aligns more with *missio ego*, the mission of the small self, more than *missio Dei*, God's mission.

An Ego in Haiti

While in Haiti a few years ago, I visited a faith-based community development project run by a physician from the United States, Dr. Michael Miller. Within the few hours it took for us to make the drive from the Port-au-Prince airport to our destination, I began to notice an obvious pattern in his style of relating to others. In his interactions with the people around him—the driver, another passenger, and myself—the doctor was continually speaking in self-aggrandizing ways and bolstering his own importance.

After spending a few days at the project site, it became all too apparent that a major impetus for Dr. Miller to serve in Haiti was his ego. Another name for the ego is the false self or the small self. It can be thought of as the mask we wear or the persona that we project to the world. Seen through a spiritual lens, the ego is the part of us that exists outside the reach of God's love. Thomas Merton calls it a disguise that we tend to worship in place of God.[1] "The false self is bogus more than bad; it pretends to be more than

1. Merton, *Waters of Siloe*, 349.

it is," writes Richard Rohr, who continues, "Various false selves (temporary costumes) are necessary to get us all started, but they show their limitations when they stay around too long. If people keep growing, their various false selves usually die in exposure to greater light. That is, if they ever let greater light get in; many do not."[2]

Wanting so badly to be seen as great, invincible, and beyond fault, Dr. Miller's false self was running the show and impacted the ways he carried out his work in Haiti. He did not have the ability to authentically listen to or be truly present with another person. He lacked the capacity to set aside his own personal agenda. Though somewhere deep inside he had the desire to be a healer—to journey with the marginalized, the sick, the outcast— he clearly had not engaged in the inner work necessary to engage from a place of authenticity. He had not allowed his false self to die in exposure to greater light. He had not undergone the process of coming to know his hidden motivations, pain, and beliefs about who he was. It was evident that he was a stranger to himself—and thus to everyone around him, as well.

The healer did not know that he, too, needed healing.

There were also two young women, twenty-something short-term missionaries, serving alongside Dr. Miller. He played the role of guru to them, holding all of the power and covertly demanding their adulation and praise within a disordered relational triangle—a mix of good intentions, narcissism, and unmet needs.

Besides that, there were the guns. Several attacks on expats and missionaries in the area over the previous few years led the doctor to decide it would be a good idea to have some handguns in the house for protection. But some of them were smuggled in from the United States, others bought illegally in Haiti. Besides that, the young women had never shot a gun before, and from conversations I overheard, were not very eager to learn how to shoot an intruder. Dr. Miller took them out to a nearby field each afternoon for target practice. He even had an acquaintance of his, a police officer back in the United States, take a trip to Haiti to train them how to shoot to kill.

Though this doctor had a bona fide desire to serve the marginalized, his level of psychological functioning led to many dubious actions and harmful relational patterns. His American task-oriented view of mission combined with a debilitating sense of shame and inadequacy were tied to the self-aggrandizing manner in which he spoke and acted, which

2. Rohr, "What Is the False Self?," lines 15–17.

resulted in harming not only himself, but also the young missionaries helping out, as well as the local people living in the community. The doctor's need for dominance and power were linked to this violence so incongruent with the gospel and of making oneself vulnerable to the needs of the economically marginalized. These are the kind of things that happen when the best of intentions are overshadowed by McMission, when *missio ego* eclipses *missio Dei*.

Sadly, Dr. Miller effectively disqualified his potentially beneficial project from being missionally valid, from being in resonance with God's mission. His false self propelled the forward movement not of a gospel-oriented engagement with a devastatingly poor community, but his own narcissistic need for constant validation and to assert power over others, the ego's mission. Eventually, the project he had dedicated himself to had to close its doors, collapsing under the weight of his false self. He ended up leaving Haiti, yet another example of a heart so desirous of serving the oppressed, yet divorced from the self-understanding that is critical in cross-cultural service work.

From its beginnings, Christianity had always been a faith whose locus was reconciliation with God, self, and other people and the radical transformation of individuals and communities. As that original focus was traded in for the dreams of empire, and later an emphasis on individualistic salvation, spiritual formation was relegated to the periphery of the church's great task. As time moved forward and the modern missionary movement came about, the motivation to rescue and save others obscured our own need for transformation, which the gospel invites us into. McMission was born and has been growing up ever since.

As we have seen, the impulse to serve is a natural desire, a corollary of the *missio Dei*. We are wired for compassionate service. But divesting ourselves from the inner spiritual life precludes us from doing helping work in ways that can catalyze real change. Mission and spirituality were meant to be intimate allies, but instead became divorcees. It was this great schism between action and contemplation—one that has persisted into the present, which we will look at more closely in a later chapter—that has made McMission so culturally acceptable.

McMission hasn't been scrutinized or questioned because we are so familiar and comfortable with the American cultural pursuit of progress. It is what we see and participate in every day. Mission work that has the same familiar cultural flavor and scent fits within our expectations and our norms.

Why would something we're acquainted with so well need to be changed or even questioned? After all, what could possibly be amiss with something so well-established?

The Risks of Using (Poverty) Pornography

I recently watched a television feature on the Democratic Republic of Congo. DRC rarely makes the news and when it does, it is usually about the ongoing complex humanitarian emergency in the eastern part of the country, one that has persisted for over two decades and has resulted in more lives lost than in any other conflict since World War II. I figured the program was going to be related to this and was surprised to hear the reporter begin talking about entrepreneurship and movie theatres. The program showcased a Congolese filmmaker, Petna Ndaliko, who is also the artistic director for *Yole! Africa*, the organization he founded to "empower young people to see themselves as agents capable of thinking critically and acting non-violently to shape their own realities."[3] He hosts a film festival each year and has a vision to create a state-of-the-art cinema in his hometown of Goma, the epicenter of DRC's entrenched armed conflict.

When was the last time you saw the words "Congo" and "artistic director" in the same sentence?

We usually don't associate this country, or many other countries in Africa or the rest of the Majority World, as places where social entrepreneurship is thriving, where people are chasing their dreams, where hope is flourishing. That story is rarely told in the West. The media tends to focus on disasters and tragedies. The press sub-Saharan Africa receives has been reduced to about five things: political chaos, war, genital mutilation, child soldiers, and lions. But it can't all be blamed on the media. Another major factor is *pornography*: poverty porn.

The ubiquitous images of the poor seen in so many missions and NGO fundraising campaigns objectify human beings for the sake of eliciting an emotional response, just like real porn, with the exception that its "users" are praised, not told to join an accountability group and confess their failure. Advertising works by eliciting an emotional reaction. Fundraising campaigns do the same thing in order to be effective. It looks something like

3. Ndaliko, "Art of Empowering Youth," lines 9–12.

this: we receive a letter in our mailbox or inbox from a missions organization or relief agency. We open it up and front and center is an image of a black baby in Africa with a distended belly and flies swirling around her head. Seeing the picture gives rise to the feeling of wanting to do something about it combined with a sense of guilt, causing us to reach for the checkbook or type in our credit card number. Now, we feel we've done our part to help, the guilt is relieved and tension reduced as a cascade of neurotransmitters like dopamine and serotonin are released in the brain. Pleasure circuits in the brain light up, similar again to real porn.

There isn't anything inherently wrong with this. Perhaps we should donate, especially to an organization we trust for a cause we are passionate about; that is for each of us to discern. And there is no point in going to war with our neurobiological circuitry; it is simply how our brains are wired.

It is important, though, to identify the degradation taking place, as it does with actual pornography. The poor in the images are objectified, portrayed in a way that makes them objects of our compassion. Objectification strips people of their inherent dignity and worth. It also crushes the image of God within. Poverty porn reinforces stereotypes by telling a skewed story about who people living on the edges really are and labels them as powerless victims who can't help themselves and thus need rescuing. Theologian and philosopher Kierkegaard noted that when you label someone, you negate them. The process of labeling negates individuality and personhood. People in grave predicaments in foreign countries are not powerless, inept, or incapable, passively waiting for rescue.[4]

The West has been shown a single image of Africa and the Majority World. Alongside that has come what Nigerian writer Chimamanda Adichie refers to as the single story.[5] The single image and single story go hand in hand. We are presented with an incomplete picture, an image that both creates and sustains the narrative that the economically marginalized are helpless and need *us* to rescue *them*. Treading that fine line between a candid pictorial representation of the inhuman condition of poverty and the sensationalistic, one-sided narrative that these images articulate is not an easy task. There is a tension between an accurate portrayal of the ignominy of extreme poverty and utilizing the degrading "flies in the eyes" images for fundraising campaigns. Many of these organizations that use these questionable photos in their fundraising campaigns do great work in

4. Gharib, "At What Point Does a Fundraising Ad Go too Far?," lines 15–17.
5. Adichie, "Danger of the Single Story."

some extremely difficult places—there is a difficult tension between telling the facts, accurately depicting the human faces and telling the human story while simultaneously maintaining people's dignity.

Local people know better than anyone else the abysmal nature of poverty and systems of injustice—more so than any Westerner ever can because it is their personal context, not a place they visit. They know intimately the conflicts that rage on their home soil, the food insecurity issues that stunt their children's growth, the lack of means to send their children to school. They also see the vast potential within their communities—again, more than someone from elsewhere can. Local leaders know intimately the latent capacity for radical transformation. And they also realize that the door to liberation opens from the inside out.

Yet, Western journalists and NGOs haven't challenged the one-sided narrative of Africa as a place of hopeless starving people ruled over by ruthless demagogues. And continued growth of international nonprofits has created increasing competition for limited funds. According to the head of a large American humanitarian organization in Kenya, "When you're fundraising you have to prove there is a need. Children starving, mothers dying. If you're not negative enough, you won't get funding."[6]

As activists and development professionals began to critique the latest wave of poverty porn incidents, a few organizations responded by focusing solely on the positive, ignoring the abysmal realities of the places they were working. The single story can quickly swing the opposite way. That is precisely what one-sided narratives do: they bifurcate complex situations into the false opposites of good or evil, poor or wealthy, war or peace, saved or lost, civil or savage, pain or pleasure. To stay in the middle is challenging. To remain in the tension is not an easy task; how much easier it is to narrate only the extremes, to have views that are situated at one pole or the other.

In physics the word polarize means to restrict the vibrations of light to one direction. Something that is polarized—whether an object in physics, an ideology in politics, or an image of a person in advertising or a fundraising campaign—is loaded with energy in a single direction, to either one of the extremes. The single story acts as a gradient that pulls attention toward either one side or the other of these opposing extremes, deliberately utilized to harness either the positive or negative power of a story line in order to fulfill a specific outcome. The NGOs and missions organizations that use humiliating pictures of brown- and black-skinned people from the

6. Rothmyer, "Hiding the Real Africa," lines 62–64.

Majority World to elicit an emotional response are polarizing the narrative to be charged negatively in order to get people to donate. Showing helpless victims awaiting rescue from the West helps them meet their fundraising goals. The NGOs and missions organizations that show only happy-go-lucky brown and black people in their fundraising campaigns and on their Facebook walls are, likewise, polarizing the story toward the positive—a false positivity rooted in ephemeral hope and cheap contentment. This form of the single story is epitomized in the often-used phrase "The people I met were so poor but so happy!" The misrepresented stories about who people are which are told and spoken into complex situations of poverty and injustice are, unfortunately, the norm rather than the exception.

As poverty and helplessness became the single story of sub-Saharan Africa, AIDS, famine, war, and violence became the dominant images that the media, churches, and organizations show us. The single story of Africa is accompanied by images that visually narrate that story. This single story has become the central narrative that guides faith-based sojourners, shaping the ways we view marginalized people.

Seeing the African, for example, as a victim that needs rescuing can reinforce paternalism and ideas about helplessness, which leads to a belief that we must do things *to* and *for* others. At best, this results in projects and programs that are oriented toward charity, rather than biblical justice, which seeks to undermine the very roots of oppression and marginalization. At its worst, harm is inflicted, dignity is robbed, and the opportunity for mutual transformation is forfeited.

Charity and Justice

The word charity has two primary meanings. The first is the American cultural understanding, which involves charitable acts, such as giving handouts to "the needy," money to the homeless, clothes to people who can't afford any, and also includes models of mission based on helping people who lack. The other meaning associated with charity is found in the Book of Acts, 1 and 2 Corinthians, as well as in the Gospels. Here, it is understood as a theological virtue, closely associated with "love." For our purposes, we are looking at the former meaning of the word—charity as a model for engaging social and economic ills.

Engaging in charity-based mission and development work can, at least for a while, seem to be quite efficient and practical—two qualities, coincidentally, highly valued by American culture. However, going beyond a surface-level glance, we soon recognize how limited the "handout" worldview really is. Gena Thomas, author and missionary in Mexico for five years, writes, "Charity makes us Santa Clauses. But then depression hits when our plush red bags have nothing left in them."[7] Charity models often appear to be working according to their Santa Claus–oriented design in which those who have give to those who don't, and those with more help those with less.

Charity is rooted in paternalism. Generally speaking, charity work is unimaginative and not very creative. Mission models based on charity are a dime a dozen. Charity builds a house for a family. Justice engages the root causes of why a family can't afford a home in the first place, advocates and works to create a sustainable way for a family to find long-term housing, and connects the family to other resources they need beyond the housing issue—all of which are generated through relationship and presence.

Biblical justice is rooted in incarnation, radical presence with people who have been marginalized and despised by society. Responding to people's concrete needs through a paradigm of biblical justice is first and foremost rooted in relationship and faithful presence. But the work of justice is more than theological. Justice work is profoundly practical as well. Authentic relationships lead to action that seeks to undermine the systemic structures of oppression that allow marginalization to occur. But justice never does for someone what they can do for themselves. Justice honors the divine image at the heart of every person and works for the irruption of shalom in our midst. Biblical justice is what the kingdom of God looks like here on earth.

Biblical justice is about the creation of shalom and working to eliminate the need for charity to even exist. It is about bringing heaven to earth through power redistribution and addressing the relational roots of poverty. Models rooted in biblical justice refuse to play God in the lives of the poor.

Biblical justice has to do with Jesus. Charity has to do with Santa Claus. And there is no such thing as charity in the kingdom of God.

Story Physics

Newton's first law of motion states that an object in motion remains in motion unless acted upon by an outside force. Something similar can be said

7. See Thomas, *Smoldering Wick*.

regarding narratives. A story that has been told and retold remains in motion unless acted upon by an outside force. This story-in-motion remains in motion, just like the law of physics states for objects, and impacts how we perceive who and what we encounter when our Boeing 777 touches down in Port-au-Prince or Phnom Penh.

An outside force—often a powerful experience of great love, great suffering, or great disorientation—disrupts the motion of the usual story and acts as a catalyst for a shift in perception. The same story that had been narrated countless times and accepted with veracity is now questioned; an alternative is presented where previously none had existed. It is within this space created by the recognition of an additional valid narrative that the danger of the single story is mitigated.

How I see myself is based on stories I consistently tell myself about who I am. How I view another, whether my wife or best friend or the naked man begging on a Mumbai street corner, is directly correlated to the narrative that is operating inside of me—perhaps below the surface of the conscious mind—that tells me who that other person is. We make sense of the world through storytelling. We make meaning through narrative—and we have a choice in the stories we tell and thus the meaning we make.

Stepping back from the need to perform acts of charity, achieve "great things for God," make a difference in the world, or save the "lost" creates the space to begin engaging our personal assumptions, biases, and beliefs as well as the collective cultural milieu. Without entering into those places and bringing what has been hiding in shadow into the light, we forfeit the hope of leaving our inner colonialist behind and actually participating cross-culturally in ways that are good for us and those we want to see flourish. We cannot be catalysts for authentic change unless the McMission archetype shifts into something more sustainable and more holistic, consisting of the real thing rather than an imitation.

Recognizing one-sided narratives and the images that go with them and staying in the tension between the polarization is a place to begin, wherever we find ourselves, which can help facilitate one of the most important aspects of mission rooted in a framework of biblical justice: listening to the stories of local leaders who are deeply invested in their communities. Between the negative charge and the positive charge, we find space for authentic relationship based on mutuality. Entering this place is the cure for the single story and helps cross-cultural servants become aware of the stereotypes and misconstrued understandings we often impose onto places and people we are unfamiliar with, whose stories we don't intimately know.

Petna's wife, Dr. Chérie Rivers Ndaliko, said, "It's incredible to see people . . . who have no sense of confidence, no sense of their own self-worth because they have only seen images of themselves that portray them as worthless. It's incredible to see what happens when they learn they can tell their own story and in their version of the story they can be the hero."[8]

The hero, not the helpless victim.

To see someone in that light means first naming our desire to play the role of hero and savior—a role that the single story claims we can be.

How (Not) to Be a Savior

Not long ago I came across the website of a faith-based organization working toward access to clean water in the Majority World. Apparently, they were holding a contest to win a trip overseas. It read:

> Contest for a Trip to Africa
>
> Have you longed to travel to Africa?
>
> Would you like to change people's lives forever?
>
> How about saving lives?
>
> A six-night all-expenses-paid trip to Africa and a rainwater-harvesting tank with YOUR name on it!

People in many areas of the African continent, particularly south of the Sahara, do not have access to clean water. It is one of the persistent global inequities that continues to persist, catalyzing morbidity and mortality at alarming rates. There are some stellar organizations doing incredible work to change this, work they have learned to do well because they understand the particular contexts in which they are working and partner directly with local leaders and local organizations. I am not very familiar with the ins and outs of how the organization running this contest approaches clean water projects, but their marketing strategy reveals a great deal about the single story many North Americans have been told—and so continue to re-tell—about Africa and Africans: it's a place of miserable poverty that needs

---

8. Ndaliko, "Film Students in Congo."

saving. And we can save it, all the while getting credit for it by claiming ownership of the project.

This marketing material is playing directly into our deep need to have meaning and purpose in our lives, as well as our desire for ownership. "A rain-water harvesting tank with YOUR name on it!" Having our name on it fulfills the need for ownership, which is a balm to the ego's sense of insecurity. The message this organization is giving is, "Hey, this is your opportunity to be the savior of Africa," while tacitly communicating underneath that, "And then you can feel good about yourself. Then your life can be meaningful. Then you will matter to the world." But it's all a facade, because a water tank with our name on it cannot fill our deepest needs.

We can't save lives here in North America. We can't be white saviors in our own white culture. The nagging sense of purposelessness that commonly haunts us is given the analgesic of an opportunity to rescue, to save—and thus to matter. It makes us feel better about who we are. This advertisement is doing what any other form of good advertising does: touching a deep human need and promising fulfillment of that need through the product being offered. Except in this case, it isn't that drinking a certain type of beer will make a man desirable to a beautiful woman or the new car that will bring a sense of adventure and freedom from the daily grind. This organization's trip to rescue the poor, save lives, and provide clean water is framed as being part of the gospel, of the narrative of God's redeeming work in the world, when in reality, it is much more about getting our own needs met. It is a promise that we can attain a sense of self-worth through becoming a savior, a dangerous message that, once again, is not centered on God's mission but the ego's mission.

By helping, we feel better about ourselves, relieve existential anxiety, and strengthen our egos—all in one fell swoop. We call it sacrifice, leaving the comfort of our homes and families to enter places of entrenched poverty. Indeed there is a sacrifice at play, but it's not what we think it is. If we haven't looked deeply within ourselves, we can end up sacrificing the marginalized on the altar of our own unmet needs and participate in McMission rather than *missio Dei*.

Missio Dei Meets Missio Ego

Witnessing poverty, disease, and oppression affects us, all of us. The most common experience is a sense of compassion for the individuals who are encountered living in squalor and inhuman conditions. Often this feeling is combined with a strong desire to do something, to alleviate some of the suffering. These emotions and the desire they give rise to are a very good thing. The desire to bring justice is a profoundly sacred desire that wells up from deep within which can lead to acts of mercy and a commitment to expand one's concept of the truly cruel nature of poverty and injustice. When we talk about going somewhere to serve the poor, we often speak about our willingness to suffer on behalf of others, to sacrifice our lives for those who live in the anguish of poverty—a holy desire that rises up from the divine DNA that forms the spiritual substrate of our beings. Yet, the ways in which we respond to this impulse aren't as unblemished as the desire itself. Helping work carries with it a shadow side, something we must engage if we are to participate in cross-cultural work in mutually transformative ways resonant with the gospel and *missio Dei*.

The energy moving within the "helper" to alleviate suffering often turns into an action that unwittingly results in two consequences. First, it may unintentionally create harm to the vulnerable population. But it often does more than just that. At a psycho-spiritual level, participating in mission relieves the helper's guilt, and sets their own psyche free through the declaration that "I did my part. I helped someone who needed it badly. I bought medicine for a sick man. I bought a meal for a beggar. I held babies at the orphanage. I helped build a house for a poor family." It is all about *me*.

The helper is now free from a psychological standpoint. They feel good about themselves. Their ego is satisfied. Back at home in North America, they are wondering when they can get their next week off of work or when their next church mission trip is, so they can go back to Nicaragua or Kenya and see their new "friends" who they "fell in love with."

I have a friend who works for a large international faith-based NGO. One day, we were discussing short-term mission with a group of Seattle-based leaders. The participants were offering their thoughts on short-term missions, why they do and don't work well, and how we can reshape and reimagine mission to be more in line with the gospel. My friend said, "But short-term mission works for us. For those going, it works." He is right. In many ways short-term mission offers many benefits for those traveling, including exposure to the inhumanity of poverty, a new perspective on suffering, and experiences that can invite us into deeper commitments to global justice. Yet, exposing ourselves to poverty for an experience of growth isn't necessarily mission at all if it doesn't align with the *missio Dei* and God's dream for restoring the world. In many circumstances, mission trips shouldn't be labelled mission at all. Perhaps service learning or volun-tourism would be more appropriate. It isn't mission unless it squares with the mission of God.

So how do we know if what we are doing squares with God's mission? What is the litmus test?

Asking ourselves a few simple questions can be extremely helpful in discerning this: Does it actively promote the coming of shalom? Is it about relational flourishing and the restoration of all things? Does it carry the scent of humble service on behalf of others?

Or is it more aligned with the small self and getting our needs met? Is it more about the whole condescending to serve, save, and sacrifice for the broken? Does it seem like charity or biblical justice? Does it carry the flavor of *missio Dei* or *missio ego*?

These are just a few of the questions we can ask each other and our-selves as we wrestle with the tension between being motivated by God and true self as opposed to something else. It can also be helpful to remember that the major problem with *missio ego* isn't so much one of character or morality; having mixed motives is normal and natural in human beings, and the call isn't to do things perfectly. Rather, the main issue with *missio ego* is that it isn't imaginative enough. It isn't creative enough. And it isn't in resonance with God's dream for the world.

Being outside our everyday lives working on behalf of the oppressed is a poignant opportunity for the recognition of what remains undealt with inside of us. That may be the ways we crave power and control, our in-ability to see the marginalized as anything but helpless, our deep sense of shame that we constantly defend against, or the covert racism that we have been socialized into without knowing it. Spending time across cultures can become an opportunity, a gift, a blessing for us—the ones who are serving, whether we label this work "mission" or something else—in its ability to plunge us into an encounter with ourselves as we truly are, not as we'd like to be. As we saw with the physician in Haiti, the falsity in us has a way of rising potently while overseas serving in contexts of poverty.

Facing the reality that my own participation in mission was more complex than a straightforward desire to serve the hungry, the homeless, and the sick was profoundly painful work. I had resisted the truth to such a degree that it wasn't until I reached the precipice of emotional and spiri-tual collapse that I began to turn and look at my inner world. After leaving

South Sudan over ten years ago, I entered an intense time of self-reflection that included psychotherapy and spiritual direction as I tried to navigate all that was unfolding in the inner landscape of my psyche and soul. It felt like the axis upon which my life had been rotating had begun to wobble and shake, threatening to launch me into an abyss.

Therapy and spiritual direction provided the safe space for me to begin to open up with an honesty I had rarely before articulated, divulging the utter disarray of my interior life and the profound sense of futility I had about being a missionary and aid worker. I began to consider for the first time that I had a compulsive need to do mission work that was rooted in a profound sense of personal inadequacy. Mission had given me a sense of identity. I didn't know who I was without it—I was a missionary or I was nothing at all.

This plunge into emotional and spiritual bankruptcy were the consequences of my unwitting involvement in McMission motivated by *missio ego*. The unmistakable call I felt to help the poor when I was a young boy began to pivot. The centrifugal movement outward, serving in difficult places around the globe, was shifting toward the inner landscape of the soul and into coming to see what had remained hidden inside of me—which we will look at in more detail in the final chapter.

Reflection Questions

1. McMission is more in resonance with the mission of the ego (the false self) than the mission of God. In your own work, where have you witnessed or participated in McMission?

2. It is tempting to want to be the hero in the story. Can you recall a time in your life when you were the center, the savior, the hero? How did it make you feel?

3. When you see images characteristic of poverty porn from various NGOs or missions organization, what is your usual response? How do images of the poor and "the single story" of poverty and helplessness impact your decision-making process regarding where to give?

5

Poverty, Shame, and Creation

> But the poor person does not exist as an inescapable fact
> of destiny. His or her existence is not politically neutral,
> and it is not ethically innocent. The poor are a by-product
> of the system in which we live and for which we are re-
> sponsible. They are marginalized by our social and cul-
> tural world. They are the oppressed, exploited proletariat,
> robbed of the fruit of their labor and despoiled of their
> humanity. Hence the poverty of the poor is not a call to
> generous relief action, but a demand that we go and build
> a different social order.
>
> —GUSTAVO GUTIERREZ

Psyche, Meet Pneuma

IN THE BEGINNING WAS a watery void, formless and deep. "Earth was a
soup of nothingness, a bottomless emptiness, an inky blackness."[1] The
creation poem at the beginning of the Hebrew Scriptures paints a picture of
a place devoid of life. Soupy. Empty. An abyss.

The verse continues, "and the Spirit of God was hovering over the
waters."[2] God's Spirit was present in the chaos. The watery void of nothingness wasn't all there was. There was more; God was attendant in the
very midst of this barrenness. In the next verse, God speaks into the chaos,
saying, "Let there be light." With these words, light and life, form and order
emerged right within the watery blackness.

---

1. Gen 1:2 *The Message*.
2. Gen 1:2 NIV.

Cosmos had entered the chaos.

The Spirit in the Greek version of this text is called *pneuma*, which translates as breath. It was the breath of God that hovered over the lifeless void, the breath that animated the dark waters with a life it had not yet known. The Spirit was the catalyst for life in the place of not-life. There is an interesting linguistic link between *pneuma* and another Greek word, *psyche*, which in ancient Greek philosophy meant "the breath of life." It loosely translates to English as "soul" and is the root of the word psychology. The original Greek meaning of psyche didn't refer to the mind as we understand it now. The original understanding of psyche incorporated the energy that animated all of life, the deep, mysterious core essence of humans. The ancients differentiated between that which was living and breathing and that which was lifeless, between the animate and the inanimate, between life and *not-life*.

The creation account in Genesis gives a rendition of God's first creative movement that initiated the life of the cosmos. This creative act was the divine breath infiltrating the dark formlessness and infusing it with life; the old gave way to the new by the breath of God. Simultaneously, the creation story also speaks of a broader pattern of life emerging in darkness, of the Spirit who hovers over the spaces of *not-life* in the world, in communities, and in people, renewing, enlivening, and animating.

New Creation

It was sweltering hot in the backseat of the little black Nissan Sentra where I sat. Through the windshield I saw six heavily armed soldiers in full camouflage. The high-powered rifles they carried made an AK-47 look like a kid's BB gun. The soldiers walked past the car and approached two young men standing there idly. One of the soldiers motioned for them to put their hands on the adjacent cement wall while two others patted them down.

The gang that controls this community is known to be one of the most violent on the planet. The local community leader who took me there wouldn't even utter the name of the gang aloud while in the neighborhood, a place that neither the police nor the military dared to patrol just a few short years before.

A hundred feet away was the school we were going to visit. Inside, thirty young children were coloring and drawing, their bright white collared shirts somehow still sparkling clean. The classroom was inundated

in the energy of youth, children laughing and smiling with a glorious innocence, two teachers and an assistant guiding their lesson. It looked like
it could be any other classroom in Latin America, except for one thing:
the children there are the daughters and sons of gang members. All of the
teachers and staff are from the community where they work. Many of them
grew up a block away. The teachers don't just have relationships with the
students, but their parents—the gang members and their partners, as well.
Their whole life is here, amid the violence and chaos of this place where
soldiers with gigantic guns patrol day and night and gang members have as
much power as the police.

The organization which I was visiting facilitated the birth of this
community-based education project led by passionate local leaders
through a grassroots, bottom-up approach. Their presence in the community is hidden almost, barely perceptible amid poverty and violence,
an incarnational presence that reflects the *missio Dei*. It is also a project
that would have been impossible for someone from out of the area to start;
without intimately knowing the community, having key relationships with
the main stakeholders—the gang members and their spouses—someone
from outside simply wouldn't have the sort of relationships needed to
launch such a project. Leveraging local relationships, knowing the power
brokers, and having one's whole life invested in the neighborhood were
prerequisite for this shalom-catalyzing project to be born.

The director of the organization, a Salvadoran man who had facilitated
the creation of the school, gave me the opportunity to bear witness to the
good that comes when the assets of the materially poor—their relational
networks, expertise, passion, and integrity—are identified and purposed
for the work of community transformation from the inside out.

These local people are, in turn, birthing expressions of the gospel in
rooted, incarnate, concrete ways. Seeing this made me wonder what kind
of imaginations they have that can hold a vision of transformation, of
light coming into the soggy barrenness of violence. Right in the midst of
the chaos of poverty and spilled blood, they attend to what matters most.

In every neighborhood torn apart by poverty and violence, there exists something else beyond the harsh realities that are so difficult to see past.
There is something besides the chaos and void. The Spirit is there, hovering.
God is present, working through people like these local leaders, animating
life through faithful presence, bringing cosmos to the chaos. God remains
at work generating order out of disorder. The creation story continues, even

with soldiers patrolling, gangs in gun fights, economic destitution doing all it can to quench the soul's life and overwhelm the spirit's breath. Empowered by the Spirit of God, these courageous women and men hover over the chaos, the watery void of entrenched poverty and endemic violence. They are choosing to prophetically participate in the dire realities of life in their community with the creative animating force of *pneuma* and *psyche*, divine Spirit breath and human soul together in concert, their work a tiny, almost hidden nexus point joining heaven and earth.

Life is emerging in places of *not-life*, which means creation isn't yet finished.

Ongoing Creation

Pierre Teilhard de Chardin, a French Jesuit paleontologist, wrote, "The world is still being created, and it is Christ who is reaching his fulfillment in it."[3] The universe is not yet complete. The world is still being made. Christ is still being brought to fullness in humanity and creation through the restoration of all things. Cosmos continues to be brought forth from the chaos of poverty, violence, and trauma. And we exist in the tension of it all, between the already and the not yet of the kingdom of God. Reimagining our participation in God's mission toward human flourishing and the restoration of all things means not only engaging story over strategy and process over product, but participating in the ongoing creation of the world.

Science tells us that the universe is continuing to expand. Quantum physics reveals that everything in creation is in a process of becoming, a cosmogenic echo of Paul who wrote, "The new creation has come: The old has gone, the new is here!"[4] All things are being made new and God is at the heart of this process, energizing it from within. The universe and everything in it is bending toward completeness in Christ. "In Christ you have been brought to fullness. He is the head over every power and authority."[5] Science affirms these deep intuitions of Christianity. The universe isn't simply matter, but matter that is filled with spirit. As Rohr writes, "Nature clearly renews itself from within. *God seems to have created things that continue to create and recreate themselves from the inside out.*"[6]

3. Teilhard de Chardin, "Cosmic Life," as cited in Rossiter, *Shadow of Oz*, 69.

4. 2 Cor 5:17 NIV.

5. Col 2:10 NIV.

6. Rohr, "Creation Continues."

This inside out creation and recreation is how the process of the reconciliation of all things unfolds. It is emerging through Christ who underlies the whole process. Everything is reconciled in Christ. God holds all things together in him, as Paul again put it.[7] Though a cosmological scope may not ordinarily be considered in regard to mission and justice work across cultures, when we're talking about the restorative mission of God, we are inextricably referring to cosmology, the development and *telos* of the universe and where it is all heading in Christ.

Rohr again articulates an important but usually overlooked aspect of the new creation: the difference between "Jesus" and "Christ," a helpful reminder of the origins of our faith tradition, and why it matters for us today:

> On the day of Pentecost, after recognizing the eternal presence of the Holy Spirit, Peter stood up and proclaimed that God "had raised up Jesus" to reveal him as the Christ (Acts 2:32, 36). This is a different way of thinking for most of us, I suspect. Jesus and Christ are not the same; Christ is the much larger and older frame. The three synoptic gospels (Matthew, Mark, and Luke) are mostly talking about Jesus, the historical figure who healed and taught. Paul never met the historical Jesus and hardly ever quotes Jesus directly. In almost all of Paul's preaching and writing, he is talking about the Eternal Christ Mystery, rather than Jesus of Nazareth. . . . Let me put it this way: Christ is a word for the macrocosm, Jesus is the microcosmic moment in time, and all else is the cosmos—including you and me. You inherently belong to Somebody that is going somewhere! This provides ultimate and deep meaning for human existence. It settles the mind, heart, and emotions.[8]

This settling Rohr speaks of also relaxes the compulsion to serve, save, and sacrifice. It lessens the need to feel important and the compulsion to achieve. It eases the desire to create others in our own image and places us within a Christology that is orthodox, biblical, and largely overlooked. We follow the example and witness of Jesus of Nazareth, emulating how he lived, how he engaged in mission cross-culturally, how for Jesus the inner work and outer work were one work. We follow Jesus, and we belong to Christ, as Rohr says, the Christ who is heading somewhere, giving our lives inherent meaning while simultaneously revealing that our outward engagement to bring about transformation in the broken world is led by Somebody, is the ultimate work of Someone who existed from the beginning.

7. Col 1:16–17.

8. Rohr, *Moving from Jesus to Christ*, lines 1–6, 13–15.

"In the beginning was the Word, and the Word was with God, and the Word was God. He was with God in the beginning. Through him all things were made; without him nothing was made that has been made. In him was life, and that life was the light of all mankind."[9] Creation itself came about through Christ and in Christ and for Christ. Nothing exists outside of Christ as "the firstborn over all creation."[10]

Belonging to Christ means we are in Christ, through Christ, and for Christ and so participate in the ongoing creation of the world that Christ leads. The universe is heading somewhere and you and I are an integral part of that movement, that becoming. It is why we do mission. It is why we seek justice. It is why we desire flourishing for all of creation.

As Rohr noted, Paul never met the historical Jesus. And even though Paul wrote over half of the New Testament, he rarely quoted Jesus directly. Paul focused on the Eternal Christ mystery more than the man from Nazareth. The way Paul understood Christ reveals something about Paul's whole aim in his missionary journeys—how Paul understood Christ shaped Paul's self-understanding in mission and his evangelism goals in the empire.

Love as the Substance of the Universe

In his letter to the church in Corinth, Paul wrote, "If I speak in the tongues of men or of angels, but do not have love, I am only a resounding gong or a clanging cymbal. If I have the gift of prophecy and can fathom all mysteries and all knowledge, and if I have a faith that can move mountains, but do not have love, I am nothing. If I give all I possess to the poor and give over my body to hardship that I may boast, but do not have love, I gain nothing."[11] Love was the key to Paul's understanding of the Eternal Christ, of the becoming of the cosmos, of the restoration of all things—and thus how he understood mission and his role as missionary.

Love was at the center.

Love was where everything was headed.

Paul goes on in his letter to the Corinthians, "Love never fails. But where there are prophecies, they will cease; where there are tongues, they will be stilled; where there is knowledge, it will pass away. For we know in part and we prophesy in part, but when completeness comes, what is in part

9. John 1:1–5 NIV.

10. Col 1:15 NIV.

11. 1 Cor 13:1–3 NIV.

disappears. When I was a child, I talked like a child, I thought like a child, I reasoned like a child. When I became a man, I put the ways of childhood behind me. For now we see only a reflection as in a mirror; then we shall see face to face. Now I know in part; then I shall know fully, even as I am fully known. And now these three remain: faith, hope and love. But the greatest of these is love."[12] For Paul, love was the center of history, the end point of the cosmos. When completeness comes, Paul was saying, love will be how we know it. And movement in the direction of that completeness comes through transforming love—which is inseparable from the mission of God—upon which all of Paul's missionary work rested. Each one of us, regardless of where we live or the sort of work we do, is invited into this same sort of mission propelled by the "greatest of these," love.

Talk of love can come across as impractical, an ideal that cannot be concretized into action. It can seem very abstract. Love as an idea is sometimes misappropriated and spiritualized into impotency. Yet, we are reminded that "God is love."[13] Self-emptying love, or *kenosis*, is the very shape of the Triune God. The Trinitarian doctrine that underlies the whole of Christian theology reminds us that

> if we are to believe the Judeo-Christian Scriptures, then the Trin-
> ity—a circle dance of flow, communion, and relationship—which
> is the very nature of God, is the template for everything created
> (see Genesis 1:26–27). Every created thing is the self-emptying of
> God. God is constantly outpouring. The Father, the Son, and the
> Holy Spirit can trust that self-emptying, knowing that the space
> created will be filled. Like a waterwheel of divine love, the Father
> empties all of himself into the Son. The Son receives and empties
> all of himself into the Spirit. The Spirit receives and empties all of
> himself/herself into the Father. The Father receives and the cycle
> continues. . . . I can let go, because I trust I will always be filled up
> again. That is the pattern of reality.[14]

When the actions we partake in on behalf of other people are sourced from love, what we do is more than what we do: it is what God is doing in and through us. We are participating in the self-giving action of Trinity, moving along the Trinitarian shape of life.

---

12. 1 Cor 13:8–13 NIV.

13. 1 John 4:8.

14. Rohr, "Self-Emptying," lines 8–13.

The path of love is a downward path into the messiness of relationship, the earthiness of biology, the mundaneness of daily life. Loving means going down into the grit, not up into the spiritual, disembodied realm. Teilhard understood love not as a spiritual essence, but as the physical substrate of the universe itself. The world, Teilhard said, was animated by love. He goes on to say, "Driven by the forces of love, the fragments of the world seek each other so that the world may come to being."[15] Rohr describes Teilhard's understanding of the nature of love as

> the cosmic allurement of everything toward everything, a structural, metaphysical shape to the universe, most visible in the basic laws of gravity, electro-magnetic fields, and sexual reproduction. And yet there is a constant price that must be paid to be faithful to such foundational love. Everything is also fragmented and fighting this very process of reunification. For Christians, this resistance is symbolized by the cross. There is a cruciform shape to reality, it seems, and loss precedes all renewal, emptiness makes way for every new infilling, every transformation in the universe requires the surrendering of a previous "form." Nothing in the human psyche likes this pattern.[16]

Making All Things Whole through Love

"Those who follow Jesus," wrote Franciscan sister and professor Ilia Delio, "are to become wholemakers, uniting what is scattered, creating a deeper unity in love."[17] The deepest call of Jesus followers is to be wholemakers— acting in ways that bring about the wholeness that underlies the fabric of the cosmos. We seem separate but in our roots we are part of an indivisible whole.[18] There is an integral connectivity that links us. If this is how reality is construed—through a substrate of love, a fabric of connection and deep unity—than participating in mission as if this were true means looking at our task differently, through the lens of the hidden wholeness that exists in Christ prior to and beneath all things. Jesus followers are tasked with intentionally participating in completing the world; mission is nothing less than action toward the fulfillment of the cosmos itself. The

---

15. Teilhard de Chardin, *Phenomenon of Man*, 164.

16. Rohr, "New Cosmology," lines 9–15.

17. Delio, "Love," as cited in Rohr, "Whole Making," lines 21–22.

18. Delio, *Emergent Christ*, 29.

reconciliation of all things is not only a possibility, human flourishing is not only an idea, shalom not a mere word to be adopted, but realities ingrained in the fabric of creation itself.

Placing ourselves in alignment with the shape of God and thus the shape of the universe itself so that we may be conduits of shalom means bringing together the inner and the outer. It means reintegrating contemplation and action. Our logical Western-trained minds say prayer and work, spirituality and ministry are distinct, autonomous aspects of life, but that is a fairly new invention based on Western philosophy and Greek metaphysics, based on the thought of Descartes and Plato more than Paul and Jesus.

What would happen if we began to reimagine mission as relationship in which we recreate each other through a deep mutuality? Participating in the ongoing creation of the world through mending and being mended, healing and being healed, becoming wholemakers as we are being made whole?

This missional spirituality is radically grounded in materiality while simultaneously oriented toward a cosmological horizon that is coming to us from the future, a future in which "Christ is all, and is in all."[19] We experience a foretaste of that eschatological future in the present. From the very heart of reality itself, from within the messes, the brokenness, and the tragedy, Christ redeems, restores, reanimates, and resurrects. The world is being reconstituted, day by day, moment by moment, breath by breath, to reflect the new reality which Jesus referred to as the kingdom of God. It is all heading into renewal. Every act of peace, each move toward courage, every act of selfless love is an act of new creation, small and often unnoticed perhaps, but powerful nonetheless as it is a participation in God's being. In this way we don't merely believe in God, worship God, or work for God, but we participate in God's life.

The biblical text, from Genesis through to Revelation, reveals the idea that creation is being redeemed and restored, wholeness is coming into our midst, and completeness in Christ through love is the telos of history.[20] If this pattern is real and if creation is ongoing, what is the power that refutes it, that blocks the movement into wholeness and restoration, of the kingdom of God realized in fullness? If Christ underlies the fabric of the cosmos and if history is bending toward completeness, why are violence, poverty,

---

19. Col 3:11 NIV.

20. Deut 7–9; Prov 3:3–4; John 4:9–12; 15:9–10; Mark 12:29–31; Rom 13:8–10; 1 Cor 13:13; 16:14; Eph 4:2–3; 1 Pet 4:8; Col 3:14; 1 John 3:16–18; 4:7–11, 16–18.

despair, and suffering so acute and powerful? What is fighting the process of reunification and completeness in Christ? Despite God's continual pulling of humanity and all of creation toward redemption and flourishing, everything is fragmented. A force seems to be battling this process of re-unification in Christ.

Looking again to Genesis, we find some hints that reveal something about the enemy of the ongoing creation.

Un-creation

In the beginning, Adam and Eve existed in a state of connection and union with each other, God, and creation. In the garden, "Adam and his wife were both naked, and they felt no shame."[21] Upon eating the fruit from the tree of the knowledge of good and evil, which the serpent tempted them with, they realized their nakedness, covered themselves with fig leaves, and hid from each other and from God. They were no longer okay with their creatureliness, with who they were as humans. The serpent—later in the biblical text named as Satan—tempted Adam and Eve by comparing their worth to that of God, communicating the lie that they were deficient at the core of who they were. This caused the couple to view their humanity as defective and lacking, whereby they could not trust the goodness of themselves as humans, nor the goodness of God.[22] Eating the fruit had relational consequences, rupturing the once complete union between each other, God, and the created order. The self-image and self-understanding of Adam and Eve regarding who they really were was perverted due to shame. This story reveals shame as a mechanism that has infected humanity from the foundations of the world.

Brené Brown has been instrumental in raising popular awareness of the toxic effects of shame. Shame tells us that we are unworthy of connection, that we are deficient and lacking at our core and are thus precluded from the love and belonging that we so desire.[23] Shame casts a dark shadow of separation in the relational realm through the voice of accusation, "You are not worthy of love, belonging, or connection."

Brown's qualitative research linking shame and connection can be traced back to the story of Eden. When shame came into the picture, the

21. Gen 2:25 NIV.

22. Sphar, "Theology of Shame," 65.

23. Brown, "Power of Vulnerability."

relational connection was ruptured, the interpersonal bridge shattered, the divine union splintered. Where unity and connectedness once governed, separation became the new relational foundation. Shame stripped Eve and Adam of their previous sense of being okay with who they were created to be in the image of God. And following the archetypal first humans, each one of us likewise hides from each other and from God, believing that we are unworthy of mutually satisfying relationships, unfit for intimacy with the divine.

Shame is multifaceted. It involves relational disintegration, emotional dysregulation, and has powerful neurobiological underpinnings.[24] When someone is experiencing shame, the body and brain undergo impressive biochemical shifts. Shame hijacks the limbic system, the emotional seat of the brain. Access to language is also limited since the neocortex, the higher region on the brain that regulates speech and rational thought, is restricted. A feeling of exposure and smallness takes over.

Besides an acute feeling state, shame can also become a perpetual feature of personality structure which shapes a person's self-concept. This leads to a way of being in the world, a way of inviting others to be in relationship with you.[25] When shame becomes the core of a person's identity, rejection of the self results.[26]

This in turn brings about relational schism, leaving one in an isolated state of hiding like Eve and Adam in the garden. With this new distorted sense of identity catalyzed by shame, the relational rupture was cemented into the order of the world, and each generation to follow the first man and woman were destined to live into this same mechanism, one generation after the next, ruled by shame's insidious messages of unworthiness and unacceptability. Psychiatrist Curt Thompson names shame as "the emotional fulcrum around which the history of sin rotates, the fundamental source, harbinger and herald of what is to come."[27] Not only is shame emotional and relational, it also has a kind of telos, "a purpose in a larger narrative, an interpersonal neurobiological instrument that is intentionally and skillfully used to distract and disrupt the story God is telling."[28]

24. Thompson, *Soul of Shame*, 106.
25. Allender, "Shame."
26. Bradshaw, *Healing the Shame That Binds You*, 158.
27. Thompson, *Soul of Shame*, 99.
28. Ibid., 80.

It is shame which interrupts the ongoing creation of the world. Shame suspends the in-breaking of shalom through relational rupture between God, self, others, and creation. It wants nothing more than for heaven and earth to stay apart, for broken relationships to undo the mending God desires, the mending we are participating in. Shame attacks shalom. Shame interposes its false narrative onto the narrative of God through its anti-creation energy. Christian tradition points out that the source of "original sin" is found in the story of Adam and Eve eating the forbidden fruit. Another way to describe original sin is "original shame." Due to the disobedience of humanity's father and mother, each and every person is born into a world at war with shame, the energy that battles reconciliation, peace, flourishing, and the completeness of all things in God's shalom. Each of us knows what this feels like. We know shame in our bodies, in our brains, in our thoughts, in our relationships. We are like Adam and Eve. And we exist at the center of the point of opposing energies: un-creation (the energy of shame) and creation (the energy of love, which is God). We are the present-day Adams and Eves, the current generation, born east of Eden, outside the garden, toiling and struggling with shame's toxic effects.

Shame is a de-creative force. It takes order and turns it into chaos. It takes beauty and soils it with despair. It gives rise to contempt directed at self and other. Shame toils to destroy what has been made, all that God calls good. And no one escapes shame's power. Even the most confident, successful, and ethical people have hidden battles with shame.

Poverty and Creation

Seen through the story of Genesis 1, it isn't difficult to perceive how shame is implicated in issues of global economic injustice. Poverty doesn't act alone—shame is one of its key teammates. Poverty is "the result of relationships that do not work, that are not just, that are not for life, that are not harmonious or enjoyable. Poverty is the absence of shalom in all its meanings."[29] At its core, poverty is rooted in a web of disempowering relationships and systems that interact with one another, creating an inescapable situation. Disempowerment and internal oppression result from blaming oneself for conditions of poverty which leads to a shame-based identity. This in turn catalyzes a

29. Myers, *Walking with the Poor*, 86.

pattern of further disempowerment, blame and more shame, all of which reinforce the cyclical pattern of poverty.[30]

Internalizing poverty and the messages of non-value from the non-poor result in a poverty of being,[31] a shame-based identity, where people believe the lie that they are worthless. Both an individual and communal sense of unworthiness, alienation, despair, and self-rejection—the symptoms of shame, the primary driver of relational rupture—result. Augustine Musopole, a Jesuit priest from Cameroon, hints at this pattern in the African context: "This is where the African feels his poverty most: a poverty of being, in which poor Africans have come to believe they are no good and cannot get things right."[32]

If poverty is ultimately relational, the result of disempowering relationships between people, we can use this information to inform how we participate in mission and ministry. Since the roots of poverty lie in the soil of broken relationships, any worthwhile engagement with the poor will be informed by relational restoration that intentionally remains aware of the centrality of shame in marginalized communities.

Social and economic change occur locally within specific neighborhoods and communities. Looking at the interactions between persons with other persons at a grassroots level, within the interconnected, interdependent nature of a specific place, we see that "manifestations of suffering are present at the collective, relational and personal domains . . . At the collective level, poor people in the [global South] suffer from two sets of devastating experiences: (a) insecurity, chaos, violence, and (b) economic exploitation."[33] As people in poor communities struggle to survive, their social relations explicitly suffer, marked by fragmentation and exclusion.[34] Given these crippling realities—which are inflicted socially, relationally, and personally upon the inhabitants of highly impoverished places—approaches that seek to disrupt these maladaptive patterns of interpersonal and intrapersonal engagement are needed.

Shifting from vulnerable people blaming themselves for their circumstances to an indictment of broader societal injustices that impact the community as a whole as well as individual families and persons is a first step. It

30. Christian, *God of the Empty Handed*, 60.

31. Myers, "Poverty," line 102.

32. Musopole, "African Worldview," as cited in Myers, "Poverty," lines 102–6.

33. Nelson and Prilleltensky, *Community Psychology*, 189.

34. Ibid., 190.

is a trajectory change from one of shame and self-judgment to a judgment of the systemic power structures that provide the framework for this type of suffering to endure. Explicitly linking personal suffering to the external factors of oppression and exploitation is a key part of this task.

Since disempowerment and internal oppression result from blaming oneself for conditions of poverty, helping to facilitate a shift in judgment from individuals to the systems of injustice is a prophetic task. It centers on judging the principalities and powers, struggling "against rulers, against authorities, against the powers of this dark world and against the spiritual forces."[35] To begin to notice that which is difficult to see, to recognize the powers which keep people poor and, more importantly, to enter into relationships with economically marginalized persons in ways that directly shift judgment from them to the powers that bind is integral to the task of mission and justice.

One of the most profound forms of suffering for the poor in both history and Scripture is shame.[36] Shame wants nothing more than to maintain its underlying emotional dysregulation and narrative of unworthiness in order to thwart the narrative of God's kingdom of emotional, physical, spiritual and relational flourishing. How we address shame in the communities we serve is a core question for Jesus followers. If we aren't aware of how systems of dominance of the past and present have controlled people's bodies and consciousness and made them prisoners to shame, we may unwittingly perpetuate them. Asking how we can directly confront shame and internalized forms of oppression in our work across cultures is a key question.

Different contexts require different responses. There is no one-size-fits-all approach to fighting against the shame that underlies poverty. Beginning to stand in awe regarding what the poor are forced to carry is a starting point.[37] Releasing judgment and intentionally shifting blame away from individuals is in and of itself a movement toward seeing the inherent dignity within brokenness. Our compassion for suffering is not revealed in how we serve as much as in how we see ourselves, in our own way, also as poor, broken, and wounded.[38] The "us" and "them" posture begins to disintegrate as we recognize our own shame and welcome the brokenness within ourselves.

35. Eph 6:12 NIV.
36. Nolan, *Jesus before Christianity*, 22.
37. Boyle, "Barking to the Choir."
38. Ibid.

Colonization of Consciousness

Bryant Myers, professor of transformational development at Fuller Theological Seminary, tells a story of a time when he was sitting around a campfire in the Kalahari Desert. In response to hearing the news that the Son of God had died for her sins, he heard an indigenous San woman say that she could believe God would let his Son die for a white person and that perhaps she could believe that God may even let his Son die for a black person. But she could never accept that God would let his Son die for a San.[39]

Let's look at that again: she is convinced Jesus would die for a white Westerner and even a black African, but not for an indigenous San. In essence, she is saying that white people are most worthy of salvation, blacks somewhere below that, and San utterly unworthy. Remember the bartender in rural South Africa from chapter 2 who said that there were no black people in the region before white settlers came, only the Bushmen (San) were there? Both the bartender and the woman from the campfire scene understand her identity in the same way: as less than human. He spoke of the Bushmen as being less than black people. Her reply reveals the very same belief.

Why is this?

How does this deepest level of poverty that penetrates into the core of a person's identity get lodged there?

We know that colonization causes systemic ruptures in indigenous societies. The settling of the southern tip of Africa by the Dutch, followed by the British, and later governed by the apartheid system, colonized millions of people. But colonization doesn't end at the level of physicality. Its control goes beyond the body. The final frontier of the colonial project is the colonization of consciousness. Its aim is to convince people to no longer believe that they're people.[40] This final stage of colonization happens when oppression is internalized. That is precisely what we hear in the San woman's words at the campfire, she and her people having internalized the message of being subhuman, one that originally came from the European colonialists, the echo of which can be heard in the bartender's words. The evils of colonization come from the outside, like a virus, and infect the inside of a person, a village, a city, a nation. This is a sure sign of the forces of

---

39. Myers, *Walking with the Poor*, 129.
40. Twiss, "Colonization of Consciousness."

un-creation that conflict with God's purposes and act to thwart the ongoing creation toward shalom and flourishing for all.

Among the Dead

The biblical text highlights this strong agent that opposes the coming of the kingdom. In Mark 5 1:11, Jesus approaches a demon-possessed man who had been living among the tombs of a burial ground. Upon seeing him, the man asks to be left alone. Jesus responds by asking what his name is. The possessed man replies, "Legion." Jesus then casts a demon out of him and into the swine standing nearby. At the time, legion was a term used for a battalion of Roman soldiers. A demon-possessed person with the name Legion was someone who had been occupied by Roman imperial powers. This story subversively illustrates that colonization bears the quality and likeness of demon possession; to be colonized is to be possessed by an evil spirit.[41]

The Roman occupation of Judea led to this geopolitical context where a human being annihilated by imperial forces was living among the dead, both his body and consciousness colonized by Rome. In casting the spirit of Legion into the swine, Jesus was casting out the spirit of Rome and its powers of subjugation.[42] This story reveals that to have one's consciousness colonized is to be possessed by energies which are not of God. To be seized by empire is to be infected by a colonial infliction that "possesses" the entirety of a person—body, mind, soul, consciousness. To be free of the demonic in this sense is to have the image of God reemerge from its crushed state. Jesus' response of freeing the man highlights the radical subversion of colonization—and all other life-destroying forces—that he stood for.

As we saw earlier, Jesus lived and ministered under the control of Roman authority, was labeled a criminal, tortured, and nailed to a colonial execution stake. Crucifixion, the instrument of Rome's imperial control, became through Jesus' death a great paradox of the Christian faith. What once symbolized the empire consciousness of Rome was transformed in Jesus' death into an anti-empire icon. Jesus' resurrection from the dead revealed that the powers of empire and forces of death were no match for the power of God. God's life overcame empire's violence. In Jesus, the tool the Romans used to colonize people groups, individual bodies, and

41. Dube, "Talitha Cum," 125.
42. Ibid.

consciousness was transformed into the most powerful anti-colonial icon in the history of the world.

The imperial church that institutionalized colonialism missed this, blinded by the desire for land, wealth, and expansion of the crown's territory. And if we recall the papal bulls and the Doctrine of Discovery, we remember how church leaders authorized dehumanization by theologizing non-white, non-Western, non-Christian human beings into nonpersons in order to justify the colluding aspirations of church and state. That doctrine never died; it simply went underground, showing up in other forms, continually being resuscitated in contemporary iterations.

Tragically, that doctrine is alive and well, generating more shame and cementing the identities of "nonpersons" consigned to "nonhistory," like the San woman in the Kalahari. Her consciousness had been crusted over with layers of colonization, which gave rise to personal and collective shame specifically targeting her ethnicity. She had come to see herself as less than human and her people as ethnically inferior—to the point of being unworthy of Christ's redemptive death and resurrection.

The San woman and her people had been "torn away from [their] past, propelled into a universe fashioned from outside that suppresses [their values], and dumbfounded by a cultural invasion that marginalizes [them]. They had become the deformed image of others."[43] Colonization and its final stage, the colonization of consciousness, are the fertile soil in which shame reproduces, generating non-value to nonpersons.

As we have seen through the narrative offered in Genesis, following the creation of the heavens and the earth, God made human beings in his image, where they lived in a state of connection and union in Eden. They were naked and knew no shame. After eating from the tree, shame entered their beings and this connection was severed. Eve and Adam hid their nakedness in fear of each other and God. As we flip ahead to the Gospels, what we find is a strikingly similar story: a man named Jesus, who is called the New Adam, hangs on a Roman execution stake, a method of torture and death specifically designed to shame and humiliate—a tool used to turn persons into nonpersons. At the culmination of the ages,[44] he sacrificed himself to these powers of violence and death so that humanity would never again be enslaved to the forces that de-create the world. He is there utterly exposed for

---

43. Hoff, "Scramble for Africa," lines 8–10, quoting Edem Kodjo.

44. Heb 9:26.

all to see, and makes no attempt to cover himself up or hide. He is nailed to a tree, limp and bloody, allowing passersby to gaze deeply into his eyes.

The New Adam is naked and knows no shame.

Reflection Questions

Imagine sitting together with the San woman on the parched, red-hewn earth deep in the Kalahari Desert of Botswana. You hear her voice tremble as she says, "I believe that God would let his Son die for a white man. Perhaps I could even come to believe that God would let his Son die for a black man. But I can never accept that God would let his Son die for me, a San."

1. What do you feel inside as you hear these words? How do you reply to her? How do you think she came to believe this? What events in her life may have contributed to her belief that white people are most worthy of God's sacrifice, black people second, and San not at all worthy?

2. If you were sitting around that campfire and could speak her language, what questions would you ask her? What aspects of her life and her story do you want to know more about?

6

Crossing Borders

A natural effect of the missionary outlook of modern times was a certain tendency to confuse their institutionalized Christianity with Christ, to make the former the bestower of salvation.

—KWAME BEDIAKO

Unclean

DIFFERENTIATING BETWEEN WHAT WAS clean and unclean was an important facet of Jewish identity, especially for the Pharisees, who were preoccupied with making sure that they, and everyone else, followed the rules regarding handwashing and dietary restrictions with scrupulous precision. The Pharisees taught a brand of Judaism based on these rigid codes of purity, corroborated by their interpretation of the Hebrew Scriptures. In order for a person to be moral and right in God's sight, they had to follow the letter of the law.

Jesus reframed these same Scriptures and throughout his ministry we see examples of him reframing tradition itself. He broke cultural taboos when he called a tax collector to be his disciple. He negated natural law by multiplying fish and bread and by walking on water. He even tore down the divide between divine and human within himself, being fully God and fully human at the same time. It seems as though the entirety of Jesus' ministry focused on abolishing falsely constructed boundaries.

Whenever the Pharisees encountered Jesus, there was usually some sort of friction. They were constantly battling his apparent disregard for the long-held religious purity codes and accused him of breaking the cultural norms and traditions. One of these debates turned into a heated argument when a group of Pharisees noticed that some of Jesus' disciples were eating with defiled hands. They confronted Jesus and his disciples about it, asking why they did not follow the traditional practice of hand washing prior to eating. Jesus replied with a quote from Isaiah, calling them hypocrites for clinging to stringent tradition instead of the true commands of God.[1] He explained why all the purity laws weren't the thing to be obsessing about and told them that they were missing the point regarding what constitutes defilement.

The Pharisees were more concerned with their traditions regarding purity than with following God's commandments. They were following a brand of Judaism made in their own image, according to their own need for legalistic purity, which was not God's desire. The Pharisees were more concerned with religious practices that suited their own need for outward perfection rather than the inner state of the heart. Jesus responds that it is what comes out of rather than what goes into a person that matters to God.

Not long after that fiery encounter, Jesus traveled outside of Jewish territory for the very first time. He walked with his disciples into the land of the Canaanites, a people group who lived to the north of Galilee and worshipped a deity called Moloch. They were viewed by the Jews as an utterly despicable bunch, detestable to the point of being barely human. It was common for the Jewish people to refer to them as dogs. In order to differentiate themselves as much as possible from these religious and ethnic outsiders, the Jewish people would not eat some of the things that the Canaanites ate, including pigs and other animals with split hooves, weasels, mice, lizards, and chameleons. The people of Israel, like many religious and cultural groups both past and present, formed their collective identity to a large degree on who they were not, on differentiation from the other tribes and ethnic groups in the ancient Near East. "We don't eat that stuff because we are not like *them*. We are different. We are God's chosen people, special, set apart, unique."

As Jesus and his disciples arrived at their destination in Canaan, a woman showed up and cried out, "Lord, Son of David, have mercy on me! My daughter is demon-possessed and suffering terribly."[2] When she stopped speaking, Jesus' disciples asked him to send her away because she was an ethnic and cultural outsider. There are some textual intricacies in the passage that are beyond the scope of what can be addressed here, but

1. Mark 7:1–20.
2. Matt 15–22 NIV.

suffice to say, Jesus ends up healing her daughter in response to her plea, and in retort to the disciples' admonition that he make her leave since she wasn't a Jew and she didn't worship the God of Israel. Healing this woman, the first time he healed anyone outside of Jewish territory, sent a message to his disciples about the utter absurdity of religion that put up boundaries by labeling who is pure and who is impure, who is in and who is out, who belongs and who doesn't.

Just prior to Jesus' encounter with this woman in Canaan, he had been with the Pharisees, debating their view on purity, showing them that they were being blinded by their focus on categorizing according to the labels clean and unclean. Now, in Canaan, he was recapitulating a similar message with the disciples as his audience—this time regarding the notion of ethnic purity rather than handwashing rituals—teaching that one culture or ethnicity wasn't more pure or better than another, and that erecting that type of boundary was not the way of God. Jesus was saying, "There is no place in the kingdom of God for this. There is no place for this type of worldview that does nothing but create suspicion and fear. None of this is what I am about. It's not what my mission is about. In fact, my mission isn't even just about the Jews. It's about all the Gentiles, too, all people, every nation, even those who you have feared and loathed, those you thought you were holier than, purer than. Even those who you have for generations called dogs and seen as less than human, I tell you, they are as pure as any, including the Jewish people."

Why was Jesus able to do this, to see the world this way, while the Pharisees, and even his own disciples, were blind to it?

It wasn't simply because he was the Son of God who was without sin. Jesus knew where he came from. He was intimately aware of the biases and assumptions that he had been socialized into. He knew his own social and cultural location as a Jewish man. He had an awareness of the lens through which the Jewish people saw religious and ethnic difference.

Jesus knew himself. Jesus knew where he came from. The disciples had attempted to interact with the Canaanite woman according to their limited, ethnocentric worldview, proclaiming who was in and who was out based on culture and ethnicity. Their Jewish socialization had left them with bias—as all socialization does, then and now—that made them consider Canaanites inferior to Jews. They had assumed as a result of their upbringing that ethnicity was a marker of purity: they were the in-group, the divine elect, and faultlessly observing the law was the most important aspect of their religious practice. And there in Canaan, a cross-cultural setting in which emerged this encounter with the Other (the Canaanite woman), Jesus had a contrary message: "All those who you say are *out*, are actually *in*. This woman who you call defiled? She belongs. The very ones you judge as less than human because of their peculiar culture and foreign ways of thinking and believing are loved and accepted just as much as you Israelites, every bit as much as my chosen people. God's kingdom, the very one you're going to help me infuse to the ends of the earth, is about inclusivity, not exclusivity. It's not based on exclusion. It's based on embrace."

Cross-Cultural Discipleship

The word disciple in Greek, *mathétés*, means a pupil or learner. In the ancient world, a disciple was a student of a religious teacher. In the Jewish tradition, that meant a rabbi. A student of a particular rabbi would learn their lifestyle and their way of interpreting the Hebrew Scriptures.

Discipleship was very common in the ancient world, so when Jesus began his ministry around the age of thirty with a dozen pupils at his side, it wasn't anything out of the ordinary. His twelve students left their jobs and families, dedicating their lives to following him and learning his ways. Not only was Jesus' ministry about healing, preaching, and performing miracles, he was also teaching his students. He intentionally, like all rabbis did, brought them into a process of theological and spiritual formation. He used real-life moments throughout his ministry to teach his students about themselves, their worldview, the people they interacted with, as well as their future ministry. Jesus was training them for mission.

The majority of Jesus ministry took place within areas primarily inhabited by Jews. The encounter with the Canaanite woman was of particular significance because it involved encountering the ethnic and religious Other in a cross-cultural setting. The disciples witnessed Jesus act contrary to what their expectations were in terms of social norms. Their asking Jesus to send her away because she was different from them would not have shocked Jesus; refusing to interact with Canaanites was the norm for Jews. It highlighted the bias that Canaanites were impure, defiled, less than fully human.

I imagine how incredulous they were when Jesus, instead of honoring their request, continued conversing with her and, even more shockingly, healed her daughter. Doing this would have been earth shattering for the twelve because it completely breached the norms of how Jews were to relate with Canaanites. It was downright taboo to engage with a Canaanite in such a manner, let alone a Canaanite woman! I imagine some of them thinking, "What are you doing, Jesus? Why are you treating her, a dog, like one of us? Stop wasting our time."

This was a powerful teaching moment for the disciples, witnessing Jesus subvert age-old cultural expectations. It would have disrupted their worldview and planted seeds for how they would come to understand the Other. It was a definitive moment in their life of discipleship, a formational experience that shaped their own approach to mission in the following years, as they embarked on their own ministries, revealing to people the radical inclusivity of the kingdom of God. Many of them would soon go on to cross ethnic, racial, and cultural boundaries to carry the message of good news beyond Israel's borders. Jesus' interaction with the Canaanite woman was an important moment in which those who the disciples had viewed to be on the outside, impure, and defiled were actually worthy to receive all Jesus had to give. In was a harbinger of the kingdom as a reality in which every dividing line would be torn down, every notion of inferior/superior revealed for the illusion that it ultimately is. Purity laws would be abolished. Ethnic divides deemed heretical. Belonging based on ancestry considered sacrilegious.

Encountering difference often brings up anxiety. When racial, ethnic, cultural, or religious difference is encountered, it can be perceived as a threat which leads to a feeling of anxiety in our bodies and minds. Since humans have an innate tendency toward reducing anxiety, no matter what the source, we tend to utilize common psychological mechanisms, usually unconsciously, to mitigate that anxiety. One of those strategies is to turn away from difference. Another is to try to change the Other to look like us. Turning away in flight, or eliminating the threat by changing it to look like us, both function as anxiety-reducing strategies that provide a salve to the brain and body. They make us feel better as the perceived threat subsides.

In Canaan, the disciples wanted to turn away from the difference presented in the face of the woman. Jesus was likely standing face to face with her and the disciples would have been observing closely, even though they wanted nothing to do with her. In listening to the woman's plea, in choosing to hear her out, Jesus was sending a message to his students: "Don't allow your judgment of difference to rob you from being present with the person in front of you. Stay with the discomfort of difference. Don't flee from it. Don't levy your own limited understanding on the human face in front of you. Don't fall to the temptation to send someone away because of the difference you see and the discomfort that arises. Don't try to change her to look like you. Stay present."

Coming *to see how we see*, developing greater awareness of the subtle ways we view difference, can become a spirituality of encounter, a practice of mindfulness toward our responses and unconscious reactions to the Other. Our encounters with the face of those who are different from us in every way possible can become a spiritual practice through cultivating a deeper awareness of the strategies we may be utilizing when faced with difference, unconsciously turning away from or attempting to modify the Other to reflect us. As disciples ourselves, cross-cultural encounters lead us into disruptive and beautiful experiences that form us, that shape us, and that mold us to choose to respond as Jesus did.

The American Jesus in Nicaragua

Not only does encountering the Other invite us into formation, encountering Jesus—particularly how we see Jesus through a cultural lens—can shape us to respond in gospel-oriented ways while doing the work of mission and justice across cultures. Steven Prothero wrote, "To see how Americans of all stripes have cast the man from Nazareth in their own image is to examine, through the looking glass, the kaleidoscopic character of American culture."[3] American culture has a Jesus and Jesus has an American culture. We have seen in Jesus an expression of the fears and hopes of ourselves and our nation.[4]

Not long ago, I met a newly married couple from Texas, Adam and Beth. They told me about the short- and long-term missionary work they had done in several Latin American countries. Curious to learn more about their approach, I asked about how they engage cultural differences in their work. Beth replied, "We try to bring Jesus, not American culture." Her response alluded to some level of recognition of difference between Jesus and American culture. As we pressed a bit further into the conversation, however, it became clear that despite a basic understanding of culture, she didn't recognize how much her perception of the gospel was shaped and constrained by it.

As we continued to talk, Beth and Adam touched on a very common assumption widely held by North American Christians—including myself

3. Prothero, *American Jesus*, 9.

4. Ibid.

for a large part of my life: the God of Jesus Christ is not present and active in some places and it is our task to "bring" him there. Yet, the Spirit of God is *already present* before we arrive. Many theologians and lay people, from both the Majority World and the West alike, have noted that God is already understood and apprehended before missionaries arrive in a place.[5] Wherever we go in the world, God is already there. We don't bring God or Jesus anywhere. It is quite an arrogant assumption to think that God has forsaken a place before *we* arrive. The Spirit had been, and continues to be, active in each and every place this couple had visited, present and breathing new life amid the pain and inequity.

Our task is to discern the particular ways the Spirit is at work locally and participate in that, to join in what God is already doing in communities and neighborhoods around the globe. The task of the missionary is to discern how local expressions of both faith and culture have embedded within them bridges to the message of the gospel and the kingdom of God as well as a continuity with the biblical text. Having eyes to see the connectivity present between Christian and traditional/animist religion is foundational in approaching the work of discipleship. As we discern the presence of the Spirit, we bear witness to the irruption of the kingdom into our midst, not *despite* the particulars of culture, but precisely because the gospel has the power to transform human life in all cultural particularity and diversity. We go—or more appropriately, we are sent—not to bring Jesus to anyone but, rather, to discern where God is active and faithfully attend to the divine presence catalyzing life, and then discern appropriate ways to join what God is already doing in a particular place.

Nicaragua, the country Beth and Adam were visiting regularly, is a predominantly Catholic Christian country. The vast majority of locations that Western Christians visit in the Majority World, whether it be a country in the Caribbean, Latin America, Africa, or Asia, are populated by Christians. The majority of local people have already been exposed to the gospel message in some form. Yet, many faith-based sojourners tend to see themselves as the bearers of salvation, that their role is to reach "lost" people who must listen to their message, which brings up a series of questions, such as:

Is it our assumption that Catholics aren't *real* Christians?

Is it our view that local people must express Christianity as we do back home?

5. Bediako, *Theology and Identity*, 9.

Is it our assumption that Christ isn't active before we arrive bearing the message of salvation?

Do we believe that indigenous expressions of Christianity are in error?

Looking again at Adam and Beth, the Jesus they assume they are "bringing" to Nicaragua is a very particular form of Jesus. As Michael Rynkiewich observes, engaging the thought of H. Richard Niebuhr, "There is no culture-less Christ."[6] Jesus doesn't exist separate from culture. There isn't culture over *here* and Jesus over *there*, so it is impossible to "bring" Jesus and not bring culture. The Jesus we believe in and follow is not apart from culture because humans are not apart from culture.

Adam and Beth were bringing *American Jesus* to Nicaragua.

American Jesus is a very specific Jesus created in the image of American Christianity, rooted in our social and political context, just as Imperial Jesus was created in the image of Caesar and the Roman aristocracy. For example, conservative evangelical Christianity in the United States, which is as much political as it is faith-based, is largely aligned with right-wing agendas such as support for the National Rifle Association, the death penalty, and tax cuts. But if we look at conservative evangelical Christianity in, say, the Netherlands, it looks quite different. They don't support gun ownership because guns are only permitted for hunting and target practice, not self-defense. Dutch evangelicals don't prioritize the same things or have the same hot-button issues as American evangelicals. Gun rights, the constitution, and the flag are not pillars of conservative evangelicalism in the Netherlands as they are here, which means that Dutch Jesus looks different than American Jesus. Dutch Jesus isn't pro-gun or pro-Trump or in favor of corporate tax cuts or against universal healthcare. Dutch Jesus isn't patriotic like American Jesus; he doesn't carry a gun or a flag or fight for a certain interpretation of the Constitution of the Netherlands. Where we stand on political issues isn't what this conversation is about, however. It is about becoming aware that we have one specific view of Jesus, a deeply cultural view, not the only one or the right one or the best one.

Just as the Pharisees wanted their faith to be a reflection of them rather than God, American Jesus can make our faith more a reflection of our cultural conditioning—us—rather than God. There isn't a need to escape this, but rather an awareness of our cultural conditioning and how that impacts our form of Christian faith.

---

6. Niebuhr, *Christ and Culture*, as cited in Rynkiewich, *Soul, Self, and Society*, 40.

Culture is like a lens through which we view our world—and our Jesus. The Jesus that Adam and Beth "bring" to Latin America on their trips is not necessarily Jesus revealed in Scripture, but the Jesus made in the image of American nationalistic evangelicalism—in their case, even more specific: Texas Republican Jesus. Since Adam and Beth didn't recognize that Jesus is always located within culture, despite their best of intentions, they were participating in mission in an ethnocentric way, something we all perhaps have done in one form or another. Ethnocentrism involves evaluating other cultures according to our own. Ethnocentrism assumes—often unconsciously—cultural superiority. It was precisely what lay beneath Jewish attitudes toward other people groups, including the Canaanites.

The gospel is a summons for all people and all cultures to repent and look more like the kingdom. Ethnocentrism is also a summons, one that mandates the culture of the Other to convert, trying to remove the speck in another's eye while ignoring the log in its own. Ethnocentric postures in cross-cultural service work can be difficult to confront in ourselves because they usually exist below our conscious awareness.

In today's postmodern, pluralistic, and multicultural environment, ethnocentrism tends to be implicit rather than explicit. It is something we tend to be unaware of until we begin confronting it.

Adopting a posture of humility with regard to unfamiliar religious and cultural practices is a requirement of following Jesus, something that is transparent in the Scriptures. "And what does the Lord require of you? To act justly, to love mercy and to walk humbly with your God."[7] Humility goes hand in hand with the work of global mission and justice. Being humble, rather than ethnocentric, isn't optional; it is what God requires. Humility can help us see that we have one specific view from one specific point, not *the* view from *the* point. Just as Jesus invited his disciples to see beyond their own ethnocentrism, Jesus continues to invite us into this posture today.

"Christ is the humility of God embodied in human nature; the Eternal Love humbling itself, clothing itself in the garb of meekness and gentleness, to win and serve and save us,"[8] which Paul spells out in his letter to the church in Rome: "For by the grace given to me I say to everyone among you not to think of himself more highly than he ought to think, but to think with sober judgment."[9] Pride is the enemy of humility. Pride lies at the root

7. Mic 6:8 NIV.

8. Murray, *Humility*, 17.

9. Rom 12:3 NIV.

of the ethnocentric position of evaluating cultures based on our own. Pride acts as a blinder to wisdom, that is, to seeing, knowing, and acting according to the divine. As Proverbs 11:2 illustrates, "When pride comes, then comes disgrace, but with humility comes wisdom."

Awareness of the cultural lens through which we see is an indispensable facet of humble service in mission and ministry. The self that enters into mission is not just a physical, psychological, and spiritual being, but a cultural being as well. Formation and preparedness through developing cultural intelligence and intercultural competency allow those doing the work of mission and justice to be more beautiful embodiments of the gospel.

Hindu

When I was living in Kolkata, India, I spent each day at one of Mother Teresa's homes for the sick, Prem Dan, which means "A Place of Love." The Missionaries of Charity sisters brought to the home severely ill women and men from the streets, caring for them until they either recovered or died. One afternoon, I sat on a cot with one of the men, a Hindu, whose condition had been rapidly deteriorating. His gaze became distant and his breathing shallow and rapid. I held his hand as he approached death's door. A few minutes later, one of those rapid gasps of air became his last.

Before this experience at Prem Dan, I had never known any Hindus. I had rarely spent time with people, at home or overseas, who followed a religion different from my own. With its peculiar deities—one with a human head and the trunk of an elephant, another with ten arms—and names like Shiva, Vishnu, Ganapati, Hanuman, and Kali, Hinduism was the religion of the Other. I had heard pastors and various Christian leaders speak of how spiritually heavy and dark India was. Before leaving for India, an acquaintance who had visited previously wrote me an email in which she described how much evil was in the religion and Hindu people, suggesting that I prepare myself for encountering that. As I remember, she quoted Ephesians 6:11 about putting on the armor of God. I did put on some kind of armor, but it certainly wasn't the armor of God, rather the armor of vigilance and anxiety about what I was about to experience, who I was about to meet, and how I would be received.

India and its people are dark, evil, and spiritually heavy?

Hinduism is of Satan?

Where did these commonly held assumptions come from?

There has been a historical pattern in world mission involving suspicion of cultures different from ours—just like we saw with Jesus' disciples in Canaan. That bias of the past has been carried forward into the present in very concrete ways, claiming subtly or overtly, that white is better, that the West is the measuring stick, that American Jesus is *the* Jesus, that the unfamiliar customs and traditions of black and brown people are inferior. The bias can be challenging to see and confront because it is often implicit rather than explicit, hidden rather than out in the open, often operating just below our conscious awareness. Implicit bias is what lies at the root of ethnocentric tendencies.

Implicit bias isn't so much an individual moral failing as it is a systemic issue; we are products of our society, of our social location, of our history. It is a fact of what it means to be a white North American. It is part of the narrative we've inherited from the empire, from Leopold, from the Doctrine of Discovery, from our collective colonial past that has been tacitly passed down, generation to generation, arriving in our midst and shaping how we think about difference and the ways we respond when we encounter difference face to face. It also shapes everything from the way we think about the materially poor, about black- and brown-skinned people, about *us* being whole and *them* being broken. This, not surprisingly, is a legacy of the colonial era, when indigenous peoples all over the world were seen as inferior and erroneous, and told that they had to divest themselves of their modes of cultural expression if they were to be followers of Jesus. This is part and parcel of the narrative that we, the missional people of the twenty-first century, have inherited. It is one that has led many well-intentioned Christians to come to the conclusion that cultural differences become null and void when it comes to the gospel of Jesus Christ.

North Americans also tend to view dark-skinned people whose language and religion we don't understand as the ultimate Other. The acquaintance who had emailed me and the church leaders I had heard were, rather than confronting the anxiety that Indian Hindus were bringing up in their bodies and minds, translating that to suspicion, leading them to use the labels "evil," "dark," and "heavy."

Humans tend to label difference they do not understand; it is far easier to label and turn away from difference—or try to change difference to reflect us—than it is to name and stay present with. If we don't choose to turn away—like the disciples tried to do in Canaan by "sending her away"—we tend to want to change people to look like us. Remaining with peculiarity and difference, listening to the stories of the Other, and allowing for the anxiety we feel is the path forward which Jesus revealed in Canaan.

Mutual Conversion

Jesus was after the transformation of people's hearts and lives and the conversion of society to align with the kingdom of God. He continually taught about what authentic conversion was all about. In Canaan, it was his disciples who needed conversion as much as anyone. Through Jesus remaining with the woman, being present with her, listening to her, and healing her daughter, the disciples' eyes began to open. This moment wasn't just about the woman or her daughter. The disciples were shown how the kingdom works and what is important in the mission of God.

Prior to the encounter with the woman in Canaan, the Gospel of Mark tells of a Jesus who understood his mission to be primarily for the Jews. The Jews were first, the Gentiles—everyone else—second. Following this incident in Canaan, the Gospel of Mark shows that Jesus never again oriented his ministry, or even so much as spoke of his mission, as being primarily for the Jewish people. He had crossed a major geographical, cultural, ethnic, and religious boundary by going into Gentile territory for the very first time. Jesus' encounter with this woman who didn't eat, think, act, look, believe, or worship like him catalyzed a shift in his own self-understanding of what the remainder of his ministry and mission would look like.

Cross-cultural mission changed Jesus, the disciples, the Canaanite woman, and her daughter. A robust mutuality based on shared humanity was realized. There was no *us* and *them*, only *us-in-difference*—together witnessing to and receiving the kingdom of God, which is what true conversion is always about.

It is right in the midst of glaring differences in ethnicity, race, religion, and the age-old suspicions they often give rise to that God works, that the kingdom unfolds, that shalom is born. True unity, as opposed to homogeneity, is realized in difference. Yet, the *us* and *them* sentiment does not shapeshift into *us-in-difference* automatically, without a catalyst, a stimulus for the shift to occur. More often than not, the catalyst doesn't come by way of thinking over new ideas or going about daily routines. It comes when we least expect it. By surprise, we are taken by an event, an occurrence, an encounter—something that disorients. It comes by way of experience, especially the sort that disrupts.

Disorienting experience can disturb us to a degree that the Spirit can breathe new life and speak new words about what it means to be human, what it means to be a follower of Jesus, and what it means to love the Other cross-culturally. These experiences, often disguised as trespassers in our well-defined plans and goals, become the unwelcome guests essential to facilitating the inner change, the conversion God is moving us toward. It is precisely at the point when our old belief systems are shaken that enough space opens up within us that we become malleable to the point where God can gently bend us to look more like Jesus, including theologies that move us toward mutual transformation, rather than places of suspicion and judgment, to be in deeper resonance with the moral arc of the universe that is forever bending away from ethnocentrism and into justice.

Belief

Beliefs are integral to the Christian tradition. They reveal through language and symbol and metaphor who God is. Yet, it is easy to mistake belief *in* something for that something itself, as the saying, "The finger that points to the moon is not the moon," expresses. The Christian tradition is rooted in a system of beliefs which acts as the finger pointing beyond those very beliefs, doctrines, and dogmas and toward God.

With regard to the work of mission and justice, the God our beliefs point us toward is a God who is bringing about shalom for all of creation. But often, belief seems to exist for its own sake rather than for the sake of the world. It is very easy to fall into the trap of believing in our beliefs rather than allowing belief to move us toward loving others and acting for justice. There is a constant temptation to focus on and even worship the finger (our beliefs) rather than the moon (God). One of the great gifts of mission is that it will—if we let it—explode our old, limiting beliefs and show us less of our finger and more of the moon.

Belief can become an idol that can easily, though inadvertently, take the place of the divine.[10] Disruptive encounters with religious, racial, and ethnic Otherness in the context of cross-cultural mission can shock our firm beliefs that have become idols into moving into more fluid theological and spiritual forms from which God can bend us into persons who are more loving, mature, and alive and move us toward new horizons of what it means to be a Christian and an advocate for the poor. God is in the business

10. See Rollins, *Idolatry of God*.

of disruption, but not for disruption's sake, not to confuse or cofound. God disrupts in order to bless.

Faithfulness to the biblical text—reading and interpreting with a lens for justice and of the coming of shalom—combined with embracing our embodied experiences, is what God often uses to bring his people forward on the journey of spiritual formation. It is dangerous to only sit around and talk about doctrine and dogma, salvation and mission, and not be out in the world living and risking and witnessing to the diverse ways the Spirit is present and active. The open heart is the one that gets cracked open more and more, the one that bleeds and heals, suffers and mends. It is the heart of flesh that is the heart alive. The closed heart is the one that is convinced it understands everything, certain it has God completely figured out, and has reduced the unfathomable Mystery to a box that it can fit inside. This is the heart of stone that suffers not and risks not, the cold granite that is impenetrable and unbreakable. C. S. Lewis put it a thousand times more elegantly: "Love anything and your heart will be wrung and possibly broken. If you want to make sure of keeping it intact you must give it to no one, not even an animal. Wrap it carefully round with hobbies and little luxuries; avoid all entanglements. Lock it up safe in the casket or coffin of your selfishness. But in that casket, safe, dark, motionless, airless, it will change. It will not be broken; it will become unbreakable, impenetrable, irredeemable. To love is to be vulnerable."[11]

Rather than allowing Christ to shape our beliefs, we tend to let our beliefs shape our Christ. This results not in faith born of the radical love of God, but in belief that provides a security blanket of certainty and control. Beliefs are necessary and can help orient us in an uncertain world. But mistaking our beliefs *about* God for God can also further solidify the stone rather than have it burst open and return to flesh. Beliefs held with a tight fist, separated from embodied experience, often create more stone. Tightly grasped beliefs are not malleable or fluid, meaning they readily turn into ideologies. An ideology is a specific set of concepts, assertions, and opinions that inform an individual or a group. An ideology is one view from one point. Ideologies are not bad or wrong, however, they can turn into impenetrable systems of self-justifying beliefs. Ideologies often seek to prove themselves right and are not open to be being transformed or converted; they only want to be correct. Ideologies aren't made of flesh. They are not about the divine story and the interpenetration of Word and flesh.

11. Lewis, *Four Loves*, 169.

Our authentic self, others, and God can be effectively sealed off by faith-based ideology that grows forth from the skin of the finger that is pointing to the moon, the finger that comprises the doctrine and systems of belief that were designed in the first place by our tradition to help us see, know, and experience God. Belief readily moves us toward ideologies whereas faith, real faith, moves us toward the love of God and others.

Beliefs are the starting point of the Christian faith. Moving toward more mature expressions of the faith, however, means going beyond the stage where belief is divorced from embodied experience. Spending time serving across cultures provides the context for these disruptions to occur and move us toward knowing God more fully. Embodied encounters that interrupt us and threaten to shake our theological underpinnings are a phenomenon inherent to the nature of cross-cultural mission—and that is an absolute gift. It is through these experiences that God offers us an opportunity to open our hearts—to be more flesh-like—and for the stone of ideology to further disintegrate. But the opportunity is missed if we think we need to hold to our carefully laid out set of ideas about who God is, who we are, and who the other is. Many return home after their ten-day or ten-month trip, inspired by how happy the poor were who they met and helped out, relinquishing the gift of disruptive experience that is so often before us when we are confronted with radical difference in terms of race, ethnicity, religion, and culture.

Politics of Ethnicity

Exploiting racial and ethnic diversity for personal and political agenda is more potent and widespread today than at any other point in history. One of the most egregious examples of the death and destruction that it can lead to occurred during a three-month period in 1994, when nearly one million people were killed during the genocide in Rwanda. One hundred days of slaughter—neighbor killing neighbor, fellow church members slicing each other, cousins hacking each other with machetes. The violence was perpetrated along ethnic lines, Hutu against Tutsi. Yet, there wasn't a generations-old, entrenched animosity between the two groups. They lived together, spoke the same language, married one another, and worked side by side for hundreds of years.

During the period of Belgian colonial rule, the Tutsis, regarded as the superior group by the Belgians, were arbitrarily given preference by the imperial government and artificially extracted from a long-standing, peaceable existence with the Hutus. Animosity developed once their ethnic differences were politicized. Many Hutus felt disenfranchised both in the colonial period and in the years following independence from Belgium in the 1960s. Thirty-two years later, close to a million Tutsis lay dead.

When the threat of Otherness is combined with political motive, violence often ensues. Jesus knew that. He saw that cultural, ethnic, and racial differences were, and would continue to be in the future, exploited for personal and political gain. It is how power operates in the sociopolitical realm: taking advantage of difference and politicizing it to exploit Otherness for power and privilege. Difference is leveraged for the aims of one group over against another. Ethnic difference is sometimes viewed as a threat because of the social and political leverage gained when it is artificially *made into* a threat, which puts the more powerful, privileged group in the place of oppressor. It is never ethnic identity *per se*, but the politics of fear and the anxiety caused by difference that contributes to dehumanization.

Honoring and embracing diversity in terms of race, ethnicity, and culture is central to the kingdom of God. Confronting the barriers to that within ourselves and in our churches and society is a task that isn't optional as the presence of shalom depends on it.

Reflection Questions

1. Recall a time when encountering difference brought up anxiety. Can you remember what you did with that discomfort?

2. When did you have a disruptive experience through which you sensed God moving you toward a new way of seeing, being, thinking, or acting?

3. Implicit bias is something all of us have. It is a function of how our brains perceive threat. Can you recall a time when your perceptions of a group or an individual different from you (racially, ethnically, culturally, or religiously) were proven inaccurate?

4. How might stereotypes about the materially poor impact how we choose to engage in the work of mission across cultures?

7

Aliens, Athens, and Incarnation

African affirmations about God and creation have to come alive in the projects, programs and attitudes of the Church.

—Mercy Oduyoye

We usually have to recognize ourselves in others before we can acknowledge otherness in ourselves.

—Mark Amend

American Robes and African Robes

I T IS OFTEN SAID that music is the universal language, and this claim makes sense given that music is relevant to every culture and people group. Studies have shown that music often has a similar effect on people who live in different cultures. Everyone from small children to the elderly resonate with music. In this sense, music is certainly universal.

Yet, the language, grammar, and syntax of music, as well as tempo, beat, and pitch, are exceedingly particular, with vastly different expressions according to cultural context. For example, "Traditional Chinese opera is as foreign and incomprehensible to Western ears as Strauss's tone poems are to aboriginal peoples. That does not diminish either. It simply forces us to question what we mean by the universality of music. In many ways, thinking (even unconsciously) of the cultural expression with which we are most familiar as 'universal' is an ultimate form of privilege."[1]

1. Borwick, "Universality/ Particularity," lines 12–19.

Something similar can be said of the gospel. Not only do the literal language, syntax, and grammar differ in divergent cultures, the underlying expressions that are derived from the story of Jesus' life, death, and resurrection differ as well. The gospel is universal, yet it is also exceedingly particular according to context. As George Huntsberger wrote, "Identifying the gospel is both simple and challenging. No culture-free expression of the gospel exists, nor could it. The church's message—the gospel—is inevitability articulated in linguistic and cultural forms particular to its own place and time."[2]

While in South Africa a few years ago, I met the American missionary who we saw in chapter 1, Cindy, who lived alongside the indigenous Xhosa people. Discussing Christianity and mission in sub-Saharan Africa over coffee one afternoon, she said that since the Bible is God's word, it can be shared at face value with the Xhosa in the same way it would be shared back home in the United States. Cindy expressed the deeply unfortunate yet common view that the Xhosa, and Africans in general, had to renounce any indigenous cultural and religious expressions in order to be "real Christians." *Real* Christian in this case meant *Western* Christian. Like many of us working across cultures, Cindy was dismissive of "the gospel in African robes."[3] She didn't realize that the gospel, like music, is both universal and particular at the same time, and to throw out either facet is to diminish its very essence.

The African robes that adorn the gospel—necessary and unique as they are—are often seen as erroneous or plain wrong by Western Christians such as Cindy. Different cultural manifestations of the gospel are frequently viewed as either disingenuous or in error. However, robes aren't dangerous or in error. And they are always present.

North American expressions of the gospel are also dressed in robes, very different ones than the Xhosa in South Africa, the Dinka in South Sudan, or the Luo in Kenya. But we often aren't aware of the robes our gospel wears. Like the fish who doesn't know it is wet, we don't tend to see the robes at all because we are so accustomed to them.

The robes are what we were brought up with. The gospel adorned in American robes appears as the right form or the only form of the gospel because it is what we are familiar with. All other robes can seem foreign, alien, or incorrect. North Americans, like every other people and society,

2. Huntsberger, *Missional Church*, 87.

3. Bosch, *Het Evangelie*, as cited in Livingston, *Missiology of the Road*, 54.

have adopted our own cultural form of the gospel that is often viewed as the one and only gospel in existence—or at least the only correct or acceptable one—from here to the ends of the earth.

Signs of War and Peace on the River Nile

Engaging with culture can be tricky, especially since culture exists *out there* in the world and also *in here* as a lens through which we see. Because of the power that the dominant culture holds, members of this population often view their own group as being culturally neutral. Encountering the gospel in unfamiliar forms while serving overseas is a double challenge as it involves our cultural lens (*in here*) and the unfamiliar cultural expression (*out there*) interacting with one another. If we don't know what to do with that, like Cindy, there can be many less than ideal outcomes.

I've learned this lesson the hard way more times than I care to admit. One particular example occurred when I was living in South Sudan. Deng was a local Sudanese staff member working in the realm of community health at the same NGO as me. We were asked to implement plans for a new therapeutic feeding center for children afflicted by severe acute malnutrition in a village a short flight away by bush plane. One day, Deng and I were walking to the work site along a path cut into the forest immediately above the waters of the White Nile. As we walked, he began to tell me of the biblical significance of the river and of South Sudan.

"Do you know this river from Isaiah chapter 18?" asked Deng, with the tone of an intellectual.

"No. I don't. Tell me more."

"Isaiah 18, let me tell you, brother . . . Isaiah 18 speaks of this place where we walk. Do you see that river? In 1982, things began floating in it, carried by the current. When we saw them, we knew a great conflict was coming. In 1983, the war began. The north started attacking us. They started killing us, bombing us, terrorizing us."

"So what did you see floating in the river?" I asked him, part curious to hear more and part incredulous that he was connecting a passage from the Hebrew scriptures directly to a modern-day armed conflict.

"It is all right here. Let me show you," Deng said as he stopped walking and proceeded to sit down. He opened the backpack he was carrying, pulled out his Bible, and began to read from the eighteenth chapter of Isaiah: "Woe to the land of whirring wings along the rivers of Cush, which sends envoys by sea in papyrus boats over the water. Go, swift messengers, to a people tall and smooth-skinned, to a people feared far and wide, an aggressive nation of strange speech, whose land is divided by rivers."[4]

"The papyrus boats," he explained, "were here, flowing up the White Nile toward Egypt. They're not actual papyrus or boats at all, but plants. Certain plants, thousands of them flowed north on the river. We knew that meant a war was coming. The plants could be seen every day for many years. Now that the war is over, again they have stopped. There is peace now."[5]

The plants stopped flowing. The war is over. There is peace now. The symbols of both bloodshed and the return of peace were seen in the river. For Deng, the words of Isaiah were evidenced in the waters of the White Nile. His experience as a Christian was largely tied to liberation from war and the oppression perpetrated by the government of Sudan who had persecuted his people for decades. At the time Deng and I walked along the banks of the river together, I thought he was crazy for thinking an obscure passage from Isaiah had anything to do with war in his country. Even though I was living there, I did not have a robust understanding of the context and how that informed how Deng and many other South Sudanese read this passage from Isaiah.

They interpreted the passage in a manner that allowed it to come alive for them. They let the ancient words speak into their lived experience of both suffering and liberation. I had not perceived Deng's story and the broader history of the region and thus labeled him, in my own mind, as a strange African man who read the Bible in a very peculiar way, a way that was in error. Because I had missed the deep connection between African Christianity and liberation from oppression—specifically, the South Sudanese Christian context—I had missed *him*. I missed his experience of pain and his experience of freedom from the violence of war because I was focused on the wrong thing: an unfamiliar way of interpreting of the Bible rather than being present with what Deng was revealing to me about his life, South Sudan, and Isaiah's words. At that point in my life, I lacked cultural intelligence and sensitivity. I ignored the African robes adorning

---

4. Isa 18:1–2 NIV.

5. This conversation took place a year after the government of Sudan (the north) and semi-autonomous southern Sudan (the south) signed a peace treaty ending the 22-year civil war. South Sudan became the world's newest nation in 2011 following a vote to secede. Tragically, a new civil war erupted in the fledgling nation in 2013 as a result of ethnic conflict driven by political agendas.

Deng's interpretation of the scriptures and as a result, foreclosed on an opportunity to bear witness to a deep truth regarding the ways the biblical text comes alive when read with a lens that allows it to speak powerfully into people's lived experience.

Culture and Christ

Cultural intelligence isn't important only with respect to reading the biblical text in diverse global contexts. It also has theological implications, including how we perceive the incarnation of Christ. Relegating culture to a peripheral place in the story of God becoming flesh in the person of Jesus can lead us into a subtle, yet nonetheless significant, presumption that history, place, geography, and context don't really matter in God's story of redeeming the cosmos. Ignoring culture leads to making a tacit claim on Christ's incarnation that is neither accurate from a standpoint of historicity nor Christian tradition. Failing to focus on the incarnation of Christ, an enculturated incarnation, leads us to dilute the importance and centrality of the event that unfolded in the ancient Near East in Jewish robes, so to speak. Jesus was born into a Jewish family, learned to speak a particular language, Aramaic, in a particular place, Bethlehem, at a particular time in history, the beginning of the first century. He became a refugee when his parents fled to Egypt seeking asylum from King Herod's campaign of infanticide. The majority of his ministry took place in Judea among the Jews, and he was persecuted by the Roman military and executed.

These are vital pieces of the Christian narrative. Yet, they lose much of their meaning if the importance of context is overlooked or worse, denied. Missing culture means missing the crux of the salvific truth of Jesus' life, death, and resurrection by alienating Christ from culture and artificially trying to separate that which has always been and will always be inseparable. Even God didn't escape cultural context. We mustn't try to, either.

The gospel is certainly universally valid. It is for all people, all nations, the whole of humanity—but perhaps not in the way Cindy thought and the way many of us have been taught. The universality of the gospel arises precisely in the diversity of ways it is contextually present in various cultural forms across time and place. Which is to say, the gospel is universal by way of many particulars.[6]

---

6. See Bauckham, *Bible and Mission*.

A healthier, more faithful, and theologically appropriate starting point when engaging with how to share the gospel cross-culturally involves the recognition of the wide stream of cultural manifestations of the gospel, each unique and beautiful. We remember the incarnation which took place not outside of culture but at the very heart of it. There is no culture-less gospel and no culture-less Christianity because there are no culture-less people. Christians crossing cultural boundaries are given the opportunity to encounter varied expressions of the gospel and to bear witness to their truth and beauty. At the same time, encountering the gospel in robes that aren't familiar can help us begin to see the robes that adorn our North American forms of Christianity more clearly.

Confronting the Alien Inside and Outside

Over half a century ago, one of the leaders of the American Bible Society was concerned about the cultural preparedness of those traveling overseas to do mission work: "Some missionaries . . . have carried to the field a distorted view of race and progress, culture and civilization, Christian and non-Christian ways of life. . . . I have become increasingly conscious of the tragic mistakes in cultural orientation which not only express themselves directly and indirectly in translations of Scriptures but in the general pattern of missionary work."[7] These words are every bit as relevant today as they were in the 1950s. Here we are in 2018, our lack of cultural intelligence in mission still evident. But there is a good reason for that. Collectively, the church has not prioritized cultural concerns in mission.

In the 1950s and 1960s, the field of anthropology began to formally influence the practice of missions, offering new insights into language, culture, ethnocentrism, and worldview.[8] The North Americans and Europeans who undertook research among various people groups across the globe began to provide Christian mission with a more nuanced understanding of different people groups and how they function and make meaning in the world. This soon gave rise to the academic discipline of missiology as the formal dialogue between anthropology and missions theology strengthened.[9] As the postmodern turn began to take shape in the 1970s, anthropology welcomed it, and in some ways helped create it. But the church had its arms

7. Rynkiewich, *Soul, Self, and Society*, 6.
8. Ibid.
9. Ibid., 7.

crossed, unwilling to participate in the deconstruction of modernity's take on culture.[10] This has resulted in a twenty-first-century missiology that is struggling to catch up with the times and to remain relevant.

Social perception is the study of how people perceive and therefore relate to others. There are a variety of factors that influence social perception, including personal and group bias. Research in this area reveals a psychological tendency to perceive others according to the ways they are different from us. It is not uncommon to see the Other through their peculiar dissimilarities to us rather than a recognition of their deeper personhood. We become the measuring stick, the standard by which everyone else is seen. The danger in this is that we then perceive others to be alien.

It is easy to label and stereotype people outside of our group. How much easier it is for us to talk about converting "the lost" than it is to talk about our own need for conversion, to critique ourselves and the group to which we belong. It is much simpler to focus only on trying to make the Other look like us, rather than entering more deeply into the task of transformation.

The dominant culture's bias against native cultural norms shapes the way we think about poverty, about black- and brown-skinned people, about who is whole and who is broken, who is saved and who is lost. This bias runs deep. It is something we can't escape, and therefore, must confront. In encountering the Other who we see as an alien, this Other reflects all that is alien within ourselves[11]—our shadow, our fear, our shame, all that we have repressed—back to us. This encounter with Otherness is an opportunity to reverse that pattern and begin to wonder about ourselves, our histories, our stories. Traveling overseas, encountering that which is so strange, peculiar, and different from us and our culture and our norms offers us this tremendous gift. This is one of the primary reasons why mission work invites us deeper in the gospel and deeper into ourselves. This isn't to say that participating in mission is meant to be all about us. Rather, coming to see ourselves more clearly eventually leads to seeing others more clearly, as well, which might in turn lead us to also love others more fully. To love one's neighbor as oneself, as Jesus taught, means knowing neighbor and knowing self. There is an intrinsic mutuality in loving others and loving ourselves; we can't really have one without the other.

10. Ibid., 8.
11. See Rollins, *Idolatry of God*.

Indigenous people across the globe have been, and continue to be, forced to adopt whiteness because of the cultural sightlessness of the West. According to Richard Twiss, the late Native American theologian and author, "because we are all so prone to being culturally egocentric, the temptation is to consider our worldview *the* biblical and correct one, shunning all others as unbiblical and wrong."[12] We are long overdue to begin fully embracing the diversity that is reflected in the triune God, the image of unity-in-difference characteristic of the Trinity found right here in our own Christian tradition.

This conversation tends to bring up some discomfort and may cause defenses to go up. May we remember that the gospel always disrupts, but it does so in order to bless. If we can stay with some of the angst and sit with some of the pushback that comes up, it allows the opportunity to witness how we measure others against what we view as right or acceptable—that which we are familiar with. Humans generally prefer the people, practices, ways of living, and modes of belief that are most similar to their own. It makes us feel comfortable, secure, and okay about ourselves. There is a very real payoff for avoiding Otherness or wanting to change it so it will be in line with what we are comfortable with: it reduces our anxiety. A feeling of security increases. And because we then feel better, we take this to mean that making the Other change to reflect us is indeed the right way, or even the way of God. But of course, it isn't. That is exactly what Jesus was arguing with the Pharisees about, their specious assumption that faith should be a reflection of them, rather than the divine.

Phrases such as "we are going to share the gospel with *the lost*, to love *on* people, to care for *the poor people* who have nothing" highlight the sometimes subtle assumption that North Americans are the whole ones who are called to help the broken ones. Also, the hyperbolizing of poverty and the elimination of cultural specificity are some of the many defense mechanisms we turn to when faced with Otherness. It's here that psychological functioning and cultural particularity interact with one another in very profound ways. The inability to constructively deal with difference often creates an attempt to, consciously or unconsciously, eliminate these differences as a way to reduce our anxiety. The result is a flat, unidirectional caricature of cultural transcendence.

---

12. Twiss, *One Church, Many Tribes*, 113.

The Apostle Paul Understood Culture

The Apostle Paul is regarded as the greatest missionary who ever lived. He crisscrossed the ancient world, visiting Antioch, Rome, Damascus, Cypress, Malta, Athens, and beyond to invite people into the story of Jesus. He was utterly compelled by his personal encounter with the risen Jesus and wanted nothing more than to share the good news with others.

Paul grew up in Tarsus, a large trade center in the southern part of present-day Turkey which was part of the Roman Empire at the time. It was known as an intellectual and cultural epicenter and home to a major university as well as a number of well-known philosophers. Paul and his family were Diaspora Jews living outside their ancestral Jewish homeland who also held Roman citizenship.

As a young man, Paul was sent by his family to study in Jerusalem. Growing up in the urban, pluralistic context of Tarsus followed by many years in a Jewish environment gave Paul a breadth of knowledge and exposure to varying religious and sociocultural environments. He likely spoke three languages: Aramaic, Greek, and Latin. He was familiar not only with the Jewish worldview but the Greek one, as well. He followed Judaism and also knew Stoic philosophy. By spending his formative years in diverse environments, Paul had learned how to read culture. When it came time for him to embark on his missionary journeys, he had already learned that doing mission from his own cultural and religious frame of reference would not work, that his message would have no impact and may even cause harm.

Before Paul's encounter with the risen Christ, he brutally persecuted Jesus followers.[13] He dragged people out of their homes, put them in prison, and ensured they were either tortured, executed, or both. Paul's missionary zeal was first a persecutory passion. Following this encounter with Christ and his repentance from his old ways, Paul entered his missionary call.

So how did Paul approach the complexities of culture and mission? Why was he such an effective missionary?

Paul did the hard work of translation, interpreting his understanding of Jesus in a way that made sense to people. In Athens, he didn't just show up and announce a message or speak about his own experience and his personal conversion to Christ. Instead he used Greek concepts and philosophy that people could understand and resonate with. In short, Paul contextualized the message of Jesus so that it would have relevancy to the worldview

13. Acts 8:1–3 and Gal 1:13.

of the Athenians. He didn't export a message rooted in his own paradigm as a Jewish man who had become a follower of Jesus. Instead of taking an ethnocentric posture and communicating as if he were still in Jerusalem, he intentionally molded his message to both communicate effectively and to respect the community he was visiting.

Part of the reason God was able to use Paul in such a powerful way was because of Paul's cultural intelligence—his ability to take culture, both his own and that of others, into account. Without it, Paul's message would have been impotent. His preaching would have been narrow and insular. There would have been no relevancy or vivacity in his messages and he would have ended up creating social divisiveness and perpetuating cultural superiority—the very thing Jesus taught his disciples to avoid.

While in Athens to talk with the Greeks about Jesus, he spent a lot of time with the scholars and philosophers who gathered to talk and debate outside the city center at a place called Mars Hill. This is where Paul went, meeting the people of Athens on their own terms, in their own place, in their own context. Even though Paul was a missionary filled with passion to reveal the love of Jesus, he was—like Jesus had been—aware of his own cultural lens.

The Greeks were mainly polytheistic, with a pantheon of gods including Zeus, Athena, Poseidon, and many others. In Acts 17:28, Paul quotes pagan sources in order to teach that God lies at the very heart of existence and is the source of all life.[14] The Athenians could understand that type of religious paradigm. It resonated with their polytheistic worldview.

For Paul, mission and its theological underpinnings were about the art of telling and listening to stories about the divine within the context of culture. He didn't force the Greeks to renounce their heritage and espouse a Hebrew worldview in order to become followers of Jesus. Rather than coming to Athens with an ethnocentric posture and trying to bring "Jewish Jesus" to Athens, he instead used a contextual approach.

Paul was the original practitioner of the idea that there is no culture-less Christ. He had sufficient acumen to evangelize the Greeks with cultural intelligence. He knew that bringing Jewish Jesus to the Greeks would not only be ethnocentric, but also impotent. It would have missed the center of the good news of Jesus' life, death, and resurrection that Paul was so compelled by.

14. Keller, *Center Church*, 124.

Paul thought following Jesus entailed a revolution of understanding and practice about law and faith. This transformation in the way he saw his role in the world following his conversion experience led Paul to repent, to stop persecuting people and surrender his violent ways. His conversion to Christ led him to a completely different way of being in the world. His struggle against Christians was transmuted into other forms of struggle, including fighting to abolish the notion that circumcision was required for male converts to Christianity. He also resisted the popular notion that one first had to become a Jew in order to become a Christian. Paul didn't condescend to serve others. He didn't preach and teach as if he was among children in need of his rescue. He didn't see the Greeks worshipping many gods as a problem to be eliminated. Rather, he saw it as an opportunity, a place to begin conversation, a starting point from which dialogue could begin, and a place from which bridges could be constructed to link to the gospel message.

In Acts 17, Paul preaches at a meeting:

> People of Athens! I see that in every way you are very religious. For as I walked around and looked carefully at your objects of worship, I even found an altar with this inscription: to an unknown god. So you are ignorant of the very thing you worship—and this is what I am going to proclaim to you. The God who made the world and everything in it is the Lord of heaven and earth and does not live in temples built by human hands. And he is not served by human hands, as if he needed anything. Rather, he himself gives everyone life and breath and everything else. From one man he made all the nations, that they should inhabit the whole earth; and he marked out their appointed times in history and the boundaries of their lands. God did this so that they would seek him and perhaps reach out for him and find him, though he is not far from any one of us. "For in him we live and move and have our being." As some of your own poets have said, "We are his offspring."[15]

Paul doesn't begin by saying, "You're way off base, you're sinful, and you need to change." He starts by naming something which he sees as good, their dedication to a form of faith, their Greek religion, even though his desire was for them to know Jesus. He follows this by a necessary and respectful critique: you don't even realize that the "unknown god" you worship is the One God! The God who gives life and breath to everything and everyone, a concept the Greeks could understand, given the influence of Stoic philosophy which saw the world as the soul of God. Paul finishes his

15. Acts 17:22–28 NIV.

sermon by noting that Greek poets already understood the message, they were already in some way in resonance with what he was saying and what Jesus' life, death, and resurrection were all about.

What Paul doesn't say in his sermon is as important as what he does say. He could have spoken about Jesus as a Jewish man, like him. He could have said they needed to abolish all their idols, especially since the Jews were repulsed by idols of any form, let alone a whole city full of what would have been considered abhorrent. That was part of his Jewish religious heritage that was completely antithetic to the Greek one. Rather than telling them to turn from their religion, Paul saw it as a foundation from which the Greeks could experience the transformative, saving power of Jesus. He didn't try to do away with it. Instead, he included it and ultimately transcended it.

Paul honored Greek robes, knowing they could, up to a point, adorn the gospel. He certainly didn't condone polytheism or idol worship. But Paul was not afraid to critique the shortcomings of the Jews or the Greeks, saying Christ crucified was "foolish to the Jews, who ask for signs from heaven. And it is foolish to the Greeks, who seek human wisdom."[16] Paul goes on to say that Christ was "a stumbling block to Jews and foolishness to Gentiles, but to those whom God has called, both Jews and Greeks, Christ the power of God and the wisdom of God. For the foolishness of God is wiser than human wisdom, and the weakness of God is stronger than human strength."[17] He wasn't afraid to critique Jew and Greek alike.

Cultural homogeneity wasn't part of the missiological picture for Paul. That is what the Romans had done. That is what the empire's dream was about—a fabricated usurping of religious and cultural expressions through violence that stripped people of their identities in order to homogenize the *polis*. I imagine Paul teaching about this, saying, "That is exactly what the Romans have done to us and what I used to do when I persecuted the church! That is what the powers have done to our people. That is empire, not gospel. That is lord Caesar, not Lord Christ."

The skillful way Paul contextualized the gospel message invited people into the potential for what could be, how the future could look in this person called Jesus. Paul was someone who looked at the possibilities for people to know God intimately and personally. His way of doing cross-cultural mission had the citizens of Athens asking new questions about who they were and the nature of ultimate reality. I can imagine one of the Athenian philosophers

16. 1 Cor 1:22 NLT.

17. 1 Cor 1:23–25 NIV.

having a dialogue with Paul on Mars Hill, listening to Paul tell of this Jesus who had been crucified by the Romans and rose from the dead, and in response, asking Paul questions about his encounter with the risen Christ and how a Jewish rabbi could hold a cosmic power greater than the gods, saying, "So you're telling me the gods are actually One God? The unknown god is the Father of this crucified Jesus you speak of? The unknown god took on human flesh? You're telling me your deity is like a human Father who loves? Who cares for people and calls them his children?" That was—and still is—completely revolutionary. It changed everything for people.

Paul's message was so powerful and so effective because it was so creative. It wasn't ethnocentric. It wasn't coercive. And it certainly wasn't boring. Paul had a robust missionary imagination.

The Missionary Imagination

Imagination has to do with the mind's faculty to create new things, to imagine ideas, to develop images and possibilities that don't yet exist. An individual's imagination is situated within, influenced by but also potentially influential upon, the collective social imaginary, which is related to the beliefs and values of the larger society. Our imaginations are our own while at the same time being more than simply our own. They are formed in the fabric of relationships, politics, and social norms.

Imagination is a social reality as much as it is an independent function in an individual's mind. As opposed to fictitious or pretend imaginings, like when children daydream of castles in the sky, the collective social imagination is real—it has very genuine impacts on how we see the world and other people.

So what happened to the fertility of imagination exhibited by Paul in his ancient missionary journeys? If our imaginations haven't been formed by Paul and the early church, then by whom and by what?

Ever since the cross and the sword became bedfellows during the European colonial project, the Western imagination has been locked in the cell of the colonial narrative. By the time the European superpowers began their project, more than a thousand years after Paul, Christian mission had tragically been co-opted by a different imagination, captive to imperialism rather than the risen Christ. The modern missionary imagination was shaped by the imperial imagination, and Paul's ancient missional wisdom was all but lost in the Western church.

Over a decade ago, I visited a captivating village along a rugged stretch of the Indian Ocean coastline in South Africa. Taken by the traditional way of life of the village, the thousand green, undulating hills above the sea, I never wanted to leave. It was the most perfect place I'd ever laid eyes on. After the week was over, I didn't make it back there again for nearly eight years, but not a day went by that I didn't think about the old women dressed in traditional clothing, sitting together outside a rondavel (mud hut) smoking a traditional wooden pipe; the waves peeling perfectly across empty beaches; a postcard perfect existence of simplicity.

The spell it had cast on me wouldn't be broken. It was rural poverty at its most romantic. Perfect waves. Whales breaching just offshore. Rondavels on the coast. A traditional way of life much like it was a few hundred years ago.

At least that is the story I projected onto this place, exoticizing a people and a community who, largely as a legacy of apartheid, suffer from an alarming rate of HIV/AIDS, gender violence, addiction, and lack of financial resources. I had remade that place according to my romantic visions and exotic longings.

Westerners tend to romanticize poverty, especially the rural variety that appears pristine, without squalor or filth. In the quest for exotic alternatives to the commonplace, it is natural to desire the far off, the mysterious, a grand adventure. Leopold longed to flee the prosaic tedium of his existence in Europe to pursue the allure of the "Dark Continent," with its lush equatorial rainforest overflowing with bizarre dark bodies—the promised land of a beguiled imagination charmed by exoticism (though he never did set foot in Africa). I longed for the freedom and unadulterated, raw experience of a rural, traditional South African village.

Thankfully, the majority of us are not like Leopold; our intentions are good, his clearly were not. But a similarity many of us do share with Leopold is the common exotic imaginings fashioned from the Western imagination. Our imaginations are also held captive to the romanticization of foreign places and indigenous people.

And mission exerts a certain romantic pull. Images of visiting unusual places around the globe and interacting with dark-skinned people dance through the Western mind. These images are bewitching. They seduce. They generate desire.

The exoticization of "primitive" cultures, often combined with a messiah complex, creates a powerful and precarious narrative: not only do *we* have what *they* need—the answers, the expertise, the money, the salvation, the Jesus—and not only do we know what they don't know, we are also fascinated with their peculiar way of life, different language, and simple existence. We project our desire for the exotic onto them while at the same time imposing upon them our own need for purpose and our desire to save.

The beguiled Western imagination impacts the poor and the non-poor alike. The global poor exist in the Western imagination as helpless, backward, and impotent; this narrative is then internalized. The West in many ways has robbed people of their own creative imaginations so much that they can no longer imagine a life without poverty. They've become prisoners of our Western imagination.

Far from being hidden in the recesses of our minds, imagination is concretized in the messages it communicates to people. Imagination is constituted by stories. The stories that comprise imagination are communicated to others in various subtle ways. For example, the message "we have what you need" and "white is better than brown" or "American Jesus is superior to indigenous Jesus" or "we are here to help you because you can't help yourself" communicate something. All of this is, of course, unspoken, tacit, soft. The materially wealthy don't even realize we are doing it. It is not our intent. And though it is never our *intent*, it is often our *impact*. To go forward, it is essential that we go back and renegotiate the agreements we've tacitly made with the Western imagination and reclaim Paul's missionary imagination.

Reflection Questions

1. What are your initial thoughts as to how contextualization might facilitate a deeper engagement with the gospel in the place where you serve or want to serve in the future?

2. Where have you encountered the gospel in "robes" different from what you familiar with? How did you respond then? How might you respond differently in the future?

3. Reflect for a moment on the cultural lens through which you see. How might awareness of this lens facilitate new ways of inviting people into the story of Jesus? How might that same awareness facilitate knowing yourself, God, and others in new ways?

8

Called

What we plant in the soil of contemplation, we shall reap in the harvest of action.

—Meister Eckhart

Spirituality means waking up.

—Anthony de Mello, SJ

Named and Invited

T HE APOSTLE PAUL IS regarded as the greatest missionary to ever live as well as the first Christian theologian. He invented Christian theology as a reworking of Jewish thought and the Hebrew story of Abraham and Egypt around the person of Jesus. Paul believed that God's solution to the world's plight began with Abraham's calling.[1] This was the foundation from which Paul understood the Hebrew Scriptures and his own calling as a missionary to the Gentiles.

For Paul, the starting point of mission was God's calling.

The Hebrew word *qara* (pronounced *kaw raw*) is similar to the English word calling, but has a more robust meaning. It is defined as *to be called, to be invited* or *to be named*. This ancient Jewish understanding of calling, the one with which Paul would have been familiar, was to be welcomed into a certain way of living, being, and acting in the world. To be called wasn't only a summons to a task, but an invitation for everything to change: relationships, spiritual life, core identity, and work in the world. The modern

---

1. Wright, *Paul and the Faithfulness of God*, xvi.

understanding of calling in our society tends to focus on career, jobs, and work in the world, which are certainly important and have their place. Yet, *qara* is more capacious than that. Besides outward forms of engagement, calling is also an inner process that is undergone. To be called is to be invited within as well as without.

In addition to an invitation to an inner and outer way of being in the world, *qara* also relates to being named. Jesus' own calling into ministry officially began with his baptism by John in the Jordan River. "Immediately coming up out of the water, He saw the heavens opening, and the Spirit like a dove descending upon Him; and a voice came out of the heavens: 'You are My beloved Son, in You I am well-pleased.'"[2]

This was the moment when God publicly called Jesus and his kingship was officially announced. Before beginning his three-year ministry to carry out his destiny as Son of God, Jesus was named the beloved. God was saying, "I love you. I am pleased with you. You are my beloved child." It is easy to forget that Jesus, fully human like each of us, had the deep need to hear and accept that he was loved, to know his Father approved of him. He needed to hear these words that named the core truth of who he was, his deepest identity.

So much of our identity rests on the particular ways we have been named. Who we know ourselves to be is largely based on what others have told us about who we are. That is the single biggest factor in how we form identity. Being named beloved was a significant part of Jesus' identity formation. In calling Jesus to his life's work and destiny as Messiah, God could have said, "You are my Son. Do the work you are here to do faithfully" or "You will be tested greatly and suffer immensely in the task set before you" or "Persevere when you are tempted to turn from my will." But God didn't say those things to Jesus. God didn't tell him what to do or how to live out his calling. Instead, God named him. Calling always involves being named.

An accurate identity rooted in being loved and accepted was crucial for Jesus like it is for each of us. It is what every person needs to hear in their identity formation, which is what underlies all the choices we make and how we choose to live and participate in the world. What a person chooses to do is an outpouring of their identity.[3]

---

2. Mark 1:10–11 NASB.

3. Insight I gleaned during a conversation with Richard Kim on culture, identity, and agency.

Earlier in the book, we looked at the example of the physician who started a project in Haiti, using his medical skills to do good in an extremely poor community. We saw how his mission venture imploded after a short period of time, leaving everyone involved angry, hurt, and confused—including himself. There are innumerable instances such as this, where a person goes off somewhere to help solve a problem, alleviate some form of suffering, or make disciples. Hearts ablaze for the place and people in need, they do their best to help. But what was meant to help ends up hurting, both themselves and the materially poor. They return home in anger and confusion not long after, their hope and vision having gone to pieces.

Sometimes mission falls apart. Sometimes the potential for transformative justice work is miscarried.

I had many conversations regarding vocation and calling with a former therapist, and I remember him saying, "The need does not necessitate the call." In other words, the existence of a problem—be it social, political, humanitarian, or otherwise—in the world does not mean a certain individual is called to engage it or help solve it. The unique ways in which we are each made informs how we are designed to be in the world, how we are meant to live and serve. And just as the need does not necessitate the call, the call does not necessitate the readiness. Or put differently, even when we are we called, it doesn't necessarily mean we are prepared to dive in immediately and begin without undergoing sufficient preparation, including education and formation along theological, psychological, spiritual, and cultural lines.

There is no doubt that many experience an authentic draw within themselves to engage in service with vulnerable people overseas, whether it be in the context of short-term mission, community development, global health projects, human trafficking, or some other form of mission or justice work. The desire and willingness to travel to difficult places steeped in poverty can be a good place to begin pursuing these opportunities where our hearts authentically feel drawn. Yet, this is a starting point, not an end point. *Qara* leads us into a journey, both inward and outward, that is meant to be a catalyst for mutual transformation of the self and the other. The call to mission is the call to allow something to be birthed not only through us, but also *within* us.

Whether the goal is to participate in a ten-day mission trip to Haiti or move to Cambodia to advocate of behalf of trafficked girls, this call is beautiful and essential. It is the space from which mission flows. *Qara* activates something deep within that pulls us forward to pursue this vision of restoration and redemption. But the call into mission and justice work is about much more than buying a plane ticket. It is an invitation into the psyche, the heart, the soul. The call to mission bids us entry into our own pain, to engage with our own brokenness and wounds that have remained untended. If we haven't engaged our own pain, we cannot be fully present with another in their pain. If we haven't reflected deeply on our own woundedness, the best we can do is see ourselves as whole and the other as broken. We can engage in acts of charity, but not embody gospel-oriented justice. Mission divorced from formation ends up re-colonizing people through ethnocentrism, names us whole and them broken, and misses finding common humanity in suffering.

The call is an invitation into the self as much as it is an invitation into the world.

The call is a commissioning into formation as much as it is a sending outward.

Role Reversal

Imagine a Christian couple in their late twenties from Honduras who dream of coming to the United States to work in pastoral training ministry. Though they've received no formal theological education, their desire to come to the United States is strong. They have heard about the many lonely, overworked people, including pastors, whose lives they hope to make a difference in. They want to serve those who are lost in the competition and poverty of consumeristic society. So they begin fundraising through friends, family, and their local church. They follow their dream and show up in Houston and begin networking with church leaders and meeting people. They begin offering training to pastors and people who want to become pastors.

A highly motivated but unprepared couple from a Majority World nation comes to the United States to help. It sounds a bit ludicrous, right?

Here is second scenario, a real one, involving an acquaintance, Mike, who grew up in Houston. He does pastoral training work in various Latin American countries. Though he isn't a pastor and hasn't been to seminary or received any theological education, this is the work he feels called to do. So that's what he does. He fundraises and takes trips to Honduras to train pastors. No one questions his lack of preparation and formation.

Why is it seen as God's work for Mike to engage in the sacred work of pastoral formation in the Majority World and absolutely absurd for the opposite to happen?

Is Mike's work in alignment with *missio Dei*?

Does it empower marginalized people?

Does it square with God's dream for human flourishing?

Does it prophetically interrogate the sins of neocolonialism and ethnocentrism?

In many ways, those are questions for Mike to discern in the accountability of community. But they are also relevant to each of us.

The intention to do good in the world is an essential part of calling. When we look at many helping occupations, they all start with a person's intentions toward that particular type of work in the world. But is someone's good intentions sufficient for them to put on scrubs, pick up a scalpel, and perform surgery on a sick person? Is someone's deep longing to fight for just laws and policies enough for them to show up in the courtroom as legal counsel and argue a case? Is a person's desire to teach sufficient for them to begin their tenure-track position at a university? Is someone's deep passion for urban design clearance for them to begin building majestic skyscrapers based on their beautiful vision? These examples sound silly—because they are.

You can't just show up to your calling. Calling takes long years of preparation, education, training, and formation. So why is it that if we are called to serve people across cultures that desire and good intentions are license to raise support, buy a plane ticket, and show up? Why is it so different when the conversation turns to "helping the poor" and all sorts of mission work? Why can we just show up to *that* calling? Wrestling with how we assign less value to the poor in terms of excellence in preparation, education, and formation is an important part of *qara*.

The (Other) Great Commission

The Gospel of Luke ends with a passage known as the Great Commission. Luke's version looks a bit different from its parallel text written in Matthew and Mark. In Matthew it reads, "Therefore go and make disciples of all nations, baptizing them in the name of the Father and of the Son and of the Holy Spirit, and teaching them to obey everything I have commanded you. And surely I am with you always, to the very end of the age."[4] The same text in Mark reads, "He said to them, 'Go into all the world and preach the gospel to all creation. Whoever believes and is baptized will be saved, but whoever does not believe will be condemned'"[5]

The Great Commission has often been read as an edict to cross boundaries of geography, ethnicity, and religion and then place an agenda on people. This text has been misinterpreted to support ethnocentrism and misappropriate power. Many Christians have used it to corroborate a small-minded religiosity, and make disciples in our own image rather than the image of God whose very Trinitarian nature is unity-in-difference. It has been used to re-colonize in modern times, appropriated to spread American Jesus. It has given some a biblical license to misuse power and privilege. No other passage in all of Scripture has been misused in world mission as much as The Great Commission. How we read and interpret this passage matters deeply. It also sheds light on what biblical calling might look like.

The Great Commission text in Luke's Gospel emphasizes something distinct from that of Matthew and Mark: "Then he opened their minds so they could understand the Scriptures. He told them, 'This is what is written: The Messiah will suffer and rise from the dead on the third day, and repentance for the forgiveness of sins will be preached in his name to all nations, beginning at Jerusalem. You are witnesses of these things. I am going to send you what my Father has promised; but stay in the city until you have been clothed with power from on high.'"[6] Matthew and Mark emphasize immediate movement into the world: Go. Make disciples. Baptize. Preach. The Great Commission in Luke curiously omits the language of immediate commissioning into the world. It doesn't have the tone of urgency. Sending in Luke's Gospel is first about remaining, staying in Jerusalem, witnessing to the transformative events that have just unfolded, the death and resurrection of the Lord, which was beginning to change everything. In Luke's Great Commission, Jesus highlights being over doing; prior to the disciples heading out on their mission to the world, they themselves required further transformation, which would come through the Holy Spirit who would soon arrive.

4. Matt 28:18–20 NIV.

5. Mark 16:15–16 NIV.

6. Luke 24:45–49 NIV.

Perhaps the disciples needed to further journey into the process of salvation prior to offering the message of Jesus to the world. Maybe they needed their community a bit longer. Maybe they had something more to learn before they could go teach and make disciples. And unlike Matthew and Mark, Luke doesn't mention condemnation. He doesn't discuss belief. Something else mattered more to him: witnessing to the life that overcomes death, remaining in the resurrection space, staying present with people, entering into personal and communal renewal.

Even though Luke knew Jesus to be the Messiah who was reversing oppressive structures, catalyzing justice for the oppressed, and bringing heaven to earth, commissioning as Jesus articulated here is about both "being" and "doing." It was, and continues to be, about contemplation and action, inner conversion and outer transformation, spirituality and mission. Jesus seems to be saying, "You are going to go out into the world and share the good news and preach of the kingdom and baptize in my name. But don't go haphazardly. Wait. Wait for the Spirit who is going to continue to transform you. Your mind is beginning to open and everything is going to be different now."

The Great Commission can shape the ways we are thinking about mission and can form the questions we are asking about what it means to be called to serve and be catalysts for justice down the street or across an ocean. Like Luke, many of us believe Jesus was—and is—reversing the structures that have wrought suffering and oppression. As we think about what it means to be reversers of oppression and bearers of shalom, we can also begin to hear the invitation to remain, to expect, to witness, to be transformed. To remember that we need saving as much as anyone else. To know that the call to go out and make disciples is also a call to be transformed. If Jesus were here now speaking a new Great Commission relevant to our context in North America, being sent out in our missional journeys today, I imagine him saying, "Be watchful of impetuousness and the craving to save and rescue. Continue releasing your false self to God. Your true self, where you and the Spirit meet, will lead you. You are being transformed, and in turn you will transform those you meet, those you help, those you tell about me. Transformed people transform people."

Desert Spirituality

After being named the beloved by God, Jesus still wasn't commissioned directly into his life's work of teaching, preaching, and healing. Before being sent out into the world, he was sent into the desert. His calling began in isolation in the wilderness, not in ministry among his people:

> Then Jesus was led by the Spirit into the wilderness to be tempted by the devil. After fasting forty days and forty nights, he was hungry. The tempter came to him and said, "If you are the Son of God, tell these stones to become bread." Jesus answered, "It is written: 'Man shall not live on bread alone, but on every word that comes from the mouth of God.'" Then the devil took him to the holy city and had him stand on the highest point of the temple. "If you are the Son of God," he said, "throw yourself down. For it is written: 'He will command his angels concerning you, and they will lift you up in their hands, so that you will not strike your foot against a stone.'" Jesus answered him, "It is also written: 'Do not put the Lord your God to the test.'" Again, the devil took him to a very high mountain and showed him all the kingdoms of the world and their splendor. "All this I will give you," he said, "if you will bow down and worship me." Jesus said to him, "Away from me, Satan! For it is written: 'Worship the Lord your God, and serve him only.'" Then the devil left him, and angels came and attended him.[7]

In the dry isolation and desolation of the desert, Jesus faced a period of trial and testing in which he confronted the temptation to live according to the individual ego and the ways of empire. Enticed to choose that which wasn't in alignment with who he was and his destiny as the Son of God, Jesus' deep *no* to Satan was a direct refutation of empire, of Caesar as son of God, and Rome's imperial dominance. He had already given his *yes* to a life of teaching and healing, to living in alignment with God and with his deepest identity as the Father's beloved. Jesus articulated with his whole being a primal no to all that was false and contrary to his identity and calling.

As we saw earlier, not long after Constantine converted to Christianity, the still fledgling Jesus movement that had existed only on the fringes became the religion of the empire. As the Christianizing of the ancient Near East began, the foundations of the gospel began to morph to fit Rome's vision rather than the vision of Jesus and the original church. The empire began remaking the Jesus movement into its own image. As many faithful

---

7. Matt 4:1–11 NIV.

followers of Jesus witnessed the perversion of their faith concretize further and further, some chose to resist it by fleeing. Men and women left the cities for the deserts of Palestine, Egypt, and Syria. It was here that desert spirituality arose as a reaction to and liberation from empire spirituality.[8]

The spirituality of empire is rooted in the need for power, control and everlasting life, which is a reflection of the false self's need for separation, security, and survival. Ego and empire are two inseparable facets of a single contiguous process. Those who fled into the wilderness did so to nurture another way of life in community, to discern what it meant to follow Christ through humility, silence, and solitude. The desert invited a radical interiority rooted in contemplative practice focused on a complete surrender to the divine as well as a confrontation of falsity in the self and in the world. Here, the Desert Mothers (Ammas) and Fathers (Abbas) were able to have an experience of Christ not mediated by the state but by their own bodily reality.[9]

Metaphorically, the desert is a place of testing and transformation, of being divested of empire and ego. In the desert experience, the dreams, goals, and visions of the false self can be seen clearly, sometimes for the first time. The desert symbolizes the terrain in which we unlearn empire spirituality and its ways of doing mission from an imperial stance. It is a space of confronting empire's gods and the small self's narrow, self-interested visions. Desert spirituality's great power is the undoing of empire's spirituality and its temptation to live according to force, power, and control. In metaphorical desert spaces, we can practice deep truthfulness.

Facing the falsity of ego and empire is the beginning of commissioning. In the desert we are confronted with the things we normally remain unaware of. We come face to face not only with our own brokenness, but the ways our brokenness breaks others.

To intentionally enter the desert experience is to come to know oneself intimately, especially the ego, the pain, the shadow, the falsity. It is also to behold the way empire has shaped our imagination, to wrestle with colonial ghosts, duel with our inner colonialist, expiate mission's original sins that have lived on secretly inside our tradition, face the times we planted seeds of American culture when our desire was to till the soil for the growth of the gospel.

8. Wiest, "Desert Spirituality."
9. Ibid.

The desert is the environment, the inner space in which our imagination is transmuted from imprisonment to empire. It is the place where we articulate a strong *no* to who we are not and to who God is not. The false self begins to be recognized, released, and reconstituted in the image of the true self "hidden with Christ in God."[10] The Western imagination that has affected how we think about the marginalized and how we see the missional task starts to emerge from the layers in which it has been covered over. Our unconsciousness, our loss of memory begin to arise from beneath the comfort of amnesia.

The desert is the place of great undoing.

Encountering truth is disruptive. Living as an amnesiac is far easier, but it is not the way of the desert, of the gospel, or of the *missio Dei*. Truth telling is not rosy or optimistic. It is a taxing process that can threaten identity. It questions everything. It asks us to let go of all we thought we knew, our preconceived notions, our treasured way of seeing the world and our role in it and even the God we believe in. The desert invites us to go into the vulnerable places inside to face and to let go of what we find, to leave the God we know and meet a God we don't yet know and can't possibly imagine. That is the heart of desert spirituality, forming us for the work of mission by forming us into the image of the God we can't yet conceive of.

A Prophet's Vision

The desert is a major feature in the imagery of both the Old and New Testaments: the Israelites are held in bondage by Pharaoh in the desert of Egypt; following the exodus led by Moses, they spent forty years in the desert waiting to reach the promised land; Paul spent three years in the desert of Arabia; John the Baptist was an itinerant desert preacher; Jesus spent forty days fasting and being tempted in the desert.

In the biblical tradition, the desert is the place where prophetic voices are fashioned.

Prophets are those who dare to question the present ways people are living. The Old Testament is full of stories of those who spoke truth to power, interrogating what they witnessed as deeply amiss—idol worship, corruption of temple priests, religious bigotry. Men and women such as Micah, Jeremiah, Ezekiel, Deborah, Miriam, Samuel, Nathan, and Elijah were captive to a hope that transcended the popular status quo and aligned

---

10. Col 3:3 NIV.

with God's vision over the visions of unjust political, religious, and social institutions in the societies where they lived.

Their prophetic vision was born of a risky and courageous hope. Walter Brueggemann notes that "hope is the refusal to accept the reading of reality which is the majority opinion; and one does that only at great political and existential risk. On the other hand, hope is subversive, for it limits the grandiose pretension of the present, daring to announce that the present to which we have all made commitments is now called into question."[11] The prophet goes against the grain of popular opinion which puts him or her at risk for ridicule and rejection, excommunication, and even physical harm by calling popular commitments into question.

Brueggemann goes on:

> The prophet engages in futuring fantasy. The prophet does not ask if the vision can be implemented, for questions of implementation are of no consequence until the vision can be imagined. The imagination must come before the implementation. Our culture is competent to implement almost anything and to imagine almost nothing. The same royal consciousness that make it possible to implement anything and everything is the one that shrinks imagination because imagination is a danger.[12]

The prophet is transformed through the imagination, which comes prior to, as Brueggemann notes, the implementation of plans and action, before the doing of justice work. The prophet is first oriented inwardly. If the prophetic imagination bears a vision of a future of shalom, and the prophetic task is to speak truth to power, it necessitates an inward interrogation—confronting the falsity not only in society but inside ourselves.

The prophet is first born within.

Prophetic interrogation of commitments includes how we inadvertently participate in systems of injustice. This is a key aspect of the prophet's calling, unmasking that which has been disguised, letting light shine on the dark corners of our psyches, our theologies, our stories. The prophetic imagination slowly replaces the Western imagination through authentic inner transformation.

Many globally engaged organizations and churches have begun to re-conceptualize mission in new ways. There have been many noteworthy and commendable efforts toward erasing harmful patterns in mission,

11. Brueggemann, *Prophetic Imagination*, 65.

12. Ibid., 40.

development, and other forms of service work. Words like partnership, mutuality, and empowerment have become standard lingo to describe the ethos of many NGOs and parachurch organizations. This is a fairly recent opening in both discourse and practice that is leading somewhere good, where the dignity of the materially poor can be honored more fully. But despite this promising movement, much of the progress that has been forged in recent years has been focused on translation rather than transformation.

Translation is like rearranging furniture in your living room. It looks a bit different, but the underlying qualities are still there, just arranged in a new manner. Transformation is like removing all the furniture, taking out the drywall, and remodeling the room, tearing out the old and replacing everything from the studs up. New walls with fresh paint, new flooring, new light fixtures. The structure itself is new, as well as the cosmetics. It is not the same underlying form configured in a new way. In transformation, the constitution itself has changed. A full renovation has taken place and the room is recreated. If we remodel the room, everything changes. If we rearrange the furniture, we've only altered the appearance.

Prophets are in the remodeling business, not interior design.

We have so far done a good job rearranging the furniture, now it is time to remodel the room. In the case of transforming mission and development, it is not just the principals and best practices that need be addressed, but the deeper levels of narrative, consciousness, memory, and imagination. Authentic transformation recreates the inner realities that shape the outer forms (how we engage in the practices of mission and development cross-culturally).

The prophet knows that the inside work and the outside work are one.

Justice Jesus and Prophetic Hope in El Salvador

The Gospel of Luke depicts Jesus as a prophet concerned with reversing the structures of society that kept people locked in oppression. The author of Luke reveals these ideas about who Jesus was through the way he writes about Jesus' ministry. He paints a picture of Jesus as the Messiah who came for the outsider, intentionally using language like "rich and poor" to paint a picture of Jesus' radical message of justice for the marginalized and the reversal of systems that privilege some and devalue others, and artificially lift up the powerful and dehumanize the powerless. The book of Luke points to a kingdom that upends these power systems being ushered in by a God who sides with the poor, the outliers, and those living on the margins. "The strategy of Jesus," Fr. Gregory Boyle reminds us, "is not centered in taking the right stand on issues, but rather in standing in the right place—with the outcast and those relegated to the margins."[13]

Jesus sought to undermine the injustice of the systems that oppress through deliberately standing with the powerless and broken. Luke shows us that the actions Jesus took and the words he spoke were toward the creation of justice. Luke's Jesus is certainly not the Jesus of American evangelicalism, but a person of political prowess who had an incomparable longing for religious authenticity. True justice must be seen through the lens of this Jesus. As we enter into his story, we can learn to be prophetic disciples that work to catalyze this type of justice of which he is the exemplar.

In the kingdom of God, everything is turned upside down. Jesus spoke of the messianic reversal that was at the heart of the kingdom: "The Spirit of the Lord is upon me, because he has anointed me to bring good news to the poor. He has sent me to proclaim release to the captives and recovery of sight to the blind, to let the oppressed go free, to proclaim the year of the Lord's favor."[14] There have been countless men and women who've lived the prophetic call of Jesus in their own contexts: Archbishop Desmond Tutu, Dietrich Bonhoeffer, Dorothy Day, Mother Teresa, Martin Luther King Jr., and the unsung multitude who have dedicated their lives to the prophet's calling to voice the truth within iniquitous systems.

Oscar Romero was archbishop of San Salvador in the late 1970s, a period of political turmoil and severe human rights abuses perpetrated by the government, which sponsored death squads to kill those who they saw as a threat to their power. Romero spoke out sharply against government repression and the widespread assassinations that were occurring. He corresponded with the president of the United States, Jimmy Carter, requesting assistance in the form of a moratorium on US military aid to El Salvador.

While saying Mass in March of 1980, Archbishop Romero delivered a sermon condemning the widespread violence, calling on soldiers to disobey orders and stop the senseless murder. "I would like to make a special appeal to the men of the army, and specifically to the ranks of the national guard, the police, and the military. Brothers, you come from our own people. You

13. Boyle, *Tattoos on the Heart*, 72.
14. Luke 4:18–19 NIV.

are killing your own brother peasants when any human order to kill must be subordinate to the law of God which says, 'Thou shalt not kill.' No soldier is obliged to carry out an order contrary to the law of God. No one has to obey an immoral law. . . . In the name of God, in the name of this suffering people whose cries rise to heaven more loudly each day, I beg of you, I implore you, I order you in the name of God: stop the repression."[15]

The following day Romero again said Mass. After the homily, he returned to the altar, about to begin the Eucharistic prayers, consecrate the communion hosts, and recall the words of Jesus at the last supper: "Take this, all of you, and eat it; this is my body which will be given up for you. . . . Take this, all of you, and drink from it; this is the cup of my blood, the blood of the new and everlasting covenant. It will be shed for you and for all so that sins may be forgiven. Do this in memory of me."

A lone gunmen pulled up to the chapel and exited his vehicle with a rifle in hand. A few seconds later, a single shot rang out. Blood spilled from Romero's chest where the bullet had penetrated, reddening the communion hosts, his body broken, his blood shed.

Romero had earlier foreshadowed this moment, saying, "If they kill me I will rise again in the people of El Salvador. . . . If they manage to carry out their threats, as of now I offer my blood for the redemption and resurrection of the people of El Salvador. . . . May my blood be the seed of liberty and the sign that hope will soon become a reality. . . . May my death be for the liberation of my people, as a witness of hope in what is to come."[16]

Hope is a journey with God that is both long and costly, through which we are continually being transformed into new life.[17] Romero's hope wasn't cheap. It ended up costing him everything. The hope he embodied in his prophetic voice and his action toward justice in the face of violence was an eschatological type of hope—anticipation for fullness of God's kingdom manifest—in a future El Salvador where the rifles of death squads had been beaten into plowshares, where the power-brokering lions had laid down with the defenseless lambs, where government assassins lived in community with the peasants they once targeted, where a powerful neighbor nation sought mutual benefit rather than self-interested, ideological foreign policy moves. A future where shalom reigned.

---

15. Romero, sermon (March 1980), as cited in Goldston, *Year of Reckoning*, 4.

16. Romero, in a 1980 interview with the newspaper *Excelsior* (Mexico City), as cited in Keane, "Oscar Romero's Beatification," lines 12–21.

17. Katongole and Rice, *Reconciling All Things*, 101.

A Prophet's Imagination

Just a year after Romero was assassinated in 1980, one thousand civilians were massacred in the village El Mozote in the eastern part of the country. For three days, US-trained forces slaughtered men, women, and children. It was without question the worst atrocity of El Salvador's civil war and in modern Latin American history.[18]

The United States had been giving military aid to the government of El Salvador to the tune of a million dollars a day. There was a giant cover-up and denial of the event by the United States, and El Salvador granted amnesty to any soldiers who may have been involved. The families of victims, afraid of retaliation and traumatized by the slaughter, generally didn't talk about it, trying to forget and move on. Year after year, the tragedy remained buried on all sides. Then in 2008 a British nun and priest convinced the Inter-American Court of Human Rights to hear the case even though the Salvadoran courts still refused to. The nun, Anne Griffin, traveled the countryside to conduct interviews along with a psychologist. Most of the people they spoke about El Mozote were talking openly about the event for the very first time. The majority wept as if it had just occurred.[19]

In 2012, the Inter-American Court of Human Rights found the government of El Salvador guilty of the massacre and issued an order to reopen the case. As a result, immediate relatives of victims have received some monetary recompense and a memorial plaque has been installed. People are finally free to talk about what happened, to tell their stories to each other. There is now a group that meets regularly to discuss efforts to continue seeking recognition.[20]

The thirty-fifth anniversary of the El Mozote massacre was commemorated in December of 2016. Families of victims gathered. Youth learned of what happened and why. Elders in the community shared memories. There was grief and mourning. Tears were shed for what was lost then and what remains lost. Over three decades after the killings, a community continues to seek healing of that wound. They are turning toward it, facing the pain of the past, entering grief, and lamenting loss in a communal act of bringing hurt to public expression. This is the prophetic imagination at work.

18. Maslin, "Remembering El Mozote."
19. Ibid.
20. Ibid.

Romero's hope endures inside of this prophetic community, in which a new social reality continues to emerge in the midst of the old one.

As a prisoner of hope, Romero was captive to a vision of a world where violence and oppression is but a memory—a world being birthed into the midst of this broken one. Even amid egregious assaults on his people, where assassination was an everyday occurrence, where death squads were unescapable, Romero embodied this hope born of and borne by his prophetic imagination. Amid the violence of systemic poverty and the violence of murder, hope remained. That vision cost him everything. Jesus' words "Greater love has no one than this: to lay down one's life for one's friends"[21] became the archbishop's lived reality.

Romero's life testifies to the reality that hope asks everything of the one who bears the prophetic imagination. Sometimes it leads to physical death. More often, it brings another kind of death, a dying to the ego and its self-interested visions, a withering away of the infirm Western imagination for the risky way of the prophet's imagination.

The prophetic imagination doesn't casually arise. Despite Romero's active involvement in the lives of the poor and oppressed, he practiced not only action, but contemplation. He saw the work of ministry on behalf of the oppressed and the work of cultivating inner transformation as equally important, illustrated in words from one of his sermons: "The most profound social revolution is the serious, supernatural, interior reform of a Christian."[22] A radical commitment to justice, truth, and liberation didn't blind him to the necessity of spiritual formation. A devotee of St. Ignatius and the Ignatian Spiritual Exercises, Romero was engaged in spiritual direction and contemplative prayer. For Romero, action and contemplation, ministry and spirituality were two sides of the same coin. His dedication to the spiritual life in the midst of nefarious state-sanctioned bloodshed allowed him to embody a hope born of his prophetic imagination.

For Romero, inner work and outer work were one.

Mystic and Prophet Embrace

Karl Rahner said that in the future we will be mystics or we will be nothing at all.[23] The mystic is one who has experienced God for real, one who

---

21. John 15:13 NIV.

22. Romero, "Most Profound," as cited in Daly, "Transfigured by Love," lines 24–26.

23. Rahner, "Christian Living," as cited in Staub, *Culturally Savvy Christian*, 80.

knows God—not just information about God. The mystic encounters the world with a transformed way of seeing and being, of serving and loving as Romero had. The mystic is one who continually faces and accepts the small self on the journey toward prophetic action against injustice.

Thomas Merton, one of this nation's great mystics, lived in a Trappist monastery in Kentucky where he practiced the contemplative way. Through a disciplined inner journey of prayer and contemplation, he cultivated an awareness regarding the experience of God that is so relevant to spiritual formation in ministry. Coming to know God was the goal of spiritual practice for Merton. He referred to this desire for the divine as seeking "the experience of presence." This is what all spiritual practice is about, this sense of Presence with us, beyond the mind and ego. It is in these experiences that the head-based nature of our faith fades away and belief takes a backseat to embodied experience. What we had clung to so firmly we now grasp with a loose fist. In the presence of God, the mind slows and its anxious chatter gives way to the open heart's innate capacity to know, to feel, to experience divine love. Our previous clinging to cerebral concepts, ideas, and propositions about God relax while our deepest longings to experience the divine for real arise.

This is the space of silent experiential knowing that all true mystics have been grasped by. And a grasping, though gentle, it is. We are gripped by Another, held tenderly with a strength that is both feminine and masculine. The ego, the false self, for this moment has ceased to exist. The true self hidden with Christ in God[24] emerges from background to foreground.

The ego cannot experience truth, cannot fall in love, cannot taste the divine. This is why Merton was so steadfast in living and teaching about the spiritual life, for the very reason that spirituality is about transforming the small self. The ego is experienced as an isolated, separate self, the part of us that viscerally feels as though it is disconnected from God and others. And the ego has one main goal: survival. Its desire, like the empire, is immortality. The dream of the ego usurps the dream of God; the mission of the ego overshadows the mission of God—which is precisely why Jesus said one must deny oneself (ego) and follow him.[25]

The small self wants security in having the right beliefs; the soul desires the risky encounter of experiencing God for real. It is the mystic who has transformed the ego in such a way. It is also what the Apostle Paul was

24. Col 3:3.
25. Matt 16:24.

referring to when he said, "My old self [small self] has been crucified with Christ. It is no longer I [ego] who live, but Christ lives in me."[26] No longer the small self that needs to be important, that needs to be seen, that needs to live for its own agenda. The small self has been let go of so completely that Another—Christ, the divine, Presence—is leading one's life.

Authentic spirituality and the contemplative journey aren't about bliss. The spiritual path is deeply challenging because it always has something to do with death—the ego dying. "For you have died and your life is how hidden with Christ in God."[27] For you have died to your false self and your real life, your true self, is alive, hidden with Christ in God. An interior process is undergone as we transform into the new creation in Christ.[28] New creation means first dying to the old. It is the mystic whose ego has been transformed through dying. His self-importance and need for power and control has been surrendered. She has taken the risky plunge of release into divine love.

Merton, far from being hermetically sealed off from the real world of toil and suffering, was engaged in the realm of politics, including the civil rights movement of the 1960s. In fact, Merton so fully engaged in activist work that he was criticized sharply for his outspoken form of spirituality that put flesh to his words and footsteps to his prayers.

"What is the relation of [contemplation] to action?" asked Merton.

"Simply this. He who attempts to act and do things for others or for the world without deepening his own self-understanding, freedom, integrity, and capacity to love, will not have anything to give others. He will communicate to them nothing but the contagion of his own obsessions, his aggressiveness, his ego-centered ambitions, his delusions about ends and means, his doctrinaire prejudices and ideas. There is nothing more tragic in the modern world than the misuse of power and action."[29]

As a prophet and mystic, Merton's contemplative practice produced an outward orientation toward issues of justice that is one of the fruits of spiritual practice. Deep spirituality impels us to action, and action impels us to deep spirituality through a continuous circle of deepening. The mystic is fashioned into prophet and the prophet becomes mystic.[30]

26. Gal 2:20 NLT.
27. Col 3:3 NIV.
28. 2 Cor 5:17.
29. Merton, *Spiritual Master*, 375.
30. Dyckman and Carroll, *Inviting the Mystic*, 80.

Reflection Questions

1. In what ways have you sensed the call to serve others? How has your interior journey shaped your outer work and vice versa?

2. How have you sensed your understanding of calling shift or change?

3. In what ways might your calling be about identity and being named in addition to your work or ministry?

4. How have you witnessed calling unfold in positive ways in your own life or the life of others? In ways that have caused harm and hardship to you and others?

5. Imagine you are sitting with Jesus and his disciples in Jerusalem, having a conversation about the work each of you are called to do in the world. It is your turn to speak. What do you say? How does Jesus reply?

6. Where do you find resonance in the call to being a prophet? A mystic?

9

Your Brain on Mission

> The brain is the organ of destiny. It holds within its hum-
> ming mechanism secrets that will determine the future . . .

—Wilder Penfield

> I've always firmly believed that the deeper realms of hu-
> man emotion and motivation operate at the unconscious
> level, and that they are processed in the right and not the
> left brain.

—Allan Schore

American Brain

CULTURES ARE GENERALLY CENTERED around one of two organizing principles, individualism or collectivism. Individualist cultures,
which include North America, the majority of Europe, Australia, and New
Zealand, highly value personal freedom and independence. The locus of
organization of these societies is the individual self, where the needs of the
individual are more important than the needs of the group.

Collectivist cultures, including most of East and South Asia, Latin
America, and Africa, are based on an organizing principle that values the
group over the individual and emphasize the importance of community
and family. Rather than placing highest significance on independence, collectivism emphasizes interdependence.[1]

---

1. See Markus and Kitayama, "Culture and the Self."

Collectivism and individualism permeate all aspects of a given society, generally without people's conscious awareness. What we eat, where we shop, the movies we watch, and the way we greet people are all culturally mediated aspects of everyday life. The McDonald's drive-through window (and fast food in general) and elderly living separate from their families in assisted living facilities or nursing homes are a few examples of Western cultural phenomena born of individualism.

As we noted earlier, culture is a lens. It is as much something we see through as it is something we see in the world. Culture exists *out there* but it is as much *in here*—literally. Culture is wired into our brains. Researchers are beginning to find that the brain's neuropathways—the corridors along which neurons transmit information—are shaped by culture. Over the past fifteen years, these findings have given birth to a new field known as cultural neuroscience, which investigates how culture impacts brain development and, likewise, how the brain impacts culture.

The emerging neuroscientific data is beginning to tell a new and fascinating story about the brain. It isn't the autonomous, isolated instrument of consciousness that scientists once thought. The brain is culturally constituted.

People from the West, due to the nature of individualism, process objects and organize information by way of rules and categories. East Asians, on the other hand, tend to view themselves in the context of a larger whole, and as a result, process information in a holistic way in which a central object as well as surrounding context are considered. For example, one study revealed that when Japanese and American participants are shown pictures of fish swimming in an underwater environment, people from Japan recall contextual details—the environment the fish were swimming in—better than Americans.[2]

Another study measured the brain activity of American and Chinese participants while being shown pictures of a giraffe on a savannah followed by the same giraffe on a football field. The results of the MRI imaging showed that the brains of the Chinese participants were affected more by incongruence—the giraffe standing on a football field—than their American counterparts, whose brains showed no difference whether the giraffe was on the sports field or standing on the savannah where it would be found in nature.[3] This indicates that Americans don't tend to pay as

2. Ibid.

3. See Azar, "Your Brain on Culture."

much attention to context as Chinese. Because of the way our brains are structured culturally, we don't naturally focus as much on background details. It's not the way our brains are inclined due to the individualism of our society. Information regarding how things are in relation to one another takes priority for East Asians—a consequence of the structure and function of the brains of people from collectivist cultures.[4]

According to the data, it seems the brains of Westerners have to work extra hard to see context, to notice what isn't obvious. And when we travel overseas to a collectivist culture, we are likely to see things differently—literally—than the local people we will be serving and collaborating with. We are inclined, given the structure and function of the American brain, to favor certain types of approaches and ways of engaging. We are apt to focus on the foreground: the pressing issues in a given place and what we can do to help solve them. We might see lack of access to clean water or education or the absence of a church in a particular area. Focusing on the problem, we can then work to solve it, which is a good thing. That is a blessing of our Western, individualist neurological architecture.

But at the same time, our brains are not naturally disposed to noticing the background, the context in which the problem exists. It takes looking at the complexity to observe the thing behind the thing, the problem beneath the problem, since the most visible aspect of a given issue can't simply be put out like a fire with a water hose. It isn't hard to see the giraffe. But the football field, the background where the deeper issues lie, takes a bit more effort and a different way of seeing.

Because of how the Western brain is constituted, people from the West have a kind of neurological predisposition to disregarding background context. Like in the study of the fish in an underwater environment, Americans have to train our brains to see the whole picture in order to engage complex problems.

Fortunately, neuropathways are malleable because of the brain's inherent plasticity. New neural connections can be made in the American brain that modulate its deficits while maintaining its strengths. The one thing it takes is practice; repetition is key. Asking questions related to the background in which issues are embedded is one way to practice:

How is collective trauma from a decades-old civil war contributing to gang violence in San Salvador?

4. See Park and Huang, *Culture Wires the Brain*.

How is the internalization of colonialism and white, Western supremacy creating profound shame, feelings of inferiority, and a sense of helplessness in a community devastated by AIDS in Lesotho?

The more we ask contextual questions, the more we look beyond the surface, the more our brains begin to create new neuropathways that help us participate in the work of mission more like the Apostle Paul.

As we've seen, the brain is never apart from a cultural matrix; the brain and all of its neural structures are enculturated. In relation to a culture, the brain is both acting and being acted on, both shaping and being shaped. As it turns out, so is Christianity. Richard Neuhaus wrote, "Christianity is never to be found apart from a cultural matrix; Christianity in all its forms is, as it is said, 'enculturated.' In relation to a culture, the Church is both acting and being acted on, both shaping and being shaped."[5]

Our brains and our faith tradition have, surprisingly, much more in common than we thought, which raises some fascinating questions about the relationship between the brain and the church. The interface of American culture, American Jesus, and the American brain form a shared boundary of social, religious, and neurological exchange, a triad that shapes how we see and interpret the world. Christianity, culture, and the brain all interpenetrate, each shaping and being shaped by the others. It appears that since the neurology of an individual is culturally constituted, (i.e., shaped by cultural processes) the church both shapes and is shaped by culture and the brain.

Truly, there is no culture-free expression of the gospel, church, ministry, or mission because not only is Christianity never found apart from a cultural matrix, neither is the brain. To look at why this matters, we'll have to look at the two sides of the brain.

The brain is divided into separate hemispheres. The right hemisphere controls nonverbal functions, creativity, imagination, feeling, and intuition. It "begins with a relationship to the world at large, not seeing it as a separate object, ripe for manipulation. It is involved with new experience, new events, things, ideas, words, skills or music; it connects with the concrete world of experience. Its attention is in the service of connection, exploration and relation. The defining quality of the right hemisphere's world is that it thrives on relatedness. It engages each event it encounters as unique.

---

5. Neuhaus, *Religion Business*, lines 5–8.

Because of the right hemisphere, we reach out to connect, to create, to share in another's fate, or to explore the world for what it is."[6]

The left hemisphere controls logic and analytical processes. It is the "narrow-beam, precisely focused attention, which enables us to get and grasp. . . . Its attention is narrow, its vision myopic, and it cannot see how the parts fit together. It is good for manipulating the world and controlling the parts. It neglects the incarnate nature of human beings and reduces the living to the mechanical. It prioritizes procedure without having a grasp of meaning or purpose."[7]

The dominance of the left hemisphere in Western people began to be seen around the fourth century, about the same time Greek culture reached its zenith. Previous to this, going back to the sixth century BC, historical records related to art and science show more integration of the hemispheres.[8] As the left brain became more dominant in Western Christianity, "knowledge of God and the things of God began not with experience (the right brain) but with the hypothetical question (the left brain)."[9]

The Brain and the Center of the Universe

Claudius Ptolemy, a mathematician who lived in Rome around the year AD 100, developed a mathematical model for understanding the universe. According to his research, the earth was the center of the solar system. It wasn't until nearly 1,400 years later that a different model, proposed by Copernicus, located the sun as center of the solar system. There was an uproar in medieval society. Being in the center held great significance both cosmologically and psychologically. The center felt secure. It afforded meaning and a place of cosmological importance. The science behind the new heliocentric worldview brought about a collective crisis of identity.[10]

About a hundred years into the Copernican revolution, Descartes showed up on the scene in the midst of this disorientation in Europe. His most notable line, "I think, therefore I am," illustrated that, since the world no longer carried the same meaning as it once had before Copernicus,

6. Delio, "The Church and the Divided Brain," lines 30–34.

7. Ibid., 35–42.

8. Ibid.

9. Ibid., 54–56.

10. Due to limits on what can be covered here, it should be noted that I am painting the monumental developments of Western science and philosophy with a broad brush.

that displaced meaning was reassigned to the mental realm. The foundation for existence was now based on the mental faculty of thought: I have thought therefore I exist. The mental realm was seen, for the first time, as completely distinct from the physical one, not a common view in Europe up until that point.

Largely as a result of Descartes's philosophy, the unseen was completely detached from the seen. This shift in the pattern of logic was dubbed the Cartesian dualism, mind and matter forever dueling, one over against another. Not only had people lost a sense of inherent meaning and significance, estranged from their place in the center, but now mind was distanced from matter, seen placed in contradiction with unseen. This in turn influenced the dualistic separation of body and soul, spirit and flesh, divine and human—the very opposites that Jesus held together within himself.

As the hemispheres became further divided and the left brain predominance solidified, an emphasis on the systematization of knowledge and ideals as well as theoretical laws in the place of an equal valuing of embodied experience resulted in Europe.[11] As mind and matter, soul and body were placed into contravening positions largely due to Descartes, and as the divided brain continued toward a left hemisphere dominance, hard boundaries were drawn between outer and inner, heaven and earth, mind and matter, body and soul, work and prayer. The divided brain brought about a divided worldview of duality in Western society. This in turn influenced church doctrine and teaching. The inner orientation of prayer and contemplation was placed at odds with the outer orientation of mission. One of the major consequences was the great divorce between action and contemplation. The outward orientation of mission was split off from the inner posture of spirituality.

Postmodern Mission

The left brain brought with it astounding benefits, including an overwhelming amount of progress in the modern era: wide spread urbanization, industrialization, and massive technological growth. Staggering advances in medicine, education, and social services were realized. Life expectancy grew. But along with all of that good came the hyper-individualism of modern societies in the West and a period centered on "a fundamental split between divine and nondivine which stands in opposition to . . . the

11. See Delio, "The Church and the Divided Brain."

Incarnation."[12] In other words, in the modern era, the church made the impossible attempt to find truth separate from incarnation, from living, breathing embodiment and experience. Favoring the unseen realm of spirit, focusing on ethereal afterlife at the expense of the lowly, mundane, fleshly mix of everyday toil and splendor.

A departure from the modern era began to take shape in the late twentieth century, influencing philosophy, religion, art, and culture. Essentially, postmodernism reinterprets modernity's incomplete interpretation of the world. From a faith perspective, it is a response to errors of the recent past, "the outworking of mistakes in Christian theology correlative to the attempt to make Christianity 'true' apart from faithful witness."[13] This was the endeavor of making Christianity true separated from relationship, outside of incarnation as if the Word was never made flesh. The church over focused on the Word while ignoring, and sometimes even condemning, the flesh despite the whole of the Christian position resting on the Word taking on flesh and living as one of us.

Since Word and flesh became one in Jesus, the endeavor to make Christianity true apart from bodies in relationship is ultimately a futile project. It was a blunder of trying to *make* Christianity true rather than an approach where the body of Christ was *being* truth in the world.

Before Jesus was condemned to death, he stood before Pontius Pilate, governor of Judea, who posed him a question: "What is truth?" a common philosophical inquiry asked across time and cultures.

Is truth available to be known or seen or grasped?

Can truth be found somewhere?

And if so, how then shall we live according to it?

Pilate's question is one that each of us have likely asked. And yet, it is as stands a Roman question not framed in light of the life, death, and resurrection of Jesus. The Christian question pivots from "What is truth?" to "Who is truth?"

According to the Christian narrative, truth is not a metaphysical proposition, something to figure out or lay claim to having the rights to. Truth, rather, is the Person who stood facing Pilate. Truth is Jesus Christ.

The Word that became flesh and lived as one of us said, "I am the way and the truth and the life."[14] With this statement, Jesus wasn't making an

---

12. Hauerwas, *Better Hope*, 13.

13. Ibid., 38.

14. John 14:6 NIV.

identity claim. He was turning truth from a concept into a person,[15] from a disembodied idea into a flesh-and-bone reality. He turned truth upside down, from a proposition to be understood to a relational reality. If Jesus is truth as he said, it means that we don't have to look for truth somewhere out there. And if Jesus is truth, it means that truth is found in the context of relationship. Rather than something to be searched for and figured out or a problem to be solved or something to lay claim to having the rights to, truth is Someone we can look at, whose eyes we can gaze into. Truth is a Person we can fall in love with.[16]

"In Christian tradition," Parker Palmer writes, "truth is not a concept that 'works' but an incarnation that lives."[17] The incarnation that lives is the Word made flesh who dwelled among us.[18] Word and flesh, seen and unseen, immanent and transcendent interpenetrate rather than duel against one another as the church mistakenly taught for centuries, the mistake that defied the fundamental nature of Christ and the cosmos itself while deifying the dualistic split of so-called opposites which Jesus has already reconciled.

In this age of division, suspicion, fear, and violence, we would do well to return to the gospel meaning of truth revealed by Jesus. The church's great postmodern opportunity is to confess its mistakes and seriously consider Jesus' words about the embodied, relational nature of truth. As Jesus followers reclaim the Christian position of truth as incarnate relationship revealed in the Scriptures, there is a great opportunity for a new kind of Christian mission. By reclaiming what it means to be sent into relationship with those dwelling on the margins as Jesus was sent to be in relationship with the world, we can reimagine global mission with such freshness and vitality that the word "mission," with all of its baggage and brokenness, is rendered an insufficient container to hold the potential for what can be.

Within this postmodern moment, collectively we have begun to see beyond the constraints of modernity's models of mission and have begun to peer into a future in which something new is emerging. Beyond modernity's assumptions, ethos, and approaches to missiology there are fresh expressions arising. A paradigm shift is upon us in which mission is freed from the Western imagination, action and contemplation are reintegrated, a memory of

15. See Rohr, *Naked Now*.

16. Ibid., 154.

17. Palmer, *To Know as We Are Known*, 14.

18. John 1:14.

history is cultivated, empire's forces are confessed, and messiah complexes are released. Mystics and prophets embrace once again. This moment in which we are now situated is ripe with opportunity to redeem the interanimating stories of missionary, place, and gospel while looking with new eyes on what it means to be sent across geographical, ethnic, racial, linguistic, and theological boundaries. This is a *post-mission* moment.

The post-mission opportunity is not so much about going beyond or transcending mission per se. Rather, it's about reconstituting it, refashioning it from the inside out through the recognition that the old methods, guiding narratives, and approaches are limited and have a need to be re-imagined. The foundation of mission, as we have seen, is filled with patchwork repairs, and continues to crumble. Rather than attempting more fixes, it is time to pour a new foundation. In this post-mission moment, we have the great possibility and indeed responsibility to rebuild mission from the ground up. A post-mission ethos holds the matrix of history and narrative, unconscious and conscious, theology and culture as central to the task. It is concerned with our own brokenness as well as the brokenness of the world. The post-mission paradigm shift underway both honors wounds and affirms dignity. It has begun to free mission from the constraints of the past and present, and as a consequence, to free the Spirit from our intentional and unintentional errors and omissions. Ironically, a particular population of Christians who lived a millennium ago epitomized a missional paradigm that can help lead us into the post-mission future that is now arriving in our midst.

Post-Mission Pilgrim Posture

Centuries prior to modernism and the great divorce between action and contemplation, spirituality and mission, the ancient Celtic Christians of present-day Great Britain, Scotland, and Ireland embraced a deep, earthly spirituality rooted in non-duality. The Celts saw in wholes more than in parts. They viewed life in terms of union rather than division, practicing a fleshy faith that reverenced all of creation and held the entire cosmos as sacred.

Often traveling to faraway lands as pilgrims who "said yes to a risky way of living," they left their homelands in small sailboats to embark on epic sea passages, reaching foreign shores where they would remain for the rest of their lives, which they referred to as the place of their resurrection. With a posture of humility and respect, the Celtic missionaries entered into relationships of exquisite mutuality with the people they encountered on the far shores, deeply reverencing the personhood of the other while living alongside them as equals. The Celtic model of mission included offering medical care and teaching agricultural techniques, with an overall emphasis of being in community together.

The Celtic evangelists were first and foremost dedicated to faithful presence with the people who they hoped would come to embrace the ways of Christ. The Celts who left their homes were pilgrim-missionaries. Mission was pilgrimage and pilgrimage was mission. There was no separation between their embodied missional orientation and a mystical way of seeing.

The beginning of the end of Celtic Christianity came at the Synod of Whitby in AD 664. The Roman and Celtic traditions had some disagreements over the date of Easter as well as the proper length of hair of monks. The Roman church took precedence. Over the following centuries, the Celtic Christian tradition slowly began to fade as it was usurped by the Roman church. The Celtic way was all but lost, and along with it, the tradition of pilgrim-missionaries engaging communities they visited with the imaginative, right-brained spirituality focused on relational connection among each other, God, and the earth.

The pre-colonial, pre-Enlightenment faith of the Celtic Christians can be reintegrated into mission and ministry today, shaping leaders who catalyze transformation in themselves as well as the materially poor. Re-visioning the post-mission opportunity through the lens of pilgrimage in our globalized world means coming to see with Celtic eyes, re-embracing nonduality and reverencing the sacredness at the heart of all people, the cosmos, and ourselves. The integration of the brain hemispheres through contemplative practice is a key part of embracing a post-mission imagination.

The interface of mission and pilgrimage offers us an opportunity to reawaken to ancient practices. Pilgrimage can help facilitate a movement toward new models of cross-cultural engagement based on the ancient-future synergy of contemplative activism which Christians can reclaim from the obscurification of the colonial and neocolonial projects, a dualistic worldview, and empire's spirituality. Pilgrimage can give the forgotten half of mission back to itself, reinstituting the hidden wholeness that Western missional Christians need to rejoin action and contemplation, two separate aspects of a single contiguous process. Pilgrimage can become an important conduit for this merger, assisting us in telling a fresh story through which global mission can mature while simultaneously recovering its roots and begin redeeming the ghosts of the past. Integration is what lies at the core of the post-mission opportunity, this moment of grace in which we are situated, from which we can become pilgrims witnessing to the kingdom.

Pilgrim Witness

During a trip to El Salvador, I visited the chapel at Divina Providencia Hospital where Archbishop Oscar Romero had been assassinated. I stood at the altar and faced the pews, imagining him in that very spot over thirty years prior. The words he spoke foreshadowing his martyrdom echoed silently through me: "I offer my blood to God for the redemption and resurrection of the people of El Salvador."[19]

Later that afternoon, I visited the Catedral Metropolitana, where he was laid to rest. Kneeling at his tomb, I was taken by the silence and sanctity of the space. A sudden grief took me by surprise. Tears streamed down my cheeks and onto the white marble floor.

I had come to El Salvador to visit a faith-based transformational development organization led by local Salvadorans, there to learn, not teach, listen rather than speak. Without an agenda, I remained at the periphery rather than at the center, learning from local leaders about the work they were carrying out in some of the most violent neighborhoods of San Salvador. I had come to El Salvador as a pilgrim rather than a missionary.

Pilgrimage has often been used as a metaphor of life's journey, a long walk through the diverse array of landscapes, some of arduous pain and disorienting chaos, others of bliss, of glory, of dreams fulfilled. In pilgrimage, it is the journey that matters, the process rather than the product. There is no fixed strategy. Instead, there is story. There is humility in honoring the divine that is already present. The pilgrim posture is one of journeying toward inner transformation. Pilgrimage is an embodied encounter more than a cerebral experience.

To go on pilgrimage is to contemplate. To be a pilgrim is also to encounter the present through an eschatological, future-oriented lens of fullness of the kingdom. The tension between the two, what is and what is to come, is what the pilgrim intentionally bears, a vessel for unifying the duality between the "already" and the "not yet" of the kingdom.

The posture of a pilgrim is much different from that of a missionary. A focus on "What can I do? How can I help? Who can I bring Jesus to?" is

19. Romero, *La Voz*, as cited in Dear, "Romero's Resurrection," lines 3–4.

replaced with, "In what ways do I need saving? Where am I noticing the presence and absence of God in myself and in the world? In what ways is my own heart lost?" Well-planned ideas and strategies for making a difference fade. Agendas are released. Control is relinquished. The illusion of being experts who have all the answers gives way to listening to the stories of people.

Pilgrimage can also act as a conduit for exposing the places in us where we have carefully hidden pain away, neat and tidy. The emotion that surfaced as I kneeled at Romero's tomb fell forth as tears as much for myself as for Romero and El Salvador. The process of pilgriming can unzip our core and expose the places where pain is located—especially when we're not prepared. Other times while on pilgrimage, on the Camino de Santiago in Spain and in Lourdes, France, I have been utterly surprised by the potency of what has emerged from the depths. Often, it has been suppressed grief that, despite the assistance of gifted therapists and spiritual directors remained untended, is given an opportunity to rise.

The art of pilgrimage is the art of connecting stories, those stories through which we heal and the ones through which we've been broken and have broken others. Walking the inner road of transformation and the outer path of reconciliation draws us further into the core of who we are. Pilgrimage offers an intentional opportunity to touch buried pain and wounds, coming face to face, breath to breath, with darkness and light in us as well as in the world. Only in healing the brokenness in ourselves can we hope to heal the brokenness in the world. As untended emotions are processed through, we emerge more connected and integrated than previously.

Pilgrimage is a practice that is facilitating the post-mission turn. The practice of pilgrimage reflects a microcosm of the journey we are on into wholeness and healing for the brokenness in ourselves and the world through authentic spirituality, vulnerability, and real dialogue in the context of community. In the practice of pilgrimage, inner work and outer work converge, left brain and right brain are reintegrated, mystic and prophet kiss. From this posture, we become pilgrim witnesses to the kingdom.[20]

Reflection Questions

1. Given the recent findings of neuroscience which tells us that our brains are culturally constituted and that the "American brain" has certain strengths and deficits, how might you begin to practice seeing

20. Stroope, *Transcending Mission*.

context and background information more clearly? Think of a situation that you are familiar with where shifting focus from the problems of the foreground to the context of the background may be helpful.

2. Many of the countries where North Americans travel to in order to serve are collectivist cultures. What are some specific ways you might see things differently from people in the collectivist cultures you have visited? How have you seen the individualist/collectivist differences create challenges?

3. What aspects of the Celtic model of mission resonate with you?

10

Missionary Republic

> I am sorry to have to share this with you, but the impact
> of the Church's collusion with empire must be confessed
> or we will never be free from it.
>
> —RICHARD ROHR

> This God is not to be confused with or thought parallel to
> the insatiable gods of imperial productivity. This God is
> subsequently revealed as a God of mercy, steadfast love,
> and faithfulness who is committed to covenantal rela-
> tionships of fidelity (see Exod 34:6–7).
>
> —WALTER BRUEGGEMANN

In the Beginning Was the War

CREATION NARRATIVES FROM DIFFERENT cultures show us something
about the way a particular society understood how their deity brought
forth life. In the Judeo-Christian tradition, light and form emerged from the
watery void as God spoke. Speaking ordered the chaos. In the Babylonian
creation story, called the *Enuma Elish*, creation happened after a battle between two gods. The male god killed and dismembered the female god and
from her dead body the world was formed. The Babylonians founded one
of the most powerful empires in the ancient world, one that originated not
through divine word, but by divine violence.

A story from a later period, from a culture that also grew into a great
empire, reveals some similar themes. According to Roman mythology, the

founding of Rome can be traced back to a time when a beautiful princess gave birth to twin brothers, Romulus and Remus. Their father was Mars, god of war. In the region where the boys grew up lived a king who was fearful that they would oust him from power since their father was a powerful deity. So the king took the twins, placed them in a reed basket and set them on the Tiber River in hopes they would be drowned. A she-wolf discovered Romulus and Remus, caring for them until the day came when a shepherd took them in and raised them as his own sons.

Romulus and Remus grew up to be young men of honor and influence. Together they decided to leave home in order to found their own city. On their journey, they came across a suitable area with several hills. Romulus was preferential to Palatine Hill while Remus was partial to Aventine Hill. Unable to agree on where to begin building, they waited for a sign from the gods in order to decide. Each brother claimed divine favor and Romulus started building a wall around Palatine Hill. In his jealously, Remus began to make fun of his brother's wall and jumped over it in demonstration of how simple it was to scale. In a rage, Romulus killed Remus. So began the fratricidal founding of Rome and the commencement of its reign of "peace and prosperity" through war, domination, and violence, expanding throughout the Mediterranean region and beyond, lasting for nearly 1,500 years.

Of course, the founding narratives of Babylon and Rome aren't meant to be taken factually, but they hint at some common patterns. First, empires are created through violence and always create more violence to ensure longevity and, ultimately, immortality. Eternal life is the empire's eschatalogical aim. Toward this end it seeks "peace and prosperity," life, and creation, ironically, through war and violence.

Second, the leaders of empire look to the gods to bestow power and favor and then assert that "blessing" through absolute control. As we saw in chapter 1, the Romans wielded power over against their subjects—a dominion that was believed to have been given from the gods above. While ruling on earth, the emperors were seen as sons of god. Upon their death, they became deities who interceded for the success of their kingdom; the sons of god ruling for the good of the empire on earth became gods doing the same work in heaven through an eternal inheritance of divinity.

Empire also functions based on asymmetrical power dynamics; relationships are characterized by power over and against. There is no openness to the other or willingness to be exposed. In the empire's relational blueprint, any sign of vulnerability is seen as weakness, which, of course, is a threat to power. This impermeability contributes to relationships based in fear and a constant defending against perceived threats.

Empire remains violent because it is inherently numb. It doesn't feel anything except for satiation, the pseudo contentment of "uncritical laughter" and rage. Invulnerable, it cannot feel anything more—not sorrow or fear, not grief or joy. Neither can empire be empathic or compassionate, which means *to feel with*.

Empire refuses to feel pain, to be vulnerable, and so to transform itself. Instead, it projects its pain, externalizing it by choosing a scapegoat to blame for its own pathology. Depending on the time and context, the scapegoat could be religious heretics, witches, Jews, immigrants, Muslims, blacks, and so on. Empire cannot hear the cry of the oppressed.

As we've seen, the mythology of empire sheds light on how it operates and the "divinities" that create it. But God is not one of the gods. God becomes flesh and feels pain; the gods stay disembodied in the heavens. God is crucified; the gods refuse to die, instead condoning crucifixion and denying resurrection. God makes himself the nonviolent victim; the gods use violence to assert power and victimize. The gods demand sacrifice; God puts an end to the entire violent sacrificial order, becoming the forgiving victim who puts an end to all blood sacrifice in Jesus of Nazareth.[1] The gods are human projections of our rivalry and paranoia.

Tracing the creation mythology of empires and juxtaposing God and the gods may be interesting information about the fundamentals of how empire functions. But since we don't believe in the existence of gods, and since Babylon and Rome are ancient history and empire doesn't exist in those classical forms anymore, why does it matter for us today?

The British Empire was the largest and most powerful in history, reaching its zenith about a hundred years ago when it controlled twenty-five percent of the world's population and twenty-five percent of Earth's land surface. A mere four generations ago, classical empire was at its peak. India didn't gain independence from the British until 1947. Kenya in 1962. Zimbabwe not until 1980.

Empire is not a distant memory.

Since the colonies gained independence from Spain, Britain, France, Portugal, and other global superpowers, empire has certainly shape-shifted from its classic form, continually changing and being reborn in new

---

1. We will look more at the suffering of God below.

iterations. Recognizing what empire looks like in the present is particularly relevant to those who seek peace, justice, and flourishing for those living on the margins of global society.

Empire Lite

The Third Reich had come to power in Germany five years earlier and Hitler's campaign of Aryanization through systematic extermination of the Jews was in full swing. During a meeting of European intellectuals, two Austrian economists who had fled the Nazi regime coined the term neoliberalism, an economic theory that emphasized the free market and the transfer of power from the public to the private sector. This would not only create robust economic growth, they affirmed, but also stand against the dangers of the bourgeoning communism and Nazism at the time.[2] The macroeconomic policies underlying neoliberalism became the engine that would drive global interconnectedness in terms of trade, capital, and technology at a level that no one had ever dared to imagine—the phenomenon that would come to be known as globalization.

This worldwide movement of people, resources, and companies driven by international trade and aided by information technology provides abundant opportunities and benefits, including soaring profits for multinational corporations and astonishing wealth creation. Globalization is a corporate-led, government-backed phenomenon that directly benefits North America and Europe as well as many emerging economies, opening up more markets for companies to sell their products and generate profits. A trickle-down effect—the idea that wealth created at the top levels will flow downhill like water and benefit the poor—is an important aspect of how globalization can be advantageous to everyone, not just the rich and the elites. Robust economic opportunities have been created in the Majority World, and many are better off now than they were forty or fifty years ago. An emerging middle class has been created in countries such as Brazil, Colombia, and India in the past few decades. Economically speaking, globalization has benefitted hundreds of millions of people.

Pope John Paul II noted the immense potential to be found through the interconnectedness of this global village, including the generation of gospel-oriented values. "Globalization," the late pontiff noted, "for all its risks, also offers exceptional and promising opportunities, precisely with

2. Monbiot, "Neoliberalism," lines 49–53.

a view to enabling humanity to become a single family, built on the values of justice, equity and solidarity."[3] The rewards of globalization transcend economic benefits and include the advancement of human values. If the governments and corporations driving the engine of globalization are helping to catalyze these values, however unintentionally, then it is indeed something to celebrate. Many churches also see globalization as an advantage in terms of the ability to quickly and easily reach people with the gospel. "The Church must see globalization as an extraordinary opportunity to see the gospel of Jesus Christ reach every corner of the earth," expressed one congregation in Ohio,[4] highlighting one of the many ways Western Christians in global mission have utilized the vast infrastructure and networks born of globalization.

But as Pope John Paul II also noted, the benefits do not come without costs.[5] There are also dire consequences that can be easy to overlook, especially for the governments, corporations, and churches that receive much of the benefit with little of the peril. The accompanying hazards of globalization are disproportionately borne by the poor and vulnerable of the emergent global village. Economists have shown that globalization has contributed to the increasing wealth gap between people in developing nations.[6] Despite the worldwide creation of massive wealth, the rich have been getting richer and the poor have been getting poorer. Culturally, loss of tradition and widespread Americanization of societies across the world is another consequence.

Globalization isn't a phenomenon only relevant for policy makers and corporations; it is much more than *laissez-faire* economic theory that men in suits need to concern themselves with. It is an issue of global justice, which means the church's response matters. A faith-based perspective toward its promises and pitfalls is important.

Botswanan theologian Musa Dube poses a question to us: "Who is globalizing and who is being globalized?"[7] Her question invites us to look at the dichotomies in terms of those who benefit and those who lose. Who is gaining wealth by leveraging the labor of people whose faces remain unseen?

3. John Paul II, "Peace on Earth," as cited in Massaro, *Living Justice*, 175.

4. Lifepoint Church, "Globalization and Mission."

5. See Mbila, "John Paul II and Globalization."

6. See Berger, "Globalization Is Increasing Inequality."

7. Dube, "Inhabiting God's Garden," 31.

Who uses the bodies of people in a utilitarian fashion to fill their own coffers? Which people are on which side of the growing wealth gap?

Her question "Who is globalizing and who is being globalized?" echoes a parallel question asked by history: "Who was colonizing and who was colonized?" Dube's globalization question has the identical answer as the colonization question: the colonized of the past are the globalized of the present. The colonizers have become the globalizers. Glancing back at the geographical movement of the colonial powers—from Europe to the global South—we see an analogous pattern in terms of which countries benefit the most from globalization: the global North, largely at the expense of the poorest, the most vulnerable, the least of these in the global South.

One example that highlights the relevance of Dube's question involves an American corporation, the United Fruit Company, which later became Chiquita. It once persuaded the military in Colombia, where it has massive fruit plantations, to massacre hundreds of banana workers who went on strike for better working conditions. Later, in 1954, its powerful Washington lobby resulted in a military coup in Guatemala led by the CIA, which overthrew the democratically elected president and replaced him with a dictator, a move which led to genocide, civil war, and a quarter of a million people dead. And more recently during Colombia's ongoing armed conflict, Chiquita collaborated with the AUC, a major paramilitary group known for its infamous death squads and crimes against humanity, often in the form of violence against peasants, union members, indigenous people, and Afro-Colombians. Between 1997 and 2004, Chiquita paid the AUC $1.7 million to protect their business interests in the country.[8]

How many times have each of us eaten a Chiquita banana? How many times have we heard the old song, "I'm a Chiquita banana and I'm here to say, bananas have to ripen in a certain way?" Chiquita bears the marks of a reputable company: their logo is on the majority of the bananas we eat or slice into pieces for our children. Their marketing song has perhaps gotten stuck in our heads on occasion. But we don't often hear about corporate collusion in war crimes, involving Chiquita or any other company. The media doesn't tend to cover issues like these.

Blood diamonds, perhaps. Blood bananas, never.

And Chiquita is not alone. Many multinational companies have benefitted from conspiring with armed groups who evict people from their

8. Kennard and McWilliam, "Chiquita Made a Killing," line 97.

property and homes to provide land for agriculture, mining, oil and other projects in many regions of the world.

The risks of globalization also go beyond the perpetuation of poverty and the increased wealth gap between rich and poor, loss of culture, and unscrupulous multinationals. One of the core, yet largely overlooked issues involves not only the impact on the materially poor of the Majority World but also on the materially wealthy of the West. Those on the receiving end of globalization's many advantages are inclined to "internalize and reproduce its creeds. The rich persuade themselves that they acquired their wealth through merit, ignoring the advantages such as education, inheritance and class that may have helped to secure it. The poor begin to blame themselves for their failures, even when they can do little to change their circumstances."[9] The poor are blamed for their lot and the rich are commended for their hard work, gifts, and economic fitness. Any mention of systemic factors that favor one group over another are often dismissed as illusory. After all, the market alone ensures that everyone gets what they deserve—nothing more, nothing less. It is common to allude to global society, either in an inferred or direct way, as a meritocracy where each individual attains what he or she deserves.

The bearing on both the materially wealthy and materially poor have led some to consider globalization the newest form of empire. Contemporary systems of international control sans military intervention have emerged; not only can nation-states become empires, corporations can acquire the same status. Though complicity in war and violence is a reality, most players in the globalization game don't perpetrate crimes or actively disregard human life. The majority of corporate stakeholders have ethical standards that prevent participating in overt violence like Chiquita.

Even so, many multinationals are now more powerful than countries. Of the one hundred largest global economies, only forty-nine are nations, the rest are corporations.[10] If Apple were a nation, it would have the world's nineteenth largest GDP, coming in ahead of Norway, Sweden, Austria, and Switzerland.

The newfangled empire forged in the crucible of globalization is usually neither sadistic nor despotic. At a cursory glance, the economic advantages are created for everyone, little guy and top boss, CEO and assembly line, global North and South alike. The empires of the age of globalization

9. Monbiot, "Neoliberalism," lines 33–37.

10. Shah, "Rise of Corporations," lines 1–2.

originate in a soft form—empire for a post-imperial age. The contemporary forms of empire don't operate with a military. Their dominion is economic, their control social and cultural, their ethos deemed acceptable. This fresh variety of empire even adopts language that proves its ambitions are docile, righteous even. Words like partnership, freedom, mutuality, quality, and responsibility have become customary lingo.

It is *empire lite*.[11]

Empire lite is often less physical than attitudinal, its mechanism sometimes hard to discern. Empire lite doesn't enact imperial rule. It usually doesn't implement violent tactics to control dissenters like the Romans or rape, pillage, and enslave like Columbus. It doesn't take over whole regions of continents for personal gain like King Leopold. The major players in the globalization project don't perpetrate classical colonialism. But they do still annex economic and social domains. And giant multinational corporations, though the most powerful and influential players, are not the only sector involved in the empire lite project.

Buried in the Rubble of Buildings and Blame

Following the devastating earthquake in Haiti in 2010 that took 250,000 lives and further decimated the already impoverished country, faith-based and secular non-governmental organizations (NGOs) descended en masse on the island with their skill sets and expertise, spearheading the recovery process at a critical time. People were still buried alive in the rubble when the outpouring of generosity, as astounding as the magnitude of the earthquake itself, began. The world rallied around the small island nation in the Caribbean. Donations came in from private and institutional donors from around the globe for the rebuilding effort. The American Red Cross alone received a staggering $250 million in private donations for earthquake relief.

Several months into the relief effort, some major concerns began to arise. Of the quarter billion dollars designated for Haiti received by the Red Cross, only $106 million was allocated to earthquake relief, leaving nearly

---

11. I first heard the term "empire lite" in 2005 from Dr. Barry Munslow, a professor of mine at Liverpool School of Tropical Medicine in the UK. As I recall, he used it in reference to the neoconservative United States foreign policy agenda of the George W. Bush administration. I am using it here with a different meaning.

$150 million in donations unaccounted for.[12] The Red Cross donation situation is just one example of mismanagement set within a broader pattern in which neither the Haitian people, Haitian organizations, or the government had a central role in the planning and decision-making process regarding the initial relief efforts or the longer-term rehabilitation and development strategies in the country.

Circumventing the state, unelected organizations that were not accountable to the country's citizens carried out "a program of neoliberal transformation. The relationships between the NGOs and their donors continually undermine the Haitian people's right to self-determination, while the organizations are at the same time cultivating and profiting from the poverty they are entrusted to fight."[13] The relief, rehabilitation, and development strategies failed to be participatory. Despite the best of intentions, and despite the help that was rendered—some of which was certainly life-saving and dignity affirming—local people and stakeholders were largely excluded in leadership and decision-making. Local organizations weren't asked questions or listened to. The voices of the people whose land shook beneath their feet, whose homes collapsed, whose children perished, whose bodies and minds were overwhelmed by traumatic loss were not included in the planning process.

Empire lite gained more footing in the country as NGOs and their foreign experts decided the fate of post-disaster Haiti.

And then the missionaries came.

Haiti has the most NGOs per capita of any nation in the world, which led to the monikers "NGO Republic" and "Graveyard of NGOs." I'd venture to guess it has the most missionaries per capita, as well. Following the international organizations, church groups, missionaries, and various faith-based sojourners began to show up in droves, some motivated to help rebuild, others desiring to share their faith. Most wanted to help in some way, drawn by the desire to serve in some capacity. When I visited the country more than two years after the earthquake, the coach cabin from Fort Lauderdale to Port-Au-Prince was nearly full with church groups wearing matching t-shirts.

Besides the desire to serve and share the gospel, a sizeable number of North American missionaries were driven to Haiti for another reason altogether. Pat Robertson and other well-known evangelical leaders from

---

12. Edmonds, *NGO's and the Business of Poverty in Haiti*, line 25.

13. Ibid., 18–22.

North America had publicly broadcast a message that the devastation of the earthquake was God's retribution for a pact Haitians had made with the devil several hundred years earlier. Motivated to go to Haiti to share this narrative with local people, missionaries inspired by Robertson dotted nearly every flight out of Miami and Fort Lauderdale destined for that beleaguered nation. To really look at the origins of the story of the pact with the devil and the context from which it emerged, we'd have to look back to what some historians say was one of the most important events in human history: the French Revolution.

France, a monarchy under the rule of Luis XVI at the time, was controlled by a triad of king, nobility, and clergy. Economic volatility, unfair taxation, and exploitation of peasants gave rise to a sentiment of deep discontent in the country. Inspired by the American Revolution that had taken place about a decade earlier, the people of France banded together in resistance to the monarchical state.

Insurrection soon convulsed the nation. Between 1789 and 1799, feudalism was abolished and the monarchy fell. The entire structure of French society shifted and the modern nation-state model was born in the ashes of feudal society. A new constitution was instated that implemented many enlightenment ideals. And people living in France and the rest of Western Europe weren't the only ones to take notice of the changes unfolding.

Right at the beginning of the French revolution, tensions were also mounting in Haiti, which at that time was the French colony of St. Domingue. The white colonists controlled the colony's economic and political assets while the mixed-race mulattoes were relegated to the status of semi-citizens, and African slaves had hardly any rights or opportunities whatsoever, existing under the colonial shadows. Having witnessed the growing revolution in France, as well as other revolutions against plantation slavery in the Caribbean, the mulattoes and slaves were motivated by the promise of freedom. They banded together toward insurrection against the inequity and oppression that had been forced upon them by the French colonists for decades.

Tradition holds that in 1791 a voodoo ceremony launched this struggle for freedom from bondage which led to the most successful slave revolt in history and eventually to abolition. This ceremony was labeled satanic by some evangelicals in the United States who claim the ceremony was a pact with the devil, a covenant with darkness that continues to this day. Instead of recognizing a successful slave-led revolt that led to liberation for those in bondage, the people of Haiti are accused of bringing tragedy upon themselves due to the actions of their ancestors.

This idea that God punishes Haiti for that slave uprising is as pervasive as ever. It narrates a story that goes something like this: "The extreme poverty, malnutrition, lack of food and clean water, and the buildings that fell on your bodies and crushed your loved ones are your own fault. You have caused all of the tragedies that have befallen you because your ancestors participated in a voodoo ceremony." Even if these aren't the exact words that are being articulated, it is the message that is relayed, a message that catalyzes shame and disempowerment and feeds into the shame-poverty cycle. It is a narrative that further marginalizes people who call the poorest country in the Western hemisphere home.

In the aftermath of the earthquake, missionaries to Haiti told the story of the satanic pact that had doomed the nation. While people were still buried under the rubble, amid the turmoil and the stench of death, they introduced this message that blamed the victims and pointed a finger at the traumatized. An entire nation struggling with the shock of a cataclysmic natural disaster was demonized.

And those who disseminated this story called it good news.

Power and Weeping

Haiti is a nation forged in the fires of colonial rule, slavery, revolution, US military occupation, political corruption, natural disasters, and the wills of well-intentioned organizations and missionaries. Its rich and tragic history has largely been left unread and unengaged by empire lite, the contemporary crucible from which its people, made in the image of God, live and love, suffer and hope, and create their lives. In one sense, Haiti remains a colony, a soft colony, continually being recreated in the image of the Western imagination, according to the whims and the wills, the words and the narratives of the purveyors of empire lite—including missionaries and NGOs—which cover over the image of God in a people whose voices are not heard, whose cries are not answered, because they are drowned out by the voices of the powerful who have not been silent long enough to listen to them.

The story of the pact with the devil was narrated with the luxury of social distance: the Western missionaries sharing it did not experience the same traumatic loss. Buildings did not crush the bones of their children. Their families were not buried in the rubble. Their blood did not stain red the earth. The story of the pact with the devil blamed the innocent rather than proclaiming "good news for the poor,"[14] which is what social distance allows for. Those who showed up in Haiti telling this tale were insulated from its true physical, social, and economic impacts. The good news of the gospel was contorted into something else, something not worthy of the label gospel: the story of ancestral complicity was anything but good news for a people who had just experienced one of the worst natural disasters in modern history.

To forget Haitian history and the evils of colonialism and the utter complexity of poverty is to choose the power of invulnerability. Rather than facilitating greater vulnerability and compassion—*feeling with*—from Western missionaries, the story of the pact with the devil did the opposite. It was both a symptom and a cause of the numb empire—the outside voices that seek power by levying their limited understandings onto people, alleviating their own uncertainty, and projecting their own pain. It is born of the story of the gods and the power of empire rather than God and the authentic power of God's kingdom.

Finding a simplistic answer that can easily be easily understood and then set aside is one way of dealing with what is painful and difficult to understand. Rather than remaining inside the pain and complexity created by difficult questions, we tend to want to escape from it. Finding overly simplistic causes is a common psychological strategy to make sense of the senseless. Simplifying the complex, which sometimes looks like placing blame on others, offers a feeling of being in control and helps create meaning, but rarely with consideration of how that could impact others. The human need to have a sense of power and control can blind us to complex realities.

When we face and embrace these common human patterns, we take a step toward the possibility of liberation from the ills of wielding power.[15] Whether as a missionary, an aid worker, a community development specialist, or some other sort of sojourner inspired by faith or secular motivations, a gospel-oriented approach to cross-cultural service means trading

---

14. Luke 4:18 NIV.

15. See Brueggemann, *Prophetic Imagination*.

power for vulnerability. As the need for control is released, the door to true compassion is held ajar. As Henri Nouwen reminds us, "Compassion is hard because it requires the inner disposition to go with others to the place where they are weak, vulnerable, lonely, and broken. But this is not our spontaneous response to suffering. What we desire most is to do away with suffering by fleeing from it or finding a quick cure for it."[16]

Embodying the compassion of Christ through feeling with those who suffer is simultaneously "a radical form of criticism, for it announces that the hurt is to be taken seriously, that the hurt is not to be accepted as normal and natural but is an abnormal and unacceptable condition for humanness."[17] Compassion not only affirms the dignity of those who suffer, it also points a finger of blame away from the suffering and toward the systems of inequality and oppression that allow for the abnormal situation. Compassion feels with those who are in pain, takes suffering seriously, and also directly names the source of the condition that has catalyzed such anguish—whether natural disaster, war, disease, economic destitution, human trafficking, or something else altogether.

True compassion isn't easy. Feeling what another feels, journeying into the darkness together, asks more of us than offering answers, or advice, or trying to help. "Compassion is not a relationship between the healer and the wounded. It's a relationship between equals. Only when we know our own darkness well can we be present with the darkness of others. Compassion becomes real when we recognize our shared humanity."[18] To go with others into their suffering, to touch their wounds, means trading power for vulnerability.

The iconic British missionary and missiologist Lesslie Newbigin wrote, "A person who wields power cannot see truth; that is the privilege of the powerless."[19] The world's power is conceived through an ability to turn another person's world upside down, to be able to do our own will whatever its effects on another. It is for this reason that power often destroys rather than creates.[20] Within power lies both the ability to facilitate greater life or enhance the chaos. The creation story at the beginning of Genesis reveals a God who creates by speaking. Through words, the world is brought into

---

16. Nouwen et al., *Compassion*, 3.

17. Brueggemann, *Prophetic Imagination*, 88.

18. Chodron, *Comfortable with Uncertainty*, 74.

19. Newbigin, *Foolishness to the Greeks*, as cited in Mayo, *Parish Handbook*, 42.

20. Berghoef, "Well Is Deep," quoting Joan Chittister.

being. God speaks and the nothingness, the chaos, the void is transformed into the cosmos. In the Judeo-Christian tradition, this speaking is the beginning of life, the commencement of flourishing. God's power is not like the world's power; it is a "weak" power that creates without force. In the weak power of the divine, there isn't forcefulness, rather there is speaking. There is no willful agenda, rather presence amid the chaos in which we discover the reign of God present not under the form of power, but of weakness.[21] This great reversal of the world's power is revealed in Jesus, the King who was at the same time a forgiving victim. His kingliness took on a form completely contrary and utterly incomprehensible to the world. Jesus' strength was in the form of an apparent weakness in which forgiveness, meekness, vulnerability, and compassion revealed the futility of the empire's forms of power based on domination and violence.

How (Not) to Speak of Suffering

Romulus kills Remus, founding Rome and the imperial power that would rule for a thousand years. From the body of a dismembered god, the world is made. Unlike the empire crafted in the pantheon of violence, the God who brings about creation through words reveals that vulnerability is the true power of the divine. The Trinity reveals that real power has nothing to do with empire, violence, domination, or numbness. It is "of a totally different nature, one that even Jesus' followers have not yet adjusted to. If the Father does not dominate the Son, and the Son does not dominate the Holy Spirit, and the Spirit does not dominate the Father or the Son, then there's no domination in God. All divine power is shared power. This should have entirely changed Christian religion, politics, and relationships. There's no seeking of power over in the Trinity, but only power with—a giving away, a sharing, a letting go, and thus an infinity of trust and mutuality."[22]

Walter Brueggemann writes that "Jesus knew what we numb ones must always learn again . . . that weeping permits newness. His weeping permits the kingdom to come. Such weeping is a radical criticism, a fearful dismantling because it means the end of all machismo; weeping is something kings rarely do without losing their thrones."[23] If feeling with others who are suffering is what is required, in the weeping of tears or the

21. Newbigin, *Open Secret*, 35.

22. Rohr, "Shared Power," lines 9–18.

23. Brueggemann, *Prophetic Imagination*, 57.

weeping of the soul, and if that is what breaks the numbness, how do we access that place? How do we break through to it? A place to start is how we talk about suffering.

The occurrence of natural disasters and the reality of human suffering in general raise all sorts of questions about God.

Why does God allow pain?

How did evil come to exist?

Is suffering ever redemptive?

Why do bad things happen to good people?

It is a natural thing to query the heavens, to turn upward and ask why? How? For what? It is human in times of great despair to say along with the psalmist, "How long O Lord?"[24]

I don't know that there are answers to the mystery of human suffering and evil. But we can look to the biblical text to point us not necessarily to answers, but to how we might begin to speak, or *not* speak, of suffering.

John's Gospel tells a story of an encounter between Jesus and a blind man:

> As he went along, [Jesus] saw a man blind from birth. His disciples asked him, "Rabbi, who sinned, this man or his parents, that he was born blind?" "Neither this man nor his parents sinned," said Jesus, "but this happened so that the works of God might be displayed in him." . . . After saying this, he spit on the ground, made some mud with the saliva, and put it on the man's eyes. "Go," he told him, "wash in the Pool of Siloam" (this word means "Sent"). So the man went and washed, and came home seeing.[25]

Reading this text with the Haitian context in mind, well-intentioned Jesus followers like his own disciples have asked: Who sinned that an earthquake should obliterate a nation? Who sinned, Haitians currently alive or their ancestors, that the earth would shake and buildings fall? Who is to blame for this? Who is responsible?

And Jesus' response indicates that these are the wrong questions to be asking. No one sinned to cause an earthquake. No one, alive or dead, is responsible for a natural disaster. In line with Jesus' response to the disciples, neither they nor their ancestors are to blame, not in 2018, not in 2010, not at a voodoo ceremony in 1791.

---

24. Ps 13:1 NIV.

25. John 9:1–3, 6–7 NIV.

The story in John's Gospel offers an example of where Jesus not only engaged in a miracle of healing, but simultaneously taught something to the disciples about ministry and mission. Jesus takes the question—"Rabbi, who sinned, this man or his parents, that he was born blind?"—and turns their theological conjecture about the source of human suffering into an embodied encounter. He translates the disciples' attempt at cerebral hypothesizing about suffering into a moment of physical healing, making mud with his spit, rubbing it on the man's eyes, who goes on to famously exclaim, "I was blind but now I see!"[26]

This is what mattered to Jesus: seeing, healing, newness. Not disembodied theologizing divorced from the face and the eyes and the body in front of him but the person who was there, someone with a story and a family, with questions and hopes and fears and longings. A human being, not an object of speculation or a thing to be theorized about.

The Good Message

When God spoke into the void, light and life, form and order emerged from the chaos. Words are creative of something. When the divine word is spoken, it brings life. When falsity, suspicion, or fear speaks, it makes more of the void. Some words create, others *un-create*. Words of culpability regarding an earthquake, words that levy blame on those suffering, words that create more disorder among the disorder aren't divine words. They aren't the good news.

The Greek word *euangelion*, where we get the word evangelical, translates as "good message." Evangelical words create life. Divine words create worlds of flourishing. The *euangelion*, the good news, brings light and life, form and order, hope and the promise of redemption right in the middle of chaos. The *euangelion* is the divine word that continues to speak.

Being evangelical means embodying the good message, the good news of the kingdom of God. Embodying the good message across cultures in beautiful, empowering, healing ways means opening our eyes and allowing ourselves to see our blind spots. Speaking the good news, sharing it, embodying it faithfully means allowing the mud to open our eyes. The story disseminated by Robertson and other North American Jesus followers regarding the suffering in Haiti is not good news for anyone, neither North Americans nor Haitians. It exploits and feeds on the mental architecture of

26. John 9:25 NIV.

the Western imagination while simultaneously disempowering the poor. It jumps to conclusions about theodicy—the questions of how and why God permits suffering and evil—that aren't biblically rooted.

That hypothesis about suffering told by materially wealthy evangelicals to materially poor Haitians isn't good news for the suffering and the traumatized. It doesn't spit on the earth and heal people. It doesn't lift up a nation. It doesn't see as Jesus sees. It is blind. It cannot engage complexity, or colonialism's legacy, or restore dignity in the midst of trauma.

It is born of empire lite rather than the kingdom of God.

In considering the questions of theodicy, particularly the relationship between sin and suffering, the biblical story of Job offers some more clues. Job lived a righteous existence and God was pleased with him. In the story, Satan comes along and wants to make a bet with God: if Job experiences profound pain and loss, he will turn away from his faith. God accepts the bet, saying that Job will remain unwavering in his faith no matter what.

As the story continues, Job ends up losing his family, his livestock, and his health—everything is taken away.[27] He comes to the brink of giving up and giving in. Yet, none of the affliction is punishment from God for sinning. The story sketches an important theological idea: there is no connection between suffering and sin. God not only does not punish people for sin, neither does God cause any suffering whatsoever.[28] Not poverty or structural oppression. Not hunger or disease. Not earthquakes or other natural disasters.

The "evangelical" God is the God who speaks the divine word and takes on flesh to suffer and die as one of us. This God continues to speak words that create life even as he is crucified, "Father, forgive them. They know not what they do." This God speaks the good message, the *euangelion*, even at the hour of death.

This is the God who feels pain, who knows agony, and is the source of none of it.

God's suffering is an essential part of his solidarity with the oppressed.[29] The suffering God makes us capable of love, authentic compassion, and deep sensitivity to the pain of others, a vulnerability to the sorrow of the world in which there is no desire for power, control, simplistic answers, thin responses to the faces we encounter, or flat hypotheses about the agony

27. Job 1–2.

28. See Gutierrez, *On Job*.

29. Cone, *God of the Oppressed*, as cited in Bauckham, "Only the Suffering God," 7.

of a person or a nation. God's suffering invites weeping, trading power for vulnerability, and coming to newness both within ourselves and in our work with the poor.

Dietrich Bonhoeffer, theologian and active resistor of the Nazi regime, wrote, "The Bible directs humans to God's powerlessness and suffering; only the suffering God can help."[30] The God who suffers doesn't capitulate to triumphalism, but instead manifests the true power of self-giving love, which is both the shape and action of Trinity, a constant interdependent pouring out and letting go, one to the other, Father to Son to Spirit. Living inside of this trustworthy pattern, one that is generative and dignity-enhancing, gives us the freedom to embrace our own suffering through identifying with the agony of Jesus, the sorrow of the Father, the grief of the Spirit.

The suffering of God is of course witnessed in Christ crucified. The divine Word was made flesh and chose death on a cross for the sake of the world. He suffered for our sufferings, bore our pain and sin. He was pierced and crushed for our iniquities. He was a man of poverty and sorrow, despised and rejected.[31]

The suffering of the materially poor of the world bears a haunting resemblance to Jesus the Crucified One, reminding us that the poor are crucified people, an intuition of Bartolome de Las Casas, the one-time conquistador who became an outspoken critic of the Spanish mistreatment of the indigenous of the Americas following the first wave of European colonization. Las Casas prophetically spoke against the violence done to indigenous people of the Caribbean, each of whom was Jesus Christ scourged, struck, grieved, and crucified, "not once but thousands of times."[32]

The intuition of Las Casas remains relevant in the era in which we find ourselves, one that people who seek flourishing and shalom for the oppressed have sensed viscerally and rationally, theologically and spiritually. It is an intuition many Christians who have crossed borders of geography and culture on behalf of others have known in their bones, in their souls.

It brings to my mind John, the infant in South Sudan malnourished to the extent that his skin had no elasticity. Just beneath the skin, bone. Shown in his eyes was despair of a sort a little child should never possess, the look of total despondency. He had not the strength to cry or utter even a sound.

---

30. Bonhoeffer, *Letters and Papers from Prison*, 188.

31. Isa 53:3.

32. Gutierrez, *On Job*, xvi.

John, an infant of sorrows, scourged by hunger was nailed to the execution stake of poverty. He breathed his last and gave up his spirit.

The violence of global systems of injustice takes life and turns it back into *not-life*.

It de-animates the breath.

It un-creates bodies.

It turns flesh back into words, not once but thousands of times.

Reflection Questions

1. How have you sensed the suffering of God in the pain of a particular person you've known?

2. Where have you witnessed blame being cast on the innocent? How might a biblical engagement with suffering and its causes shift your own views about God's presence or absence in situations of suffering?

3. Where have you encountered empire lite in one of its many forms?

11

Wounded Healer

We re-enact the dramas of our past in our current relationships and in our current world. The reason we engage
the past is to free our heart for the future.

—Dan B. Allender

In a futile attempt to erase our past, we deprive the community of our healing gifts. If we conceal our wounds out
of fear and shame, our inner darkness can neither be il-
luminated nor become a light for others.

—Brennan Manning

Reliving the Past

THE TEAM OF LOCAL and international aid workers I was a part of in
South Sudan collaborated with the leaders of a nearby village to drill
a borehole to provide clean water for the community. One afternoon, we
had a meeting with the elders to discuss the project. It carried on for hours,
interspersed with many breaks for tea. The meeting drew to a close without
much having been accomplished. We departed just before sunset, hoping to
return before the darkness of night obscured the route back home.

I looked off into the thickets of dense brush of the semi-desert that
enshrouded us as the truck bounced along the harsh, rutted excuse for a
road, unalarmed when the vehicle came to an abrupt halt. I figured the
driver probably needed a new strategy for getting around an ill-placed rock

or gaping hole. I didn't even look up, content in my headspace—until a voice startled me out of reverie.

"What is your name? You killed my dog and you must pay!"

There was indeed an obstruction in the road of a different sort—a soldier from the Sudan People's Liberation Army (SPLA)—the movement that had taken up arms against the oppression of the government during the North-South civil war that had lasted from 1983 to 2005. He stood tall and upright, dressed in military fatigues. The last rays of the evening sun glimmered off the metal casing of the AK-47 that was slung diagonally across his shoulder. At his feet was a dead dog, laying limp and lifeless on the ground.

"I will come find you. You will pay for what you have done!" he repeated again.

The sharp inflection of his voice made a shiver go up my spine. The muscles in my limbs went weak and my stomach clamped tight with dread. While we were driving the Landcruiser to the meeting earlier that day, the driver had accidentally hit the soldier's dog. Somehow, he hadn't even realized it. In a calm and sincere tone, he apologized for the mistake he had made.

The soldier was visibly distraught as he spoke, his face contorted with scorn. A million thoughts raced across the screen of my mind. As my pulse quickened, the muscles in my arms and legs turned even more weak and lifeless, like the dog that lay there just below. Images of AK-47 bullets being sprayed through our tents that night in retaliation streaked through my mind. I felt as if I wasn't in my own body anymore, like I had gone off somewhere else in dissociation.

I had felt these same symptoms three years earlier in a different country on the African continent. It was there in the wilds of northeastern Zimbabwe that I was ensnared in a rogue political situation and abducted. That encounter with death three years prior had lived on inside of me, like a sleeping giant that was now being awoken. This chance meeting with the angry soldier was a moment of re-traumatization. It was a recapitulation of the events that occurred in Zimbabwe.

The solider eventually allowed us to proceed and we continued toward the organization's compound. Later that night I was in my tent trying in futility to squelch the anxious thoughts in my mind and fall asleep. But as the minutes passed, the tenseness in my body multiplied. The cortisol and adrenaline erupting through my veins made it impossible to relax. The more I fought the sensations, the more I was seized by panic.

An eternity later, morning came. I immediately went to the leader of our team and told her about what was going on inside my mind and body. I was utterly humiliated. At no time in my life had I ever felt so inadequate, like such a failure as a man and as a Christian.

A plane delivering program supplies arrived in the village a few hours later. I said goodbye to my coworkers and boarded that tiny Cessna. It sped down the bumpy dirt airstrip, whizzing past goats and children and into the azure sky, leaving the place that had once been symbolic of a dream realized—the dream of that seven-year-old boy—but had become for me a prison of distressing fear. My long-standing hope of a career serving the world's most vulnerable was being left behind. Everything had fallen apart.

I expected to feel better when I arrived back at the organization's base in Nairobi, but the symptoms didn't diminish. Following a conversation with the leadership team, it was decided that I would get a psychiatric evaluation. A few days later, I arrived for an appointment with a German missionary doctor. She asked me a few simple questions about the symptoms I was having and listened intently to my answers, with a clear empathic gaze that revealed a kindness far beyond the clinical. After I spoke for a few minutes, describing the abduction in Zimbabwe and how I was falling into the grips of panic, she offered a diagnosis. My symptoms were a clear indication of PTSD, she explained, and it was no surprise that my body and mind were reacting in such disconcerting ways. She recommended a course of treatment consisting of an evidence-based method of addressing trauma, Eye Movement Desensitization and Reprocessing (EMDR), which could effectively reprocess the traumatic memories that had become frozen in the limbic system, the brain's emotional center. After completing the sessions, there would be a reevaluation to determine whether or not she would recommend my return to South Sudan.

I felt a slight sense of relief as she spoke, a small but noticeable reprieve from the condemning voice of shame in my head that repeated again and again that there was something wrong with me for having these intense and painful symptoms. A spark of hope flickered within, that I might be able to heal and get back to the field where I felt I belonged.

The next day, the director of the organization I worked for received the psychiatrist's report with the diagnosis and recommended treatment plan. After reviewing it, he explained that despite the psychiatrist's recommendations, I would have to leave Kenya and return to the United States to pursue treatment. I left for home shortly after, bleeding in shame.

Upon returning home, I still held onto a ray of hope that I would return to the African continent again one day. The desire to be serving cross-culturally persisted despite my body and mind still being in the throes of severe anxiety and mounting depression. I remember the day when I began browsing the websites of international relief and development organizations to see who was hiring, plotting how I could get back to South Sudan again.

At the same time, the more rational part of me knew I couldn't keep avoiding what had happed in Zimbabwe and that if I didn't confront the trauma, I would be relinquishing any chance of getting well and any hope of ever serving overseas again. This was the impetus for me to begin reflecting on the abduction.

Gradually, I began to go into the very place inside that I was most hesitant to enter, the place where my greatest fears resided. With the assistance of a therapist who utilized EMDR, I entered that inner domain within which was buried the pain and trauma. Initially, the treatment took some of the emotional charge out of the memory of the incident. Sometime later, I began to have new insights into the reasons why I chose to return again to the African continent to serve the materially poor. Deeper realizations began to open up. Awareness came about what lay at the root of both the re-traumatization as well as my desire to engage cross-culturally.

Mission to Heal

If you had asked me back then why I wanted to endure hardships and safety risks by going to South Sudan, I would have told you about my desire to live with those at the margins, to help save lives, that my own comfort and security didn't matter all that much. At twenty-three years old, this is what I understood my life's calling to be. I was going to serve, save, and sacrifice for the sake of people who were ill, hungry, and desperate. I was on a mission to heal. Yet, the dynamics underneath this desire were more complex than I knew at that time.

Traumatized people often find themselves unwittingly repeating trauma in an unconscious attempt to work it out, a pattern Freud dubbed the repetition compulsion. Trauma specialist Peter Levine describes it like this: "The drive to complete and heal trauma is as powerful and tenacious as the symptoms it creates. The urge to resolve trauma through re-enactment can be severe and compulsive. We are inextricably drawn into situations that replicate the original trauma in both obvious and unobvious ways."[1] These words are a summary of what had unfolded deep inside of me while living in South Sudan. It was, at least in part, this unconscious endeavor to heal that had pulled me back to the ends of the earth, to the place that represented the hope of healing the trauma of the abduction in Zimbabwe. Instead of healing, I reenacted the trauma in a miscarried attempt at mastering it.

I hadn't realized that I was also on a mission to heal myself.

Unconsciously, the only way I could unfreeze, the only way to melt the unaddressed trauma, was to risk re-traumatization. Going to South Sudan was my attempt at mastering one trauma by entering into another. Without being aware of it, I sought healing by going to a setting similar to the one in which the abduction had occurred, hoping to live a new story, one that had a different ending—the ultimate paradox, perhaps, but very common in traumatized people. Because I hadn't done the necessary therapeutic work, all of this had remained buried in my unconscious.

Rarely does anyone come to profound psychological insights and growth on their own, and I was no exception. Engaging our wounds and trauma, no matter how intense or seemingly trivial, requires other people to journey with us into these disorienting places—to walk alongside us as companions through the unfamiliar territory and to be a container for the intense emotions that surface. The gender and religious framework in which I was situated had created a stigma about seeking professional help for psychological issues. In my social setting, men weren't supposed to be afraid. Feeling was feminine. Getting over things and making emotions submit to our will was masculine. This caricature of authentic masculinity relayed the message that therapy was something for people, mainly women, who had severe mental and emotional problems, and that certainly was not me, I thought.

The way I saw it, my only problem was fear. If I could just stop feeling afraid, everything would be fine. I wanted to control the pain rather than go into the wound. And the standard Christian approach to psychological issues was to either pray it away or have more faith. I memorized New Testament passages about fear and anxiety that people told me would help,

1. Levine, *Waking the Tiger*, 173.

such as Philippians 4:6: "Do not be anxious about anything, but in every situation, by prayer and petition with thanksgiving, present your requests to God"; and 2 Timothy 1:7, "For God has not given us a spirit of fear but of power and of love and of a sound mind." I thought it was all in my head, that throwing Bible verses at my pain might actually help, and felt even worse when nothing changed, judging myself ever the more harshly. I figured that there must be something wrong with me.

One of the world's leading trauma experts, psychiatrist Bessel van der Kolk, writes,

> Traumatized people chronically feel unsafe inside their bodies: The past is alive in the form of gnawing interior discomfort. Their bodies are constantly bombarded by visceral warning signs, and, in an attempt to control these processes, they often become expert at ignoring their gut feelings and in numbing awareness of what is played out inside. They learn to hide from their selves. The more people try to push away and ignore internal warning signs, the more likely they are to take over and leave them bewildered, confused, and ashamed.[2]

The past alive. Interior discomfort. Bewildered. Confused. Ashamed. Van der Kolk's description of trauma illustrates my experience with precision. At that time, I had no idea that PTSD is a normal response to an abnormal experience. I did not realize that trauma is experienced physically, mentally, emotionally, socially, and spiritually—and throwing Bible verses at it would not help, and in fact, would only add to the confusion and pain.

Meaning Making Mission

Trauma was not the only force at work during that time, however. The three years between my first and second stints on the African continent were characterized by a pervasive sense of purposelessness, like a low-grade fever that is manageable but distressing nonetheless. There was a stark contrast between the exhilarating adventure my life had been while living in South Africa and Mozambique, and its dull monotony upon returning home. Along with the sense of feeling utterly alive, the year I spent in southern Africa had offered me for the first time in my life a taste of what it meant to live with meaning. I had drunk deeply from the well of purposefulness as a result of being among the poor—and I wanted more of it.

2. Van der Kolk, *Body Keeps the Score*, 97.

For many, it seems much easier to tap into a sense of purpose when outside of North America, in contexts of poverty where opportunities to engage with the marginalized are plentiful. Of course there are plenty of options here in our everyday contexts, too, but we tend not to see them as easily as when we have departed the normal grind of daily life and the tedium that often makes our lives feel meaningless. The loss of collective meaning in North America has brought us collectively to a point of hopelessness. Consumerism and the promise of prosperity have contributed to a far-reaching sense of loss. That which truly brings life, life to the full, seems to be ever eluding us. We are desperate for our lives to be purposeful, to live for something greater than ourselves.

We all desire meaning in our lives, and we all crave a sense of connection. We know deep down that there is something more—a more that we have tasted before—in those moments when we felt a sense of connection to something beyond us, something transcendent. It's at these times when the sense of separation is suspended, whether it be for a second or a day or a week, that we can sense that we are a part of the very fabric of life. Like a time we gazed into the eyes of a newborn, or floated through fresh-fallen snow skiing in the mountains, glided across the unbroken face of a wave, or sat around the dinner table with close friends and laughed until it hurt. Experiences of connection transcend the self and tap us into the greater web of life.

But this connection that the soul is after often seems difficult to access. There is so much around us in our daily lives that proclaims a much different message, declaring that it is not meaning and connection that matter, but power, prestige, success, and accomplishment. The message is that in order to belong to something bigger than myself, I have to do *this*, have *that*, make *this* much money, go to *this* church, live in *that* neighborhood. These messages play off the human need to belong, to feel connected to something beyond ourselves. It is easy to jump from one thing that promises connection and meaning to the next, on and on, over and over again. In reality these are false promises, offering us mere parodies of the real thing, providing only a veneer of what we actually seek. We feel that. The soul is not easily fooled.

It is the desire for connection and meaning that draw so many of us into mission, community development, aid, and other cross-cultural work in the first place. Participating in work that serves vulnerable people in the

Majority World promises to return hope and purpose to our lives. It speaks to the part of us that anguishes over ever being fulfilled as we wander the hallways of our lives. A profound fear of the unlived life haunts us daily. For many North Americans, working overseas with communities of poor and marginalized people becomes the ticket out of the collective despair. What could assure meaning and purpose in one's life more than rescuing the suffering from their distress? Than caring for orphaned children? Than feeding malnourished infants?

Besides the unconscious desire to master the trauma of Zimbabwe, my need for a sense of existential purpose tugged me to go to South Sudan. Serving the poor represented a larger hope that my life could hold meaning. The pursuit of becoming an aid worker was the pursuit of meaning; a return to Africa was a promise of a return to personal significance. In my mind, Africa was the medicine I needed to treat the low-grade fever of meaninglessness.

An honest engagement with this kind of existential despair in North American culture is often avoided, as it lies buried beneath a facade of contentment. It can be challenging to acknowledge what lies just below the surface of our smiles and superficial satisfaction. Theologian Kathleen O'Connor writes that this thinly veiled despair "expresses itself in violence against the other and the world, a violence necessary to maintain the denial."[3] Destructive actions, perpetrated against another or the self, is a way to avoid the truth of what is happening deep inside, a means of keeping unconscious that which is too overwhelming to confront. Whether it is the existential despair of King Leopold needing the medication of enslaving black bodies in the Congo or that of a twenty-three-year-old American aid worker struggling with deep shame and self-contempt, when despair is masked and denied, some form of violence, intentional or not, is sure to follow.

It is in confronting meaninglessness head on and wrestling with it honestly that movement occurs. The very act of wrestling implies hope—a subtle hope that is a counterpart to the covert despair. Hope and despair have a dialectical relationship; where there is one there is the other. It is by virtue of the very existence of despair that hope can be present, but only when that despair is encountered and accepted, allowed to awaken from its latent state. Despair granted permission to rise up and be borne consciously relinquishes its hegemony on the psyche.

---

3. O'Connor, *Lamentations*, 90.

It is not just in the West, however, that there is this sense of loss and hopelessness. It is a global phenomenon, touching people from New York to Nairobi, Paris to Phnom Penh. If we read the signs of the times, we witness global society's distortion of hope manifested as rampant chaos, debilitating guilt, and crippling fear.[4]

The despair of the wealthy is something that hangs around in the back of our minds incessantly, but rarely springs forth in a manner that allows us to grapple with it directly. The despair of the Majority World is a reality that is inescapable. It doesn't remain hidden under ephemeral consumeristic contentment as it does in the West. As long as it remains repressed, the covert despair of the materially wealthy is, by the very nature of its hiddenness, as potent as the explicit despair of the materially poor.

Suffering is inevitable in all of us, no matter where we live on the globe. Suffering looks different in each context, and it certainly isn't all created equal. The suffering and poverty of the West are more tacit, hidden underneath a smokescreen of material satisfaction and personal comfort. It is a hidden poverty, not seen by the naked eye. The poverty of the Majority World is palpable. It largely resides out in the open where all can see it. But this poverty, and the people who dwell in its midst, does not pretend that it isn't there. This pain cannot be abjured. Unlike the suffering of the West, no one denies it. In North America, our sense of despair "masquerades under a guise of well-being so persuasive as to deceive the wearers of the masks themselves."[5]

Many of us, including myself, know this mask very well. It was something that I wore for an extensive period of time, one that I sometimes still reach for and pull back on. Like at a seventeenth-century European masquerade ball, so many of us go around in disguise, keeping the reality of our inner world with all of its pain and beauty hidden from those around us. Most of all, we have gone into hiding from our own selves. At no point in my life did I wear that guise more fully than while I was in South Sudan. No one even recognized that I was wearing a disguise, not even me. Removing the mask and entering the pain, I would come to learn, is the first step in participating in cross-cultural work with gospel integrity.

4. Hall, "Despair," 83.
5. O'Connor, *Lamentations*, 90.

Mutual Woundedness

Despite all the radical differences between us—race, culture, religious tradition, political preference, sex, gender, age—the common ground everyone shares is suffering. No one escapes it. Ministry leaders, justice advocates, missionaries, and other faith-based sojourners are uniquely positioned to help alleviate the suffering of those they work with. The call to address the suffering of others often, however, makes it difficult to shift our attention to ourselves and to look at our own pain. Whether we project it outward onto those around us or turn it inward in contempt for ourselves, transmission of pain is the way many of us have learned to deal with our brokenness.

The pain that remains unrecognized inside of us determines more than we might think. Denial of our suffering, according to cancer survivor and ethicist Arthur Frank, hinders our capacity to accept other's pain.[6] Instead of being truly present, we often allow the anxiety that rises up within to compel us to escape the truth of the suffering other by silencing them or by tacking a happy ending onto their story. There is a tendency in our culture to hide our wounds. As a society, North Americans tend to demonstrate a limited willingness to engage with our own pain, which impacts our ability to be present with another in their pain. The inability to be fully present with authenticity and vulnerability is usually a symptom of having covered our wounds.

Those of us drawn into various ministries, missions, and roles in the helping professions clearly have a heart to offer ourselves to others in ways that can bring healing and hope. If this wasn't so, none of us would choose to do this work. The inner process of reflection on our stories allows us to make connections between our own pain and the pain of those we seek to help. Kathleen O'Connor writes, "Without our own stories, ministry becomes a projection of wounds onto the world, mission becomes a one-way street in which the 'whole' condescend to help the 'broken.'"[7] We need our stories. They are an indispensable aspect of our work. We rarely give our own stories a cursory glance, let alone engage intimately with the hauntingly beautiful and tragic narratives that make up our lives, that shape us to be who we are.

Our stories not only impact the choices we make and the particular ways we relate to others, but they also hold the promise of blessing for

6. Frank, *Wounded Storyteller*, as cited in O'Connor, *Lamentations*, 92.

7. O'Connor, *Lamentations*, 93.

others—even the places of pain. Part of the reason many of us have such fiery enthusiasm to serve the hurting is because we ourselves know what it is to have suffered. We know what it is like to have our deepest needs go unmet and to have our voices marginalized. We know what it is to be oppressed, to be on the bottom, to feel less than. Even if we haven't suffered the disgrace of extreme poverty or the harm of an abusive relationship, it would be a grave untruth to say that each of us has not experienced profound loss and grief. Each of us in our own way knows intimately the terrain of affliction.

As Richard Rohr says, we either transform our pain or we transmit it to others.[8] Jesus' passion, death, and resurrection—what we call the Paschal Mystery—reveals a way of relating to our pain that avoids the temptation to transmit it while embracing the reality of transformation. The wounds of crucifixion that led to Jesus' death were the wounds through which redemption would come to all people. This gospel narrative reveals that the place of pain is the site of the holy; our wounds are the sacred sites of transformation, for us and for those we serve. Imagine if Jesus had covered his pain, declining to reveal his wounds to his disciples and to the world—the greatest story ever told would have never been heard.

With our wounds uncovered and honored as sacred—the paradoxical site of both death and resurrection—we enter the transformative process. To read our lives with honesty is to engage the places of harm and pain that have shaped us in very particular ways. Our own stories, especially the places of darkness, then become our greatest gift to the world. God uses the bleeding places in us as the locus of our personal transformation and that of others. Our wounds, like those of Jesus, are the conduit not only of suffering, but of redemption.

The process of owning our pain and knowing ourselves allows us to serve people from a stance of mutuality. In this space where suffering meets suffering there is the potential for true transformation to be born. Mutually we are hurting and mutually we are transformed. By holding our gaze on the woundedness of ourselves, others, and Jesus, we allow the injured places in our psyches and souls to breathe, to have a voice, to be welcomed in love. This process allows us to go out into the world as wounded healers, not as invincible saviors. We enter into difficult contexts as people who have known what it is to suffer, and therefore offer our wounded selves and in doing so receive the wounded other back as a reflection of our own self.

8. Rohr, "Transforming Our Pain," lines 2–3.

This "exquisite mutuality" spoken of by Fr. Greg Boyle[9] goes far in tearing down the staircase of hierarchy that continues to harm the personhood of the "whole" and the "broken." As the ways in which we view ourselves shift, so too do the ways in which we view the other. It is in brokenness that we come to recognize that we are all connected.

It is from this realization of shared humanity in brokenness that we can begin to lead with our wounds, like Jesus did. Exquisite mutuality arises out of the sense of shared humanity through the union of suffering. Rather than something that must be hidden, brokenness becomes a uniting essence. As different as we are, woundedness becomes the very catalyst for transformation, allowing the ladders of hierarchy and walls of division to naturally begin to decay into the common ground of suffering—a suffering that can and will be the very site of new life. Our own stories, especially the places of darkness, can become our greatest gift to the world.

In the words of Henri Nouwen, "We all are wounded people, whether physically, emotionally, mentally, or spiritually. The main question is not 'How can we hide our wounds?' so we don't have to be embarrassed, but 'How can we put our woundedness in the service of others?' When our wounds cease to be a source of shame, and become a source of healing, we have become wounded healers."[10]

Becoming wounded healers is the way forward in global mission and justice work. The journey to a place of mutuality and shared brokenness takes us to the heart of the gospel narrative and the very center of the mission of God.

Touching the Wound

After Jesus' resurrection, he appeared to the disciples.

> Now Thomas (also known as Didymus), one of the Twelve, was not with the disciples when Jesus came. So the other disciples told him, "We have seen the Lord!" But he said to them, "Unless I see the nail marks in his hands and put my finger where the nails were, and put my hand into his side, I will not believe." A week later his disciples were in the house again, and Thomas was with them. Though the doors were locked, Jesus came and stood among them and said, "Peace be with you!" Then he said to Thomas, "Put your

9. Boyle, in an interview with Salai, "Saving," line 21.
10. Nouwen, "Wounded Healer," lines 1–8.

finger here; see my hands. Reach out your hand and put it into my side. Stop doubting and believe." Thomas said to him, "My Lord and my God!" Then Jesus told him, "Because you have seen me, you have believed; blessed are those who have not seen and yet have believed."[11]

Thomas was incredulous. His beloved Rabbi—whom he had followed, dedicated himself to, and deeply loved—was dead and yet somehow alive. Thomas could not make sense of that. He couldn't hold together woundedness with risenness, death with resurrection. How could Jesus have been executed by the Romans, laid in a tomb, and yet somehow be living? How is it possible the Lord was crucified and risen?

The Greek word *pistis*, used over one hundred times in the Gospel of John, is customarily translated as "believe." It can also mean "faithful" and "to put one's trust in" as well as "to have confidence in." *Pistis* doesn't mean assent to a proposition, but a complete commitment or dedication to something or someone. Interestingly, the Greek word for doubt is not used in this story, which is another indication that this story isn't about a simple linear movement from disbelief to belief, as it has often been interpreted.

Thomas, it turns out, isn't "doubting Thomas" at all. "Despite what millions of sermons by thousands of preachers have told you, doubting Thomas didn't doubt . . . In John's Gospel, belief isn't about an intellectual assent to some list of facts, but instead, belief is about a relationship. When Jesus died on the cross, so too did his relationship with Thomas. Thomas believed Jesus, he gave him his heart and his hope, and that belief couldn't live beyond the grave."[12]

Jesus invited Thomas: "reach out your finger and put it in my side." The Greek word translated as "put" closely resembles the English word "plunge."[13] Part of what Jesus was saying was, "Go into the wound all the way. Plunge your finger into it, Thomas. It still bleeds. It's not crusted over with the scab of denial or projection."

Thomas needed to physically touch the wound. And Jesus knew that. It wasn't until Thomas met Jesus in his physicality, until he engaged in a kinesthetic manner, touching Jesus' body with his own body, that he could "see and believe."

---

11. John 20:24–29 NIV.

12. Pankey, "Doubting Thomas," lines 12–15.

13. Rambo, "Wounds Resurrecting."

This story of Thomas's encounter with the risen Christ seems to be about Thomas' ability to have a different sort of encounter with woundedness, more than about his capacity to confess belief in the unseen. In plunging his finger into the wound, Thomas was committing himself to the wounds of the crucified-resurrected Lord. He felt the blood that was not yet dry, the puss that still oozed. It was as if Jesus was saying, "Do not distrust the power of the crucifixion wound to be transformed into a resurrection wound."

The wound is the very thing that joins us to the crucified God. But the walls, defenses, and protective mechanisms that we build up around wounds to protect ourselves from feeling their pain can separate us from connection to God, others, and ourselves. Our work is to let the defenses fall in order to feel the pain. Allowing pain to surface means feeling it rather than avoiding it. It is touching pain, and allowing others to touch it, that transfigures it. Wounds are allowed to surface through touch.[14]

What is our relationship to our wounds?

Do we see truth arising from the sites of suffering?[15]

Do we hear Jesus' words "I am the way, the truth, and the life" come alive in our relationship both to his wounds and to our own?

Can we touch the bleeding Way, the wounded Truth, the crucified-resurrected Life?

Can we bring ourselves, like Thomas, to plunge our finger into the blood that is not yet dried, and in the act of turning toward and touching, be faithful to the power of the wound to become the site of new life?

Read through the gospel lens, crucifixion wounds are continually becoming resurrection wounds. And Jesus continues to invite us to commit ourselves to touching the pain, for our sake and for the sake of the world.

Rebirthing Mission

As we saw, world mission was originally organized around colonialism. We looked at how this pattern has continued into the present. Finding ways forward beyond neocolonialism, messiah complexes, McMission, ethnocentrism, the Western imagination, and the helping that hurts means reorganizing mission around something new.

14. Ibid.
15. Ibid.

We also looked at some practices that can help facilitate movement forward, such as pilgrimage, desert spirituality, and contemplative prayer. But the real crux of entering into mission in new ways lies in how we relate to our woundedness. As wounds surface, as we touch them and let them be touched, as we peel back the scabs of denial and projection and come to know and love our pain, we can reorganize mission around the wound. That is the way forward.

To move in a new direction in cross-cultural mission and justice work, away from the continual resuscitation of colonialism, ethnocentrism, theologies that disempower, and messiah complexes, we are invited to move toward rather than away from the wounded places inside of ourselves and our stories. In turning toward the pain and plunging our finger into the wounds, allowing them to be transformed in Christ, we can go beyond ministry as a one-way street. We are no longer the whole helping the broken. Instead, there is mutuality. When wounds carried by relatively wealthy Westerners meet the wounds of the materially poor, something beautiful is birthed in the space between us. Exquisite mutuality arises. Wounds meeting wounds doesn't have to equal more pain; it can be a catalyst for reciprocal healing.

Touching our wounds is the way, the only way, into the new. Going into the sites of the wound is to go beyond new iterations of the old patterns and be part of the rebirthing of mission from the inside out.

When tended, touched, and surfaced, the wound becomes a canal[16] through which mission is rebirthed. When the wound is touched, the future of global mission is radically open.

The inner work of touching our wounds and the outer work of touching the wounds of the world are one work.

The Invitation

Together we stand at a threshold. The God who is coming to us from the future is beckoning us to cross over into a new territory of unknowing, a liminal space in which we discern a better path forward. It is a challenging invitation that asks us to let go of all we thought we knew about mission in a global context to create space for something authentically new, built upon a different foundation.

16. Ibid.

Saying yes to the invitation will depend on our ability to face the sites of suffering and to touch our wounds, to know them and love them, and allow them to be transfigured—for our sake and for the sake of the world.

Saying yes to the invitation will depend on our willingness to de-theologize colonialism and Americentrism, prophetically engage history, think constellationally in connecting past with present, remember the cries that were never heard and the speaking that was never answered—and listen, hear, and respond.

Saying yes will depend on our ability to reclaim Paul's missionary imagination from the Western imagination and recognize, interrogate, and resist empire lite in all of its iterations.

Saying yes will mean a willingness to live in the tension between the "already" and the "not yet" of the kingdom of God and discern the particular ways each of us are being called to transform and be transformed.

Saying yes will mean a willingness to name what is hard to talk about, including the imperial theologies of the past that persist in subtle ways into the present—and to take seriously the task of doing mission in ways that restore dignity, confront shame, and birth shalom in the places we inhabit.

Saying yes will mean a willingness to embrace the prophetic tradition of naming what is at stake at this moment in history and being captive to a hope born of the vision of completeness, fulfillment, and shalom realized.

Saying yes will be a matter of embracing a deep spirituality, rejoining action and contemplation, remarrying inner life and outward action, embracing the desert spaces, and allowing the false self to be transformed.

Saying yes will require letting ourselves be challenged to give up power in the spaces of cross-cultural engagement and allow marginalized voices to rise to the center.

Saying yes will mean a capacity to listen, to become attuned and attentively present to the stories of people who dwell on the underside of global systems of inequity. Their faces and their stories will heal us and bring us nearer to the heart of God, and closer to the center of salvation through an exquisite mutuality realized in shared brokenness.

Epilogue

IT'S A LOVELY SUMMER morning on the coast. I'm sitting on my surfboard in the blue expanse of the Pacific Ocean, waiting for another wave. A seal pup surfaces a few yards away, dives back underneath the water, and resurfaces right next to me, his gaze fixing on mine. My heart feels light. Hope has become a friend to me through this missional journey. Yet, the memories still find their way into mornings like this. Maybe it's the sun's glimmer on the water or the look in the eyes of the playful sea creature, but I can still see their faces.

An image of Jeremy's grime-covered hands emerges in my mind when I least expect it. I hear the buzzer ring at the gate of the house where I lived in Cape Town, the distinct odor of the streets wafting off his body. Sometimes on a sleepless night I am visited by Abijek's countenance, radiant one moment, distressed the next at my refusal to touch the wounds within and instead continue numb, an amnesiac, forgetting again that he was never the lost and I never the found. On occasion during a moment of boredom a fleeting image of John's sunken eyes coalesces in my mind as he breathes one more breath, one last determined attempt to remain, to defy poverty's crucifying power.

I want to forget his face, their faces, and go back to being an innocent seven-year-old boy watching television with no concern for the complexities of poverty, the sins of mission, the ghosts of history, or shame's deception. Sometimes I want to forget the calling, the hope, the vision and pretend I never cared, never felt anything when I saw the images that interrupted my cartoons.

But there is another face that tells me I must never forget.

One evening, a few weeks after John's death, four men arrived in the village carrying a pregnant woman on a makeshift stretcher crafted out of tree limbs. Since no health facility was nearby, they were forced to make a several-hour trek down a rock-strewn path along a tributary of the White Nile.

Upon arrival, the life of mother and baby hung in an uncertain balance due to a complication. The same nurses who attended to John made haste to solve the issue and deliver the child. As they tended to the pregnant woman laying on some blankets on the floor of a large white storage tent where program supplies were kept—a makeshift emergency room in the bush—she suddenly began to bleed excessively, losing pints of blood to the soiled tent floor. An already tenuous situation worsened. One of the nurses yelled in my direction, asking me to go find the medication that would create the clotting factor needed to cease the profusion of blood. A few minutes after that injection, the mother stabilized. Another several minutes passed, and she gave birth to a healthy baby girl.

In precisely the same spot on the tent floor where John breathed his last, she breathed her first.

The mother named her newly arrived daughter Sophia after the Kenyan nurse who led the tiny human from womb to world under such precarious circumstances. In Greek, *sophia* is a term for the feminine aspect of God. Sophia's birth was a reflection of the caring, compassionate, motherly Presence in the aftermath of John's traumatic loss. Breathing her first breaths, each inhalation and exhalation was a covenant with the Spirit who hovers over the chaos of food insecurity and the darkness of systemic poverty that haunts places like South Sudan.

The hope present in Sophia's birth was an experience of survival, an interlude in coming to grips with tragedy.[1] The hope that her arrival into the world represented was not a panacea for pain nor a victory that wiped away loss. It was a fragile affirmation of life remaining in the wake of John's crucifixion, a reminder that something remains beyond death. Sophia's tiny body was a word made flesh. The Word is always seeking flesh, even as the forces of poverty and injustice seek to turn flesh back into words.

Still I am haunted by poverty. Still I am haunted by mission. But because of Sophia, still I dream of renewal and rebirth. Her face also materializes in my mind from time to time when I least expect it. Rather than haunting, her face blesses. Her eyes anoint. In them I read a covenant in which life is relentlessly emerging from God's womb into a broken world. In Sophia, I glimpse a promise that despite the presence of brokenness, disease, and death, all things are being reconciled, restored, and reborn.

The world is being recreated from the inside out.

1. See O'Connor, *Lamentations*.

Bibliography

Adichie, Chimamanda. "The Danger of a Single Story." TED Talk. Recorded July 2009. https://www.ted.com/talks/chimamanda_adichie_the_danger_of_a_single_story.

Alexander VI. "Inter Caetera." Papal bull, issued May 4, 1493. http://www.let.rug.nl/usa/documents/before-1600/the-papal-bull-inter-caetera-alexander-vi-may-4-1493.php.

Allender, Dan. "Sexuality: Gender." Class lecture at The Seattle School of Theology and Psychology, September 31, 2013.

————. "Shame." Class lecture at The Seattle School of Theology and Psychology, October 7, 2013.

Apple, Michael. *Official Knowledge: Democratic Education in a Conservative Age*. 3rd ed. New York: Routledge, 2014.

Azar, Beth. "Your Brain on Culture." *Monitor on Psychology* 41 (2010) 44. http://www.apa.org/monitor/2010/11/neuroscience.aspx.

Bantum, Brian. *The Death of Race: Building a New Christianity in a Racial World*. Minneapolis: Fortress, 2016.

Bosch, David. *Transforming Mission: Paradigm Shifts in Theology of Mission*. New York: Orbis, 1991.

Bauckham, Richard. *Bible and Mission: Christian Witness in a Postmodern World*. Grand Rapids: Baker, 2005.

————. "Only the Suffering God Can Help: Divine Passibility in Modern Theology." *Themelios* 9 (1984) 6–12.

Bediako, Kwame. *Theology and Identity: The Impact of Culture upon Christian Thought in the Second Century and in Modern Africa*. Eugene, OR: Wipf & Stock, 2011.

Berger, Nahuel. "Theorist Eric Maskin: Globalization Is Increasing Inequality." World Bank. June 23, 2014. http://www.worldbank.org/en/news/feature/2014/06/23/theorist-eric-maskin-globalization-is-increasing-inequality.

Berghoef, Bryan. "The Well Is Deep." Sermon delivered at Holland United Church of Christ, Holland, MI, March 19, 2017.

Bonhoeffer, Dietrich. *Letters and Papers from Prison*. Edited by Eberhard Bethge. Rev. ed. New York: Macmillan, 1967.

Borwick, Doug. "Universality/Particularity." *Engaging Matters*, an *Arts Journal* blog. February 8, 2017. http://www.artsjournal.com/engage/2017/02/universalityparticularity/.

Bosch, David. *Het Evangelie in Afrikaans Gewaad* [The gospel in African robes]. Kampen: Kok, 1974.

Boyle, Gregory. "Barking to the Choir—Now Entering the Kinship of Heaven." Presentation delivered at Spiritual Directors International Conference, San Diego, CA, April 8, 2016.

———. *Tattoos on the Heart: The Power of Boundless Compassion*. New York: Free Press, 2011.

Bradshaw, John. *Healing the Shame That Binds You*. Deerfield Beach, FL: Health Communications, 1988.

Brown, Brené. "The Power of Vulnerability." TED Talk. Recorded June 2010. https://www.ted.com/talks/brene_brown_on_vulnerability.

Brown, Emma. "Texas Officials: Schools Should Teach That Slavery Was 'Side Issue' to Civil War." *Washington Post*, July 5, 2015.

Chester, Andrew. "The Pauline Communities." In *A Vision for the Church: Studies in Early Christian Ecclesiology in Honor of J. P. M Sweet*, edited by Markus Bockmuehl and Michael B.Thompson, 105–20. Edinburgh: T. & T. Clark, 1997.

Chodron, Pema. *Comfortable with Uncertainty: 108 Teachings on Cultivating Fearlessness and Compassion*. Boston: Shambhala, 2008.

Christian, Jayakumar. *God of the Empty-Handed: Poverty, Power and the Kingdom of God*. Monrovia, CA: Word Vision International, 1999.

Cohen, Shaye. "Legitimization under Constantine." PBS. April 1998. https://www.pbs.org/wgbh/pages/frontline/shows/religion/why/legitimization.html.

Cone, James. *God of the Oppressed*. New York: Orbis, 1997.

Daly, Greg. "Transfigured by Love." *Irish Catholic*, May 20, 2015. https://www.irishcatholic.com/transfigured-by-love/.

Dear, John. "Romero's Resurrection." *National Catholic Reporter*, March 16, 2010. https://www.ncronline.org/blogs/road-peace/romeros-resurrection.

Delio, Ilia. "The Church and the Divided Brain." *Global Sisters Report*. July 21, 2014. http://globalsistersreport.org/church-and-divided-brain-7086.

———. *The Emergent Christ: Exploring the Meaning of Catholic in an Evolutionary Universe*. Maryknoll: Orbis, 2011.

Delio, Ilia. "Love at the Heart of the Universe." *Oneing* 1 (2013) 21–22.

Dube, Musa. "Inhabiting God's Garden: Are We in the Global Village or God's Garden?" *Ministerial Formation* 96 (2002) 29–35.

———. "Talitha Cum: A Postcolonial Feminist & HIV/AIDS Reading of Mark 5:21–43." In *Grant Me Justice: HIV/AIDS & Gender Readings of the Bible*, edited by Musa Dube and Musimbi Kanyoro, 115–40. Maryknoll: Orbis, 2004.

Dyckman, Katherine, and L. Patrick Carroll. *Inviting the Mystic, Supporting the Prophet: An Introduction to Spiritual Direction*. New York: Paulist, 1981.

Edmonds, Kevin. "NGOs and the Business of Poverty in Haiti." North American Congress on Latin America. April 4, 2010. http://nacla.org/news/ngos-and-business-poverty-haiti.

Eichstaedt, Peter. *Consuming the Congo: War and Conflict Minerals in the World's Deadliest Place*. Chicago: Chicago Review Press, 2011.

Frank, Arthur. *The Wounded Storyteller: Body, Illness, and Ethics*. Chicago: University of Chicago Press, 1997.

Gharib, Malaka. "At What Point Does a Fundraising Ad Go Too Far?" *Goats and Soda: Stories of Life in a Changing World*. NPR. September 30, 2015. http://www.npr.org/sections/goatsandsoda/2015/09/30/439162849/at-what-point-does-a-fundraising-ad-go-too-far.

Goldston, James. *A Year of Reckoning: El Salvador a Decade after the Assassination of Archbishop Oscar Romero.* New York: Human Rights Watch, 1990.

Guder, Darrell L., ed. *Missional Church: A Vision for the Sending of the Church in North America.* Grand Rapids: Eerdmans, 1998.

Gutierrez, Gustavo. *On Job: God-Talk and the Suffering of the Innocent.* New York: Orbis, 1987.

———. *A Theology of Liberation: History, Politics, and Salvation.* New York: Orbis, 1988.

Hall, John Douglas. "Despair as Pervasive Ailment." In *Hope for the World: Mission in a Global Context*, edited by Walter Brueggemann, 83–93. Louisville: Westminster John Knox, 2001.

Hauerwas, Stanley. *A Better Hope: Resources for a Church Confronting Capitalism, Democracy, and Postmodernity.* Grand Rapids: Brazos, 2000.

Hein, Laura Elizabeth, and Mark Selden, eds. *Censoring History: Citizenship and Memory in Japan, Germany, and the United States.* New York: Routledge, 2015.

Hoff, Meladie. "The Scramble for Africa." https://history.libraries.wsu.edu/spring2016/2016/01/20/witch-hunting-in-africa-compared-to-other-parts-of-the-world/.

John Paul II. "Peace on Earth to Those Whom God Loves." World Day of Peace message, January 1, 2000. https://w2.vatican.va/content/john-paul-ii/en/messages/peace/documents/hf_jp-ii_mes_08121999_xxxiii-world-day-for-peace.html.

Katongole, Emmanuel. *The Sacrifice of Africa: A Political Theology of Africa.* Grand Rapids: Eerdmans, 2011.

Katongole, Emmanuel, and Chris Rice. *Reconciling All Things: A Vision for Justice, Peace and Healing.* Downers Grove: InterVarsity, 2008.

Keane, Jim. "Oscar Romero's Beatification." *America: The Jesuit Review*, May 23, 2015. http://www.americamagazine.org/content/all-things/en-la-manana.

Keller, Timothy J. *Center Church: Doing Balanced, Gospel-Centered Ministry in Your City.* Grand Rapids: Zondervan, 2012.

Kennard, Matt, and Nick Macwilliam. "Chiquita Made a Killing From Colombia's Civil War. Will Their Victims Finally See Justice?" http://inthesetimes.com/article/19834/chiquita-multinationals-killing-colombias-civil-warparamilitary.

Kuja, Ryan. "The African Woman's Suffering: Hermeneutics, Geography, and Liberation Theology." *The Other Journal*, January 5, 2015. https://theotherjournal.com/2015/01/05/the-african-womans-suffering-hermeneutics-geography-and-liberation-theology/.

Lester, David. "The Role of Shame in Suicide." *Suicide and Life-Threatening Behavior* 27 (1997) 352–61.

Levine, Peter. *Waking the Tiger: Healing Trauma.* Berkeley: North Atlantic, 1997.

Lewis, C. S. *The Four Loves.* New York: Harcourt Brace Jovanovich, 1960.

Lifepoint Church. "Globalization and Mission." August 18, 2015. http://www.lifepointohio.com/blog-missions/globilization-mission/.

Livingstone, J. Kevin. *A Missiology of the Road: Early Perspectives in David Bosch's Theology of Mission and Evangelism.* Eugene, OR: Pickwick, 2013.

Maitland, Sarah. *A Big Enough God: A Feminist's Search for a Joyful Theology.* New York: Holt, 1995.

Markus, H. R., and Shinobu Kitayama. "Culture and the Self: Implications for Cognition, Emotion, and Motivation." *Psychological Review* 98 (1991) 224–53.

Maslin, Sarah. "Remembering El Mozote, the Worst Massacre in Modern Latin American History." *Nation*, December 13, 2016. https://www.thenation.com/article/remembering-el-mozote-the-worst-massacre-in-modern-latin-american-history/.

Massaro, John. *Living Justice: Catholic Social Teaching in Action*. Lanham, MD: Rowman & Littlefield, 2012.

Mayo, Bob. *The Parish Handbook*. London: SCM, 2016.

Mbila, Louison Emerick. "John Paul II and Globalization." https://sedosmission.org/old/eng/mbila.htm.

Merton, Thomas. *Thomas Merton: Spiritual Master; Essential Writings*. Edited by Lawrence Cunningham. Mahwah, NJ: Paulist, 1992.

———. *The Waters of Siloe*. New York: Harcourt, Brace, 1949.

Monbiot, George. "Neoliberalism: The Ideology at the Root of All Our Problems." *Guardian*, April 16, 2016. https://www.theguardian.com/books/2016/apr/15/neoliberalism-ideology-problem-george-monbiot.

Murray, Andrew. *Humility: The Beauty of Holiness*. Old Tappan, NJ: Revell, 1972.

Musopole, Augustine. "African Worldview." Paper presented at Changing the Story: Christian Witness and Transformational Development, World Vision International, Pasadena, CA, 1997.

Myers, Bryant. "Poverty as Disempowering System." Originally printed in *MARC Newsletter*, September 1998. Available at http://www.cscoweb.org/myers.html.

———. *Walking with the Poor: Principles and Practices of Transformational Development*. Maryknoll: Orbis, 2008.

Ndaliko, Cherie. "Film Students in Congo Seek a Cinema to Bring Their Stories to Life." *PBS News Hour*, October 13, 2015. https://www.pbs.org/newshour/show/congos-hope.

Ndaliko, Petna. "The Art of Empowering Youth." *Yole! Africa*. https://yoleafrica.org/2306-2/.

Nelson, Geoffrey, and Isaac Prilleltensky, eds. *Community Psychology: In Pursuit of Liberation and Wellbeing*. 2nd ed. New York: Palgrave Macmillan, 2010.

Neuhaus, Richard John. "The Religion Business." *First Things*. https://www.firstthings.com/web-exclusives/2008/12/the-religion-business.

Newbigin, Lesslie. *Foolishness to the Greeks: The Gospel and Western Culture*. Grand Rapids: Eerdmans, 1986.

———. *The Open Secret: An Introduction to the Theology of Mission*. Grand Rapids: Eerdmans, 1995.

Nida, Eugene. *Customs and Cultures: Anthropology for Christian Missions*. Harper & Brothers, New York, 1954.

Niebuhr, H. R. *Christ and Culture*. New York: Harper & Row, 1951.

Nolan, Albert. *Jesus before Christianity*. Cape Town: David Philip, 1962.

Nouwen, Henri, et al. *Compassion: A Reflection of the Christian Life*. Garden City, NJ: Image, 1983.

———. "The Wounded Healer." http://henrinouwen.org/meditation/the-wounded-healer.

O'Connor, Kathleen. *Lamentations and the Tears of the World*. New York: Orbis, 2002.

Palmer, Parker J. *To Know as We Are Known: Education as a Spiritual Journey*. San Francisco: Harper, 1993.

Pankey, Steve. "Doubting Thomas Didn't Doubt." *Christian Century*, April 5, 2013. https://www.christiancentury.org/blogs/archive/2013-04/doubting-thomas-didnt-doubt.

Park, Denise C., et al. "Culture Wires the Brain: A Cognitive Neuroscience Perspective." *Perspectives on Psychological Science* 5 (2010) 391–400.

Prothero, Steven. *American Jesus: How the Son of God Became a National Icon.* New York: Farrar, Straus & Giroux, 2004.

Rahner, Karl. "Christian Living Formerly and Today." In *Theological Investigations,* translated by David Bourke, vol. 7. New York: Herder and Herder, 1971.

Rambo, Shelly. "Wounds Resurrecting." Lecture at the Seattle School of Theology and Psychology, November 3, 2015.

Rohr, Richard. "Creation Continues." Center for Action and Contemplation. February 25, 2018. https://cac.org/creation-continues-2018-02-25.

———. "Moving from Jesus to Christ." Center for Action and Contemplation. March 22, 2015. https://cac.org/moving-jesus-christ-2015-03-22.

———. "A New Cosmology." Center for Action and Contemplation. October 29, 2017. https://cac.org/a-new-cosmology-2017-10-29.

———. "Shared Power." Center for Action and Contemplation. March 6, 2017. https://cac. org/shared-power-2017-03-06.

———. "Transforming Our Pain." July 3, 2016. Center for Action and Contemplation. https://cac.org/transforming-our-pain-2016-07-03.

———. "Whole-Making." Center for Action and Contemplation. November 21, 2016. https://cac.org/whole-making-2016-11-21/.

Rollins, Peter. *The Idolatry of God: Breaking Our Addiction to Certainty and Satisfaction.* New York: Howard, 2013.

Romero, Oscar. *La Voz de los Sin Voz. La palabra viva de Monsenor Romero.* 2nd ed. San Salvador: UCA Editores, 1986.

———. "The Most Profound Social Revolution." *Diario de Oriente,* no. 30867, August 28, 1973.

———. Sermon delivered in San Salvador, March 23, 1980.

Rossiter, Wayne. *Shadow of Oz: Theistic Evolution and the Absent God.* Eugene, OR: Pickwick, 2015.

Rothmyer, Karen. "Hiding the Real Africa: Why NGOs Prefer Bad News." *Columbia Journalism Review,* March/April 2011. https://archives.cjr.org/reports/hiding_the_ real_africa.php?Pag%2oe=all.

Rynkiewich, Michael. *Soul, Self and Society: A Postmodern Anthropology for Mission in a Postcolonial World.* Eugene, OR: Cascade, 2011.

Salai, Sean. "Saving Gang Members from the Street? Q&A with Father Greg Boyle, SJ." *America: The Jesuit Review,* August 20, 2014. http://www.americamagazine.org/ faith/2014/08/20/saving-gang-members-street-qa-father-greg-boyle-sj.

Shah, Anup. "The Rise of Corporations." GlobalIssues.org. Last updated December 5, 2002. http://www.globalissues.org/article/234/the-rise-of-corporations.

Sphar, Asa. "A Theology of Shame as Revealed in the Creation Story." *Theological Educator* 55 (1997) 65–74.

Staub, Dick. *The Culturally Savvy Christian: A Manifesto for Deepening Faith and Enriching Popular Culture in an Age of Christianity-Lite.* San Francisco: Jossey-Bass, 2008.

Stevenson, Bryan. "Just Mercy." Presentation at the Seattle Public Library, November 6, 2014.

Thomas, Gena. *A Smoldering Wick: Igniting Missions Word with Sustainable Practices.* CreateSpace, 2017.

Thompson, Curt. *The Soul of Shame: Retelling the Stories We Believe about Ourselves.* Downers Grove: InterVarsity, 2015.

Teilhard de Chardin, Pierre. "Cosmic Life." In *Writings in Time of War.* New York: Harper and Row, 1968.

———. *The Phenomenon of Man.* New York: Harper Perennial, 2008.

Twiss, Richard. "The Colonization of Consciousness." AskQuestions.tv. June 19, 2012. http://askquestions.tv/richard-twiss-the-colonization-of-consciousness/.

———. *One Church, Many Tribes: Following Jesus the Way God Made You.* Grand Rapids: Baker, 2000.

Van der Kolk, Bessel. *The Body Keeps the Score.* New York: Penguin, 2015.

White, L. Michael. "Legitimization under Constantine: From Persecuted Minority to Official Imperial Religion—What Caused This Extraordinary Reversal for Christianity?" PBS. April 1998. http://www.pbs.org/wgbh/pages/frontline/shows/religion/why/legitimization.html.

Wiest, Gregory. "Desert Spirituality." Lecture at Hesychia School of Spiritual Direction, Tucson, AZ, February 2015.

Wright, N. T. *Paul and the Faithfulness of God.* Minneapolis: Fortress, 2013.

Zinn, Howard. *A People's History of the United States: 1492–Present.* New York: Harper Perennial, 2003.